Black Gurl Reliable

BLACK LIVES & LIBERATION

SERIES EDITORS

Brandon Byrd, *Vanderbilt University*
Zandria F. Robinson, *Rhodes College*
Christopher Cameron, *University of North Carolina, Charlotte*

BLACK LIVES MATTER. What began as a Twitter hashtag after the 2013 acquittal of George Zimmerman for the murder of Trayvon Martin has since become a widely recognized rallying cry for black being and resistance. The series aims are twofold: 1) to explore social justice and activism by black individuals and communities throughout history to the present, including the Black Lives Matter movement and the evolving ways it is being articulated and practiced across the African Diaspora; and 2) to examine everyday life and culture, rectifying well-worn "histories" that have excluded or denied the contributions of black individuals and communities or recast them as entirely white endeavors. Projects draw from a range of disciplines in the humanities and social sciences and will first and foremost be informed by "peopled" analyses, focusing on everyday actors and community folks.

In the Shadow of Powers: Dantes Bellegarde in Haitian Social Thought, by Patrick Bellegarde-Smith

Race, Religion, and Black Lives Matter: Essays on a Moment and a Movement, edited by Christopher Cameron and Phillip L. Sinitiere

Continually Working: Black Women, Community Intellectualism, and Economic Justice in Postwar Milwaukee, by Crystal M. Moten

From Rights to Lives: The Evolution of the Black Freedom Struggle, edited by Charles W. McKinney and Françoise N. Hamlin

BLACK GURL RELIABLE

Pedagogies of Vulnerability and Transgression

Dominique C. Hill

VANDERBILT UNIVERSITY PRESS
Nashville, Tennesee

Copyright 2025 by Vanderbilt University Press
All rights reserved
First printing 2025

Library of Congress Cataloging-in-Publication Data

Names: Hill, Dominique C., author.
Title: Black gurl reliable : pedagogies of vulnerability and transgression / Dominique C. Hill.
Description: Nashville, Tennessee : Vanderbilt University Press, [2024] | Series: Black lives and liberation ; vol. 5 | Includes bibliographical references.
Identifiers: LCCN 2024038390 (print) | LCCN 2024038391 (ebook) | ISBN 9780826507570 (paperback) | ISBN 9780826507587 (hardcover) | ISBN 9780826507594 (epub) | ISBN 9780826507600 (pdf)
Subjects: LCSH: African American girls--Psychology. | African American girls--Race identity. | African American girls--Social conditions. | Gender identity in children--United States. | Body image in girls--United States. | United States--Race relations.
Classification: LCC E185.625 .H49 2024 (print) | LCC E185.625 (ebook) | DDC 305.23089/96073--dc23/eng/20241202
LC record available at https://lccn.loc.gov/2024038390
LC ebook record available at https://lccn.loc.gov/2024038391

Front cover image: © 2024 by Nettrice R. Gaskins

*To Black girls young and youthful, youthful
and seasoned, and not yet, us*

Contents

Acknowledgments ix
Preface 1

INTRODUCTION. Storying Black Girls Reliably: Black Feminism, Groove[ing], and the Self   9

1. "Sing a Black Girl's Song": A Code for Black Girlhood Studies   41
2. Reverse Osmosis to Awaken Flesh: An Experiment in Undressing   73
3. my Hair, my Mirror, my Own: A Lesson in (Self) Recognition   98
4. Willful Touch: An Experiment in Body-Activation   135
5. Teaching Black Girlhood: A Lesson in Cultivating Rigor   161

CONCLUSION. Gifts of Being with Black Girlhood   185

Notes 201
Bibliography 227
Index 245

Acknowledgments

The appreciation I feel and people for whom I give thanks are far and wide. I find it fitting to begin with gratitude to Divine in all of its forms and names and continue in honor of ancestors whose names I know and know not. To the village of womn who raised me on the eastside of Blo as well as those from afar, who imparted fundamental lessons to me through their firsthand actions, writing, and archives. I wrote this book with a hopeful heavy heart as one of those, in the words of June Jordan, who did not die. And because I am still here and like Badu, I too am an artist and sensitive about my *ish*, I extend appreciation to everyone, every thing, and every place that offered a word, gesture, affirmation, knowingly and otherwise, to encourage me along the way. For day one enthusiasm and support toward birthing this project, I give gratitude to Colgate University with special thanks to the Research Council.

Pasta, Christa, Deena, Unique, Mik, Phillipi, Nicole, Sunshine, Victory, Liz, Vanessa: you helped me see Black girls be dancing wind and purple skies, that to be a Black girl—young and youthful, youthful and seasoned—is loaded with imagined, real, and in-the-making realities.

To the leaders and students at Classic Upward Bound and the girls who took College Readiness classes with me who kept in touch over the years, thank you for trusting me with your dreams, stories, and critiques.

Vanessa and Ms. Sabrina for your insistence on creating platforms for Black girls to be affirmed, honored, and to own their volume—hair and otherwise, thank you.

Ntozake Shange, June Jordan, Toni Cade Bambara, Pat Parker, Audre Lorde: That you believed in the brilliance of youth, girlhood, and Black people. That you knew and said it so that the living of Black youth is where the soul of a society lives. And that you came to me in serendipitous ways (and stayed), I'm most appreciative. This book is a tracing of your presence in me and the wisdom you gifted to me, like the insistence to say what's on my heart, to feel before and as I move to pen any of it down, and to make space for the difference between what I don't yet know and what I might be seduced to pretend not to know.

To the galaxy that is SOLHOT, thank you for raising me on Badu, Incense circle, homegirl meetings, snacks, and Batty dance; they and other rituals incited my (re)membering of myself textured and complexly me. Thank you for the space to confront fears and old scripts, defy gravity, grow, and begin again.

For patience, attention to voice, and sheer care extended to me by editors, anonymous reviewers, and colleagues, I am heartened. Katie, Gianna, much appreciation. Natasha, working with you has been fire and salve. Your music and measure offered unimaginable grounding to such a loaded venture. We felt held.

To the places, homes, parks, Airbnbs and hotels, coffee shops, and people I crossed paths with—some names on recall, all experiences alive inside me, bless up for the color, scenery, and comfort.

Jaclyn, Renai, Becca, Dora, curious and critical students turned research assistants turned college graduates, always gamechangers—thank you for asking questions, holding onto my ideas, and carrying them with you.

To Inkwell Writing Retreat, Blacktastic Diasporic weekly writing accountability, and the "Writing what is" stay phresh crew, I salute. Writing accountability has proven oh so necessary and it is in your presence that I have kept honest, vulnerable, and in progress.

Mama Crystal and BJ, for always appearing in the randomest of places, usually in the wee hours, and eternally on time, to insist that I keep going and move on what I know; I needed that. And beloved Alice Walker for being a spiritual anchor and meditative prayer in text form to ground me and still encourage flight.

To the colleagues who, in brief encounters, offered a suggestion, food for thought, and/or a look of confusion, you aided in the refinement of my words. 'Preciate you.

For the gift of being seen reaching toward theatrical jazz aesthetics (TJA) and then directed toward practitioners (Sharon Bridgforth and Omi Osun Joni L. Jones) and experiences (Urban Bush Women's Summer Leadership Institute); for encouraging phone conversations; for Cynthia Oliver's attention to my then writing with an eye toward how it could sprout; for the felt support and recognition across time and space of Omi Osun Joni L. Jones: for these gifts and these happenings I firmly plant myself in ethos, spirit, and pathway of TJA that since 2012 continues to summon me deeper into myself, vulnerability work, and transgression.

To the people who facilitated and those who sat beside me on a deck, in boxes online, in the sun, in a hotel room, on a carpeted floor, working on and through our visions for poetry chapbooks, academic books, here's to saying what we needed to say and doing it in communion.

To Bernstein and the LoveWell Headquarters, for the peaceful cave to lay, cry, dance, refuel, tighten sentences, question, surrender to the process, and regroup.

To Lighthouse, for seeing me and for the shotgun on my back on the road to unbecoming.

To The Girlhood Project, for your willingness to engage vulnerability and trust in my ability to guide.

To Waters, for collectivity, gentle reminders to befriend grace and rest in the process while tenderly urging me to say the thing I need to say the way I need to say it.

To Warrior, for consistent encouragement, raw responses to a line or five, and on time reminders to say it plain as possible.

To Village, 'nuff said.

To those whose names I know not but who read, commented, and helped to extend the ideas bound here.

To those whose names escape me in this moment.

I pen these words and take a breath in deep thankfulness for all who tarried with me along this journey. I extend my arms and open heart to Universe for being in agreement with me that this book be.

Ase'.

Preface

I begin this book as I end it—in a letter and with deep gratitude.

Dear Witness,

Welcome. I write this book while immersed in a journey of becoming luscious soil for birthing and building. Imagine being barefoot or naked in nature. I am sticky in places, coarse in some, and untilled in others. Thank you for joining me here and walking my grounds. Whether your motivation comes from a desire to better understand a niece, student, or embodiment; for professional development; some academia-related contract; a dope reading club; strolling a local bookstore; some intuitive guidance received or an attempt to address a prompt from your therapist; some combination or none of these, I am encouraged you will find something here of use. In the pages that follow, I stage a layered conversation about Black gurl embodiment. Through a series of performances, I put on front street structural impediments, cautionary tales, and personal experiences that thwart aliveness. Alongside these, I advance the idea of *reliability work*, which I define as unending action, watered sensibility, and becoming that amplify one's capacity to be with/in oneself in order that one can be with/for spacious Black girlhood. But before we go there, I want to share with you a few "how I got here" moments. Come closer so I can whisper, not for the sake of secret but sacredness. The origins below are lasting occasions that handed me lessons about my body. They are also instances where I learned the arbitrary nature and harmful effects of being marked wrong. Unintentionally, these experiences and their logics took root inside my entire being and sprouted into lifework on Black girlhood, embodiment, collective worldmaking, and vulnerability.

Origin: It's 1999, a li'l after six in the morning. I'm minding my business, when I'm invited to take a "ride." Standing at the corner of Genesee and Hickory, adorned in a heather gray kilt with navy blue stripes, blue micro-ribbed tights, a puff coat, and bookbag nearly half my weight, a white man looking like popo slowly rolls down his window and summons me to get in his car. This street, and particularly this block, known for then-called street walkers, is where people I called auntie worked. My uniform, there, I now fancied, read costume to him. Fastened to the fence behind me and gripping the straps of my bookbag at the perfect angle to throw a punch, if necessary, he plays a game of lure for which I shared no interest. Eventually, his pout turns cold and his dark gray Chevy Caprice roars down the street.

Origin: My mother marries. I sense I am debris of an old other life of hers. Alongside feelings of not belonging, being in-the-way, and general sadness about the union, I learned the meaning of being a brown Black girl. Following in my mother's footsteps, the one family calls "brown bomber," I become the darkest on my family's matrilineal side, while in my hood and at school my big lips and gapped teeth afford me the signature African booty scratcher. In this new world of hers, where people adorn beautiful, almost Jacobean, Ebony skin, I become light skinned, "think you all that," a target. I turn my dark-skinned Black girl card in for a brown-girl-in-the-middle one.

Origin: I arrive in Urbana, Illinois, excited to begin graduate school and work with Black girls through Saving Our Lives, Hear Our Truths (SOLHOT). I liken this creative intergenerational praxis to the underground railroad sojourning in the name of Black girlhood and liberation. Summer 2008 and I thought myself ready to work on the behalf of Black girls and Black girlhood. I won't recant my readiness that I'd describe more fittingly now as interest. I will say, I entered with ideas acquired through enrichment and etiquette programs, assumptions about how and the need to reduce my visibility along with my "at-risk" appearance. I'll also say that radical in those places and SOLHOT were not the same. And while I yearned for a space like SOLHOT, I entered guarded and with an obsolete toolkit. I eventually discontinued certain orientations such as default deference to adults, waiting to be called on before contributing, assuming appearing unpolished in front of young girls an error and violation of Black womnhood—but not before committing multiple faux pas. The first, happening that same summer I began my journey in SOLHOT. Grounded in the aforementioned orientations that stripped youth of agency and created Black/white interpretations of action, I poorly framed a conversation about Black hair. I made no room for multiple perspectives, vilified permed and processed styles, and ignored what I already knew about Black girls—we are varied in stylization, adornment, and texture.

Under the skin of these encounters live larger systematized ideas about aesthetics and gaze. More, they reveal a set of social rubrics about bodies, how they're read, and on what terms. Within this matrix, individuals marked Black and female though not inherently cisgender, femme, or feminine are appraised based on hierarchies and politics organized by anti-Blackness and male and/or masculine preference, as well as a binary thinking.[1] These experiences surfaced contexts where my sense-making journey of my body in relation to people and places and others' bodies in relation to my own occurred; they catalog experiences within geographies that contribute to the making of Black girlhood and how Black girls' embodiment is formed. This book is about a practice of seeing and embodying Black girlhood anew; about assumptions and histories brought to interpreting Black bodies and girls; about maneuvers and knowing engendered to fend off what is later discussed as "stuckness."[2]

Black Gurl Reliable documents happenings at the nexus of Black girlhood, bodies, and justice while presenting and reflecting upon what reliability work might look like. Reliability work is intimately connected to embodiment or the labor undertaken to stay whole amid obstructions to survival, self-definition, and experiencing pleasure. To share my concern and advance embodiment as an urgent matter in Black Girlhood studies and more broadly in global liberation, I visit places and processes that create barriers to wholistic embodiment for Black girls. Additionally, I utilize re-memory, personal accounts of confinement—experienced and enacted—to exhume and interrogate textures of confinement while advancing exercises for retooling the body.

Through a personal but not individual account, I craft a series of performances mounted on the page for you to affectively peruse. By performance I mean an accumulated iterative set of events that make more visible social and cultural methods of exclusion and punishment. Presented beside them are acts of dissent and emergent practices that make perceptible other possibilities for how Black girls can be treated, interpreted, and regarded.

Related to these other opportunities of how Black girls are handled in the world is an insistence that Black girls get to live sprightly and pleasure-filled lives—a foundational principle of Black girlhood within a celebration paradigm.[3] Black Girlhood studies is a political imagining project that takes seriously the rehearsal and assignment of materializing Black girlhood as something real, dynamic, unsettled but sturdy, and indispensable to Black life and social transformation.

I enter the field and these pages through the corridor of "practicing Black girlhood" and as a homegirl of SOLHOT. It is through one of its outgrowths, Black Girl Genius Week (BGGW), and time with homegirls like poet Nikky Finney and DJ B.E. that I accessed seeds for what I pen and write about here as *Black gurl reliable*. A method for seeing and being with Black girlhood, Black gurl reliable is an orientation and iterative process that requires practice and time. Further, Black gurl reliable upholds girlhood as something exercised intergenerationally to honor Black girlhood in the present tense while writing it into the future. Black gurl reliable embraces *gurl* as an "us" inhabitance not dictated by age or developmental stage. The cultivation of this sensibility requires the adoption of contradictions, multiple truths, and divestment in conventional configurations of order. Unlike the orientations I initially brought to SOLHOT, Black gurl reliable is queer in that it is grounded in "ideological nonconformity."[4] Black gurl reliable denounces barriers that reinforce dominance and fosters new potential intimacies all the while establishing new aims, terms, and happenings in Black girlhood.

Reliability work is about working from an "us" position that acknowledges individual responsibility for one's contribution to expanding Black aliveness through Black girlhood. It is acceptance that the letter *u* symbolizes collective responsibility to Black girls and Black girlhood. Reliability work can take place in familial relations, during policy creation, at the hair salon or the neighborhood community center. As Black girlhood scholars increase in numbers, it's a timely juncture to think about how we study Black girls, ways we archive and represent Black girlhood, how it is taught, what tools are used to study Black girls and girlhood, and what nutrients we give its soil, as well as how we stakeholders (in all our variety and contexts) orient ourselves to our embodiment in Black girlhood.

Drawing on the practices of Black church and Black artistic production, *Black Gurl Reliable* positions readers as witnesses. To be a witness is to feel (*not just look*) as well as reflect and connect with what's unfolding on the pages that follow. Connection can look like revisiting memories of girlhood; reflecting on your beliefs about Black girls and the body; tracing assumptions back to their many origins; widening your frame to see yourself as a stakeholder in messages and stories on repeat as well as those truths about Black girls and girlhood that remain underground, tucked away, and/or unbelievable. The move from reader to witness is about a recognition that the processes of seeing and reading are interconnected acts that involve us—our histories, experiences, beliefs, memories, bodies. And whether you walk this soil alone or with others, outside or within academia, I recommend a somatic approach where you take time to notice your body's response throughout. Where you decide to give in to an urge that emerges while reading and where you pause to ask questions of yourself. Questions like: How am I feeling right now? What am I noticing about my body? What assumptions did I bring with me? In what ways am I resisting or leaning into this story? What messages and baggage do I bring with me here about bodies, Blackness, Black girls, Black girlhood? Where in my body do I feel these stories? How do I contribute to Black spaciousness? How do I carry Black girls with me presently and how do I want to carry them with me going forward?

A Note on Language: Vernacular Lexicon

To ground what follows in specificity, I briefly introduce some foundational concepts that I elaborate upon in future chapters. First, Blackness is vast in meaning and experience. *Black* here refers to the racial, cultural, imaginative, and historical collective heterogeneity shared by African ascendant people.[5] *Black* as a racial designation is diasporic because "as a descriptive category 'diaspora' refers to the dispersal and movement of a population (defined by race, religion, ethnicity, nationality, or another coalescing identity)."[6] While specific cases and places discussed occur primarily in the United States, the texture of Blackness is mixed and multiple. Moreover, the girls who appear, as well as the framing of Black girlhood throughout, is informed by ethnic backgrounds and cultural complexities related to being US-born, Nigerian- and Togolese-born, mixed race, and African American. To add, the notion of identity and naming is quite complicated and must account for one's background as well as how bodies are read in various contexts. Diaspora speaks to interconnection and expansion even as it sometimes produces fragmentation and displacement.

Femininity is also diasporic and structured by race, culture, and context. To acknowledge its expansiveness and contestation, I drop the letters *e* and *a* in relation to categories *woman, women*, and the experience of *womnhood* throughout the book. I make this move after decades of grappling. *Womn* signals resistance and capacious expression of gender and sexuality. This shift comes from deep observation of complexities presented by students and colleagues about identity, labels, and agency. *Womn* acknowledges that not all individuals who identify as womn identify their personhood as necessarily "she" and that not all individuals organized by a binary system of gender and classified as womn self-regard in this specific way. Aligned with nineteenth- and twentieth-century feminists who challenged the fixed nature of the category *woman, womn* discontinues a linear relationship with the traditional categories of girl and woman. This turn in spelling enmeshes individual and group while broadening the scope of who is assumed present and integral to the term. *Womn* therefore magnifies possible journeys to as well as who can participate in Black girlhood.

The body is a sociocultural text that is read and appraised based on context, the reader, and time. Throughout, I emphasize the reading of bodies and refer to bodies marked, read, or regarded as Black and female. This phrasing is not an embrace of the gender binary nor a denial of expansive gender identity. Rather, I use the phrasing *Black and female though not inherently cisgender, femme, or feminine* to connote how Black girls' and womn's bodies are physically read, to render personal identity sacred, and to make room for it despite others' attributions. Therefore, being marked as Black and female unfolds a process of experiential treatment and navigation that is then flavored by one's self-understanding. Someone regarded as Black and female is not inherently cisgender, femme, and/or feminine. Importantly, when phrases connected to being bodily interpreted emerge, they highlight the bigness of gaze on lived experience and treatment.

Black Girlhood studies is a gathering place for spatial, cultural, and ethnic dimensions of Blackness as a happening of dispersal, rebellion, and creation. The term *girl* is political, historically situated, and contested as a category made and ordered by legacies of colonialism, liberation, and humanitarian efforts.[7] *Girl* is a noun, verb, cultural idiom, and "intracommunication methodology."[8] Continuing the work of widening the function and formation of Black girlhood, I introduce a *u* in the spelling of girl. The *u* is an adoption of Black vernacular and a written way of marking a merging of the individual and collective. It is an *us* assertion and an indicator that one is writing with/as/for and confirms an *us*—young and youthful, youthful and seasoned Black girls. Specifically, its citational expansiveness is signified through curled or puckered lips (depending on what follows) and tickles in the back of the throat to hit the gurgling sound on time. *Yes, I slowly repeated the word using different speeds to feel the word.* At the present moment, however, girl is spelled with a *u* when applied to practices, states of being, or orientations like Black gurl reliable and Black gurl embodiment. More than semantic, the *u* within these practices and pedagogies stresses a within location and signals personal accountability to ensuring Black girlhood something possible, lived, and made through multigenerational convening. While *girl* is category and an individual, *gurl* is an aesthetic, a sensibility, a way of being in the world. *Black gurl reliable*, for instance, is an enduring fervent ownership in creating space for girls to cast vision; in seeing girls' dreams come to pass; in womn and femmes, despite our sexual orientation or sartorial decisions, befriending their girl selves; in crafting spells and recipes that enlarge the terrain of Black girlhood; in seeing Black girls whole and Black girlhood a site of worldmaking. Black gurl reliable is work that requires tending to y/our soil, digging up weeds, planting seeds, and watering the collective garden of Black girlhood. *Black gurl embodiment* is about the journey and results of traversing carceral landscapes that seek to deny wholeness and self-definition; it is about the process of attuning to and honoring one's body, despite social cultural understandings of bodies. It is a fashioning of self that practices full presence—to be consciously in body. I must note, these specificities I outline here derive from a particular exploration of embodiment in Black girlhood curated here. I imagine my indexing of the meaning of the *u* will evolve with time and experience and that by the time you read this I will have more to say. Take this offer as a provisional one.

INTRODUCTION
Storying Black Girls Reliably
Black Feminism, Groove[ing], and the Self

"I would probably pick one of the whitest names I know."

This was Christa's immediate response to me about pseudonyms and renaming herself in my study on Black girls' bodily experiences in educational contexts. On a Baltimore (or Bmore) Saturday afternoon in 2012, I sat across from a peanut-butter-toned, beautiful, then-seventeen-year-old Black girl. Following an almost two-hour arts-based workshop (discussed further in Chapter 4), we sat in a counselor's office of a Trio program, where I asked her about the workshop and school. Leaning back in the chair, folding her arms, studying me, grinning until sound squeezed through her teeth then lips, she leans forward, and rules out the name Melanie. Minding my belief that youth know what they need, even if people don't consult them, I insisted that participants chose their pseudonym. Settling into the seat, crossing her arms and legs in a figure-four lock position she firmly states, "Call me Christa." Unsettled, in awe of her firmness, and committed to learning from her, I accepted her determination and moved on to questions about school.

Unknowingly, Christa compelled me to "put on [my] good bra" and practice deep listening.[1] Christa challenged me to consider my ability to honor in real time self-definition practices of youth. Could I go beneath social meanings of names and their cultural significance to hear Christa? Could I revere how she Black gurl without correcting or turning away from the category altogether?[2] Could I complexly interpret her truths? Was I capable of sensing for and listening to, in this case, Christa's spirit? Could I suspend what I know about racialization and names? Could I dream with her? Not initially. Through revisitation of various moments with Black girls like the one described above, time and continued practice of being with Black girls, I arrived at the principle and practice of Black gurl reliable. Reliability here refers to an ability to demonstrate trustworthiness when Black girls reveal what they need, who they are, and how they want to be in the world. Reliability work requires a withholding of judgment or evaluation based on personal perspective (perhaps wisdom) rooted in conventional hierarchical adult/nonadult power relations. Black gurl reliable demands a will to be honest in one's body, to engage in play, and hold space while girls figure life out, try on, and go in directions opposite those we as womn, social workers, (other) mothers, practitioners, stakeholders, homegirls, teachers, lovers recommend. Black gurl reliable is an enduring practice that recognizes young and youthful girls as knowledge creators.

When initially interviewing Christa, her choosing a name she understood to be designated for white girls, including her firmness that it be spelled with a *C*, perplexed me. I only sensed that the mismatch between Christa and I—my heart sinking and her smirking and settling into her seat—meant I was missing something. Uncomfortable and puzzled, I fumbled and my stomach churned. Within my research design, I made room for expression, choice, change of direction (or groove[ing]) and paid close attention to how autonomy and agentic assumptions organized our interaction. I did not, however, foresee the lesson Christa presented. From the act of asking girls to choose their pseudonym, a pedagogical pathway emerged. Like Beyond C'est in episode seven of the series *Lovecraft Country*, Christa offered to show me what worlds are possible when Black girls are consulted.[3] Her grin and full-bodied deliberations exuded confidence. Her movements indicated resolve. Christa, a self-described "creative, open to new ideas, and musical because there's always a song in my head," named herself. Akin to Hippolyta Freeman's decision, after her multidimensional time travel in *Lovecraft Country*, to declare "mother" as who she was, in Christa's selection of the "whitest name" possible, she chose from a position of vastness—a political and purposeful move.[4] Christa was building a world where her actions and essence garnered meaning on their own terms, or at the very least called for detachment from their current set of cultural norms. Nestled in Christa's decisiveness are the seeds of a world where she could take on the whitest of names and it not be "white" but hers. Black gurl reliable is a framework for understanding the complexity of embodiment in Black girlhood.

Worldmaking requires vision, thought, and capacity to practice actions that bring the world not yet and the one materialized into closer proximity. Christa's intentional bodily enactments alongside her words stewarded me to meditate on the ways bodies ingest and digest narratives, events, and norms. My discomfort prompted me to think about the varying ways bodies get assessed, the ways movement in Black bodies invoke connotation that sometimes result in violence and other times physical death, and how in Soul II Soul fashion, Black people "keep on movin."[5] This book is an outgrowth of Christa's reliability lesson that clarifies pathways and strategies exercised by and created for Black girls to remain embodied (or whole) amid violences, injustices, and simultaneous hypervisibility and disappearance. Related, it exposes *pedagogies of foreclosure* or mechanisms of constriction that obstruct Black girl self-determination and feature performances of defiance, or *pedagogies of transgression*, that trouble normative boundaries and ways of being.

Black Gurl Reliable attends to the following questions: How are Black girls becoming amid modes of confinement? What sites and procedures incite "spirit murdering"? How do race and gender, minimally, sculpt the look and approach of these actions of foreclosure? In what ways are embodiment and justice work interconnected terrain? Ultimately, I argue that embodiment is an indispensable barometer of justice and underemphasized feature of Black liberation. *Black Gurl Reliable*, therefore, documents racial-sexual tactics of foreclosure (i.e., spirit-murdering vis-à-vis dress code and hair policies) and illuminate how Black girls' bodies archive and retool them. Further, I assert that Black girlhood, as an intergenerational training ground, is a necessary geography and portal to Black liberation where new ways of being can be imagined, rehearsed, and normalized to boost social transformation. To scaffold reliability work, I introduce a lexicon and set of practices that guide how Black girlhood and girls are storied, curated, and regarded.

Black gurl reliable grows out of the paradigm of celebration.[6] It is one filter and ethic for seeing, narrating, and being with Black girls and girlhood. To offer examples for how this orientation might look in practice and the beautiful tensions it raises, I provide firsthand accounts of my journey toward penning *Black Gurl Reliable*. I describe lenses knowingly and unconsciously adopted that resulted in me being less complex in my thinking and less able to see all Black girls, including the one here/in/as me (see origins in Preface). Although *Black Gurl Reliable* requires engaging in and remaining attentive to historical origins and ideologies, this book is primarily concerned with ways forward into new bodily relations that ascend from a deep study of Black girlhood, of sitting with/as/because of Black girls.

Black Girls Are Black Matters

Mattering is a complex project tethered to justice manifested. Throughout world history in different ways and for varying reasons Blackness is appointed a contested site of importance. From the fight for abolition in the northern hemisphere and especially in the United States, to independence and present day civil wars of African countries, to Black power in South Africa and the United States, to the contemporary movement for Black lives, Black life and value endures attack and duress. Built into these protest performances and demands for justice and equity are these questions: Under what classification of matter is Black life? To whom do Black lives hold relevance and significance? Under what conditions is Black life reduced to nonmatter, and what avoidable happenings occur from such determinations? Be it Abbey Lincoln asking, "Who will revere the Black woman?" or Aisha Shaidah Simmons concerned with Black LGBTQ people, asking, "Who will revere us?," demands are made to pay attention to the ways race, gender, and sexuality conjoin to underwrite Black bodies wrong.[7] Unpacked in Chapter 3, mattering is more than what happens after Black life is snatched by productions of state violence and unable to be resuscitated. For Black lives to matter, life, in all of its breadth and expansive expression, need be respected and cared for in the active present tense.

As early as five years old, teachers presume Black girls' are more informed, mature, and justifiably liable for their actions.[8] The process of designating Black youth culpable actors and therefore more responsible than white peers of their same age results in kindergarten-age girls handcuffed and escorted out of school for a temper tantrum.[9] Adultification offers one frame to describe the lack of care and outcry denied Black girls around endured sexual and state-based violence, which sometimes leads to death; it should not, however, justify it.[10] When standing up to injustice, Black girls are indicted and placed on trial.[11] And when Black girls receive in or outside school suspension, it is more often for acts deemed disobedient or defiant. Increasingly, these "offenses" relate to dress code infractions in the form of hair stylization and result in denied participation in rites of passage ceremonies and practices (e.g., yearbook photos, prom, recess, graduation), and school suspensions.[12] As of September 2024, twenty-seven states plus Washington, DC, had passed the Create a Respectful and Open World for Natural Hair (CROWN) Act or some version of it.[13] A law intended to generate legal recourse for racialized hair discrimination, the CROWN Act is evidence of the evolution of anti-Blackness and its pervasiveness in social institutions and convention. According to the 2021 CROWN research study for girls, 53 percent of Black mothers whose daughters have experienced hair discrimination express these occurrences happening as early as kindergarten.[14] Nationwide, Black youth are about five times more likely to be incarcerated than their white counterparts. And nationwide, "Black girls are more than four times more likely than white girls to be arrested at school."[15] While some reports attend to the distinct experiences produced through race-gender analysis, the collection of data on physical death, incarceration, and education largely in some way bypasses the specificities of Black girls. Instead, Black girls get used as padding for race or gender disparity discussions and research.[16]

Mattering and increased airtime in the twenty-first century about issues informing Black girls' livelihoods are not synonymous. In *We Want to Do More Than Survive*, Bettina L. Love writes, "Mattering cannot happen if identities are isolated, and students cannot be their full selves."[17] Voicing an urgency to see Black youth as human, Love's statement draws connections between the physical body, the project of mattering, and embodiment. The work of mattering honors one's humanity and requires acknowledgment of a person in their fullness. When Black girls are criminalized, denied spaces safe enough to share their ideas, and punished for self-fashioning, mattering is unrealized. More, the possibilities of becoming fragmented, unexpressed, and disembodied are heightened. When reduced to something that only transpires at scenes of Black death, mattering becomes an experience Black folk access through death, if at all. There now exist platforms like Justice for Black Girls, Black Girls Rock, and the African American Policy Forum that cover wins, issues, happenings, deaths, and injustices related to Black girls and womn. There are also national reports and academic scholarship that document Black girls' academic achievement, encounters with zero tolerance policies, and overall faring in the education system. What remains less known are interior dimensions of such realities. In what ways does the criminalization of Black girls, for instance, materialize in Black girls' physical movement? How do stories told about Black girls and girlhood absorb into bodily archives? In what ways do such stories stay with us? What strategies do Black girls employ to stay whole? What spaces are created by youthful and seasoned Black girls to hear, feel, and retool with young and youthful Black girls?

Indeed, mattering ought to include redress for filmed and unrecorded murders, botched raids, and physical lives taken at the hands of the police, the prison industrial complex, and other forms of institutionalized injustice. Mattering must also attend to everyday violence; violation undermined and presumed trivial, and the tax and time necessary to recalibrate from such incessant disembodying experiences. This book is one account of the ways Black girls are exposed to what Toni Cade Bambara refers to as "terrible educations," how physical bodies and spirits absorb such lessons, and the potential state of "stuckness" that derives from repeat encounters with mechanisms that block Black gurl wholeness. *Black Gurl Reliable* expands the narrative of Black mattering by detailing textures of confinement fostered by the soil of racial-sexual entanglements and promotes embodiment as a nonnegotiable feature of liberation and justice. Black mattering is life and life-giving work; it needs to be evidenced at the site of Black aliveness.

Geographies of Confinement

Confinement is multifaceted with material and discursive consequences and necessitates a roomy understanding of punishment, space, and constriction. Feminist geography, at its inception, aimed to broaden the scope of human geography, in particular what sites receive "legitimate" status. This shift ushered in a framing of bodies as knowledge sites where resistance is enacted and tensions unfold.[18] Bodies become battlegrounds where "individuals fight for recognition of their authentic selves, their autonomy, their full potential. They attempt to reconfigure normative practices and processes, fighting to redefine narrow scripts."[19] It is therefore also and precisely at the level of the body that wars are waged and inform the proliferation of carceral logics. According to Richie, "carcerality refers to all things punishment. The 'things' encompassed in this definition are those institutions, policies, and ideological positions that are involved or invoked in response to situations when 'laws' have been broken, 'crimes' have been committed, or norms have been violated."[20] In a society organized by carceral and capitalist logics, bodies are preset as carceral geographies sculpted and impacted by social norms, institutions, and ideologies. As a result, according to Ruthie Gilmore, "understanding bodies as places, then criminalization transforms individuals into tiny territories primed for extractive activity to unfold—extracting again time from the territories of selves."[21] All bodies living under such auspices are subject to being a battleground, the bodies of some people are *more* likely to be criminalized by some, and decided less legible.

Black girls withstand insidious forms of confinement. These types of constriction and the processes embedded in them warrant attention because they contour Black embodiment. Moreover, they are systemic and institutional mechanisms that encourage everyday Black despondence experienced in the body. No doubt anti-Black racism contributes to the literal and figurative suffocation of Black life. The *how* of this asphyxiation is indexed by Black scholars whose work expands feminist theory, critical legal studies, cultural studies, literary studies, and more. Recognizing both the legal holdings of racism, its visceral, continuous effects in terms of how "the legacy of killing finds its way into cultural expectations, archetypes, and 'isms,'" Patricia Williams introduces the concept of "spirit-murdering" into legal theory to depict the pervasiveness of anti-Black racism.[22] Defined as a "crime, an offense so deeply painful and assaultive," by definition spirit-murdering is iterative and built into body politics or "the practices and policies through which powers of society regulate the human body, as well as the struggle over the degree of individual and social control of the body."[23] Spirit murdering has compounded effects on the self-concepts and embodiment of Black people. Far from being innocuous, spirit-murdering results from quotidian, systemic, cyclic or not, productions built into policy, cultural practices, and unremarkable events that as repeat offenses wear on the spirit. And although this crime Williams names does not produce physical death and the cessation of breath, it suppresses quality of life, deters pleasure pursuits, and constrains people's internal knowing.

In a special issue of *Ethnos* on sites of confinement, Jefferson, Turner, and Jensen explore the concept of stuckness in relation to confinement and the carceral. They assert, "we propose the term stuckness to refer to the way confinement is experienced, sensed, and lived. The experience of 'stuckness' is not simply an expression of physical confinement and spatial closure but expresses the way people make sense of confining dynamics and practices."[24] Confinement, therefore, occurs in and is maintained beyond physical carceral structures. Additionally, confinement has residual impacts in that "to be existentially and socially stuck is not just a question of being stuck in place but equally about being stuck in time. Not seeing a future, a way forward, leads to a sense of stuckness that may linger."[25] Even when someone leaves the cell—whatever form it may take—it remains in tow. A change of landscape does not erase the sentiments, reinforced messages, nor the acquired and digested information about life and what is possible. Moreover, in a society ordered by punishment and carceral logics, stuckness describes a persistent cycle of reduced to being and embodying *wrongness*. As "a set of political commitments independent from data about actual occurrences of lawbreaking," carcerality sustains and produces conditions that differentially place people and bodies in holding patterns.[26] Further, "carcerality can be understood to be a condition or set of social arrangements that advances a reliance on punishment or incapacitation. It includes the ideological, political instincts, and public investment in deploying the state's punishment apparatus to control nonnormative behaviors from aggressive physical harm to minor nuances that inconvenience people in power."[27] Part of this project is value designation to behaviors and bodies that determine rubrics for out of pocketness, out of placeness, or wrong subjects (discussed in Chapter 1). Through this arrangement, increased criminalization of certain people and bodies is procedural, whether or not their "crimes" result in time in the legal system, and is justified as maintaining law and order. One's proximity to and familiarity with carceral dynamics is thereby refereed by one's bodily appraisal within the aforementioned matrix.

Interested in de jure sex discrimination and committed to a nuanced analysis of race alongside sex, twenty years before the introduction of spirit-murdering, Pauli Murray presented the concept of "Jane Crow" to describe labor inequality and injustice experienced by womn.[28] Various scholars utilize the concept to highlight how Jim Crow laws impacted Black womn.[29] Murray's analysis, however, confronts patriarchy broadly alongside a narrow focus of race attributed to Civil Rights activism.[30] Implicitly, Murray also challenges androcentrism within Black culture, asserting, "that manifestations of racial prejudice have been more brutal than the more subtle manifestations of prejudice by reason of sex in no way diminishes the force of the equally obvious fact that the rights of women and the rights of Negroes are only different phases of the fundamental and indivisible issue of human rights."[31] The concept of Jane Crow originally provided an analytical framework for interrogating legible and illegible forms of violence and discrimination, and thereby injustice. Further, Murray's critique shines light on the function of a binary orientation oppression discourse, wherein more overt and perhaps aggressive forms of violence are masculinized, readable, and therefore worthy of recourse. In contrast, those forms that fall outside of those are feminized and therefore inconsequential. I continue Murray's noticing of varied styles of sanctioning race and gender differences in the context of Black girlhood with a focus on textures of violence and injustice endured.

Black girlhood is a site of Black geographic imagination, space-making, and a place where harm is named without being the sum total of experience. As a space consciously named and enlarged in the twenty-first century through social initiatives and an academic field, Black girlhood is and is not yet, and is an integral space to Black Geographies.[32] Black Geographies "entail the study of the spatialities of Black life and the plurality of Black spatial imaginaries, with the goal of unsettling racist and colonial forms of spatial organization."[33] As such, Black Geographies are attendant to power relations sewn into the acknowledgment and denial of space, knowledge-making, and space-making practices. Since the creation of space, as well as the metrics and meaning of difference, is produced, geography is intimately tied to ways of knowing and being known.[34] Black feminist thinking and activism across space and time provides intense interrogation of and counterstrategies to human confinement responding to a frame of wrongness. Extending the theorization of Black feminist poets, I flesh out a theory of wrongness to catalog processes of containment. More, I outline how the assumptions of wrongness, when inversed, become a vehicle for liberation, what is discussed throughout as wrongness embraced or transgression. Black Geographies illuminate dimensions of Blackness by disentangling racism and oppression, which is to demand accountability to mechanisms that degrade and superintend the quality of Black life without defining Blackness as the projects that vilify it. As a site sometimes reduced to an absence, something hijacked, and/or fleeting, Black girlhood is Black spatiality of great potential for Black geography, life, and futures.

Black Girlhood Studies

Black Girlhood studies is lavish soil for persistent practice of collectivity, love, and worldmaking. It is a meeting ground between the lived experiences of and ideas generated (internally and externally) about Black girls. Two primary aims of the field include "a better understanding of how they [Black girls] survive and thwart systemic violence and persistent inequalities, and a celebration of their ingenious approaches to real and imagined social change."[35] Like Black Women's studies and Black feminist theory, Black Girlhood studies is a mattering project that emerges to consciously give name to experiences, ways of thinking and knowing otherwise tucked away from view or masked under more familiar guises; it is absolutely political. Penned in *Black Girlhood Celebration* as "Black Girls Studies" alongside Girls studies and one of its foundational works "Reviving Ophelia," Brown's articulation of (Black) girlhood is distinct in that it transcends traditional configurations of girl.[36] More than inserting a population qualifier (Black), she declares girlhood a political category and not contingent on age. Brown defines Black girlhood as "the representations, memories, and lived experiences of being and becoming in a body marked as youthful, Black, and female . . . [and] is not dependent, then, on age, physical maturity, or any essential category of identity."[37] From this framing, and discussed further in Chapter 1, Black girlhood is possible through being as, (re)membering, being with, practicing, and unbecoming. Celebration, Brown posits, is the extent to which recognition is endowed regardless of achievements, behavior, or social circumstances. Through this paradigm, spectacle is rejected.

Celebration is a paradigm of Black Girlhood studies and a principle that informs Black gurl reliable as it commands Black girls be seen whole. Black gurl reliable requires an ability to navigate complexity and paradox, along with the nerve to transgress manufactured boundaries that potentially produce dismemberment and people who move through the world in a fractured manner. Part of living fractured is where a person is not in intentional and aligned relationship with the self because they are disembodied while moving, literally and figuratively, through life, with firm barricades between dimensions of the self.

Black Girlhood studies is a response and call back to Abbey Lincoln's "Who Will Revere the Black Woman?" It is also a practice of "rever[ing] ing us," as Aisha Shahidah Simmons states, because beyond varying in age, Black girls are LGBTQIA* identifying, not always assigned the designation of female at birth, and do not all express any sexual or romantic interest.[38] Futuristic and trans/disciplinary, Black girlhood expands the landscape of girlhood as well as who Black girls are and can become. Here, the prefix *trans* follows the travel and formation of the Black figure through processes of colonialist projects and their ever-unfolding effects. Black Girlhood studies is a pliant field that abandons discipline allegiance to leave room for new questions and tools to surface. Attendant to a framing of Black girlhood as an intergenerational space, one that is not static, girlhood Blackened is a passage that travels *with* and with travel, changes. More, Black girl scholarship to date documents examples, outcomes, and reflections on partitioning—some self-initiated and some socially and culturally organized. In Chapter 1, I introduce the metaphor of "corridors" to configure and think about the field's roots, growth, and futures beyond disciplines of study. Increasing groundwork done by Black feminist thinkers who often draw on experiences and sensibilities developed in their youth, I propose that Black Girlhood studies be engaged as a maker's lab where perimeters that maintain distance and hierarchy are collapsed and girlhood is discussed, studied, practiced, and communicated as intergenerational.

Pedagogical Landscapes

In its broadest sense, pedagogy is a multilayered process of cooking, ingesting, digesting, and excreting lessons. In and beyond school-based classrooms, pedagogy informs what is learned, irrespective of the specific content engaged. Utilized to codify sets of principles, theoretical frameworks, varied approaches to school instruction, pedagogy, in some ways, becomes a catch-all phrase for teaching/learning dynamics. Often times, it is reduced to a distinct function and concern of formalized education, or something that happens solely in schools. And while pedagogy is practiced in school buildings, its presence both precedes and exceeds the traditional classroom. My thoughts on and gestures about pedagogy throughout this book derive from intense study of Black feminism, critical performative pedagogy, practicing Black girlhood, and deep (re)memory.

Pedagogy describes lesson dissemination, tools utilized to diffuse seeded teachings, and outgrowths of its circulation. To clarify the intent and potential reach of Black feminist pedagogy, Barbara Omolade writes, "Black feminist pedagogy aims to develop a mindset of intellectual inclusion and expansion that stands in contradiction to the Western intellectual tradition of exclusivity and chauvinism."[39] Within the context of cultivating an energy in the classroom that honors the knowledge of Black womn students, Omolade's work in Black feminist pedagogy speaks to its epistemic imperative. Pedagogy is about attitude nurturance; it cannot be reduced to visible content nor modes of instruction. Rather, pedagogy is both crevice and creation inside fissures. "Intellectual inclusion" as an outlook and aim of Black feminist pedagogy requires ontological and epistemological shifts, interrogation, and firming up "What is real?" and "How do I know what is real?"[40] Following this recalibration is reconsideration of what it means to know and how one does knowing.[41] Through an exploration of the tension and geographic imaginary between the spiritual and sacred, M. Jacqui Alexander frames pedagogy as "something given, as in handed, revealed; as in breaking through, transgressing, disrupting, displacing, inverting inherited concepts and practices, those psychic, analytic and organizational methodologies we deploy to know what we believe we know so as to make different conversations and solidarities possible."[42] Pedagogy, then, is symbiotic and without programmable effects.

Pedagogy regulates space—literal and figurative. In *A Bound Woman Is a Dangerous Thing*, poet DaMaris Hill presents a rework to the idea of being "bound" to emphasize willful commitment of Black womn to freedom and a quality of life that only individual Black womn can determine. Describing deliberations made to open the book with her grandma's photo, she shares, "These oppressions were rooted in false ideas of social superiority that could make one 'feel' imprisoned. Jane Crow types of oppression could also affect one's mental health, inciting mania or mental illness. Fracture a wise one's intellect."[43] In Hill's statement is a keen sense of the multimodal nature of oppression and the ways "different sites of confinement do not only resemble one another. Sometimes they share genealogies or morph from one type to another."[44] Further, Jane Crow oppressions encapsulate the idea that the state of being trapped entails processes that communicate to/through bodies future possibility and worth. "Stuckness" as a state of being where confinement surpasses physicality and enters the realm of mindset is a result of pedagogy. Proposing "engaged pedagogy" as a transgressive approach to learning, bell hooks in *Teaching to Transgress* problematizes status quo boundaries between teacher and student as well as classroom and community. From an insistence that education must not create stifled spirits, hooks acknowledges, "I celebrate teaching that enables transgressions—a movement against and beyond boundaries. It is that movement which makes education the practice of freedom."[45] Here, hooks writes about education as an always unfolding process and hallway toward freedom where students practice modes of being that enlarge possibilities for community, social change, and new ways of being in relation with power and people.

Unpacking "Terrible Educations"

To be taught self-abnegation, that Black is criminal, that Black girlhood is not possible, or that certain kinds of bodies are mere collateral damage for "more pressing ventures" are examples of what Toni Cade Bambara calls "terrible educations."[46] Since the business of pedagogy is about the *how* of a lesson, it is also about aesthetic quality. "Terrible education," therefore, is a pedagogical approach and outcome of pedagogy geared toward social reproduction and incapacitation in the self-determined sense. Without a reflection practice, including communal dialogue, these educations can go undetected and unaddressed.

Introduced in the essay "Education of a Storyteller," to offer lessons on "terrible educations," Bambara stages a conversation between her young self, li'l Toni, and a familial elder, Grandma Dorothy. Li'l Toni returns from school eager to share with Grandma Dorothy Einstein's theory of relativity. Open to participating in the lesson and grounded in a different pedagogical form than that taught in school, Grandma Dorothy urges li'l Toni to "do it, Honey, and give me a signal when it's my turn to join in the chorus" and "be sure to repeat the 'freedom part' two times."[47] Hands on hips, li'l Toni informs Grandma Dorothy of the seriousness of the lesson, asserting that what she learned is "not a song or singing tale" nor "a call and response deal but a theory."[48] Li'l Toni's choice of words register a hierarchical misperception between geographies of education and the nature of theory. Grandma Dorothy introduces practical ways for li'l Toni to communicate the lesson, things—like the cosmos—to which Toni could connect the theory. However, li'l Toni was unable to translate the theory using the other contexts Grandma suggested. More concerning is that she remained prideful about being the only one to possess this knowledge. Seemingly concerned about li'l Toni's developing epistemological frame, Grandma Dorothy insisted, "Madame, if your friends don't know it, then you don't know it, and if you don't know that, then you don't know nothing."[49]

Pertinent here are the ways pedagogy forged a moment of mediation. Grandma Dorothy's pedagogical bones showed up in the connections she made between li'l Toni offering a lesson and her embodiment saying, "Well get on with it and make it lively, 'cause I haven't tapped my foot or switched my hips all day."[50] Grandma Dorothy's excitement to participate in li'l Toni's demonstration of what she learned in school turned to a counter lesson about where knowledge lives, how it's communicated and disseminated, what knowledge has to do with culture, and where knowledge can be stored. The lesson acquired but not digested at that moment was a lesson in critical theory, that education happens everywhere and through varied and multiple pedagogies. Without Grandma Dorothy's intervention, terrible educations may have taken root in li'l Toni. Terrible education "is dangerous. It teaches us, trains us even, to act against our self-interest, against actualizing our gifts."[51] These educations teach us how to compartmentalize our being and quietly train us to see higher value in things outside of us. Grandma Dorothy continued, "Then too, the terrible educations you liable to get is designed to make you destruct the journey entire," suggesting that "terrible educations" occur within engineered landscapes and geographies that make their way inside of all layers of the body, the self.[52] Akin to Bambara's exposure to terrible educations, such processes are ubiquitous and therefore built into the same terrain traversed by Black girls and contribute to stuckness. Since pedagogies come in different forms and designs, Black girls navigate pedagogies imposed on them and craft pedagogies for surviving, even changing the world.

Theatrical Jazz Aesthetics

Theatrical jazz aesthetics materialized from the garden of Harlem's Sounds in Motion dance studio during the 1970s' Black Arts Movement. An '80s baby raised in the second biggest city in New York state after "the city," I was brought into the realm of this artistic practice birthed by revered creatives like Diane McIntyre, Ntozake Shange, and Laurie Carlos (to name a few) by divine intervention. As a form, theory, pedagogy, and method, theatrical jazz aesthetics is concerned with how to make art and life spirit-filled and useful to one's personal purpose and human posterity. In her reflection on the Austin Project (tAP) she founded to help artists birth new iterations of self, Omi Osun Joni L. Jones shares, "The jazz aesthetic as used in the Austin Project is a way to forestall the erosion of human connection by bringing to voice women of color and those white women who are able to learn the role of allies . . . and the use of safer geographic and psychic spaces all work to create the method of social reconstruction known as the jazz aesthetic."[53] Grounded ways of knowing that sprout from Black ancestral communing and an embrace of nonnormativity (or queerness), theatrical jazz aesthetics is a process of undoing and worldmaking. As applied theory for creating art that changes artists and those gifted to experience it, this form often lives underground, may operate without or under many names, and is always kept sacred. Audacious and respected practitioners and elders like Omi Osun Joni L. Jones have stepped outside of the craft domain to pen its theory, orientations, and aspirations into the skins of academia and futures to come.

In December 2010, I completed a dance course, "Theories of the Body," with professor and performance artist Cynthia Oliver. Unbeknownst to me, when she suggested I study it, after reading my final paper, she knew theatrical jazz aesthetics as a doer and practitioner of the form. During office hours, she heartily expressed connections between my work and the form. Nervous and intrigued, I believed her. When Black womn see me and offer guidance, I do my best to do something, if I can, with the information. She suggested I contact Sharon Bridgforth and Omi Osun Joni L. Jones, revered Black queer elders and practitioners of theatrical jazz aesthetics, and now people I've seen and experienced face-to-face, heart-to-heart. Already satiated and approaching stuffed, I leave with recordings she gave me of performances to watch and her advice that I apply to the Urban Bush Women Summer Leadership Institute. After that two-hour meeting, I took to studying and locating all I could to understand the form, as well as trying to understand what I channeled in my writing. It took me some time, but I watched the performances, applied, and began the Summer Leadership Institute (SLI) in summer 2011. And despite my fear of rejection, uncertain of what was to come, and doubt they'd respond to me, I contacted Dr. Jones and Sharon Bridgforth. Following my conversations with them, I returned to my final paper to be with the words, their layout on the page, and the overall energy of the piece. Unable to attend an in-person workshop around the form nor an art installation immediately, I created an organic course of my own to study and distill qualities and ingredients to envision their living outside of staged performance and script.[54]

Submission was the first quality I had to befriend. After she agreed to be on my dissertation committee, I shared some of my developing writing with Professor Oliver and, in kind, received some advice about full presence and writing from the edge. She responded: "I have just said a whole lot and I want you to know this is all offered in a spirit of generosity, not only critique. Your writing is powerful. I just want you to be rigorous in your uncovering of self and in the prescription for healing that you are summoning. If you are going to do it. You gotta DO IT. You can't retreat."[55] I respected her guidance and translated her wisdom into a set of agreements that became part of my regimen: be fully present, establish and maintain flow, and submit to unraveling. At every turn, I needed to choose to submit, to be actively present, and to locate and work within my rhythm or what we call in Nia technique "the body's way."[56] Though not yet willing to assume full responsibility of unlearning, unbecoming, and what these decisions might open up, I took my time and focused on just being in space physically or via phone with Omi Osun Joni L. Jones and Sharon Bridgforth, as well as deciphering for myself ingredients I saw and their applicability to my work in Black girlhood. First, the sensibility of the form is felt, recognized, and voiced by an elder or someone in intimate relationship with it. Though seeds of this form existed in me and in my writing, the recognition from my then professor is what called me to the study, the decision to adopt this "distinctive way to make work and life."[57] Secondly, theatrical jazz aesthetics is a rigorous counter-discipline sustained by revolutionary work at the level of the person from the inside out. I needed to be with myself intimately and honestly to generate my own lane and manifestation of the form. The particularities of my encounter with Professor Oliver are pivotal to my genealogical entry. Equally, it offers a glimpse into my intimacy with theatrical jazz aesthetics to trace the bridge I am mounting between the form housed primarily within written artistry and theatrical performance-specific spaces to its usability as a pedagogical tool toward facilitating (w)holistic resets that recalibrate the self, invigorate the body, and enrich spirit.

As pedagogy, theatrical jazz aesthetics offers lessons in *enthusiastic embodied vulnerability* toward a cultivation of cherished expansive queer spaces for artistic creation, practicing freedom, and self-fashioning. It is through my deep and individualized not siloed study of it, which meant using it in my everyday living, that I came to see and claim that enthusiastic embodied vulnerability is the deliberate reckoning with external and internal meanings assigned to one's body aimed at transgressing habitual movement, or repertoire (see Chapters 2 and 4) in the name of spiritual alignment and meaningful connection. Enthusiastic "embodied vulnerability" started in 2008 in resistance to the common perceptions and effects of white students reading my body in college classrooms. Seeking to curtail the weight of the white imaginary and help students understand bodies as sociocultural texts and their perspectives as political goggles, I began a set of experiments around this practice to make accountability in the classroom multidirectional. I developed the concept "embodied vulnerability" and expanded its enactment to other exercises like *undressing in public* (see Chapter 2).

As metaphor, theatrical jazz aesthetics is what watered the plant that is *Black Gurl Reliable*. As Jones describes it, "An aim of the jazz aesthetic is for the courageous choices of the artist to evolve into everyday habitual acts of freedom. . . . The transformations they experience in tAP inevitably make their way to the larger world as the women practice, at every turn, the power they have learned."[58] My particular entry into and the journey that followed foregrounded conditions where the evidence that theatrical jazz aesthetics and I know each other showed up first in my body and actions regarding how I presence my needs, yearnings, and pain. Since agreeing to be in relationship, I am better able to work in the erotic. Our initial meeting occurred in the academic arena. As I crafted a dissertation on Black girlhood, education, and embodiment, its resonance sparked immediate translation of its foundations into other activities and principles that enhanced my being with Black girls and midwifed my birth of *transgressngroove*.

Groove[ing] and Transgression

Groove[ing] and transgression are orientations and reorientations. To describe the process of orientation, Sarah Ahmed asserts, "To be orientated is also to be oriented toward certain objects, those that help us to find our way. These are the objects we recognize, such that when we face them, we know which way we are facing. They gather on the ground and also create a ground on which we can gather."[59] Orientations, as process and philosophy, aid people in getting their bearings; in nature, they also create a value system. To be oriented in this book is to be turned toward the body. Moreover, it is to devise measures that are context-specific. Adopting theatrical jazz aesthetics' commitment to artistic expression as a form of spiritual tilling, transgressngroove is a heuristic approach for retooling bodies. Drawing from Jones' particular theatrical jazz aesthetics presets of virtuosity, collaboration, and body-centeredness, transgressngroove is a process of (re)orientation to contend with what lives and festers in the archive of self and retool the body.[60]

As one of its orientations, groove[ing] joins theatrical jazz aesthetics precepts of listen, improvise, and be present to the work of embodiment and vulnerability.[61] Groove[ing] is a non-prescriptive sensing mechanism that emphasizes the what, who, and feel of a given moment. Raised on music by the group The System, my first awareness of the word was from their song "Don't Disturb this Groove." To *groove*, in the song and here, is to be present to the now and make decisions based on what arises in real time vibrationally, verbally, and movement-wise. One's next move is based on the actual conditions, feeling, and people present. *Groove[ing]* requires nonrational sensibility and is connected to the erotic.[62]

The second orientation is wrongness embraced. Growing out of Black feminist practices of resistance, like poetry, that explicitly or indirectly through their application dwell within a queer state of being, transgression denotes a break from dichotomies, juxtapositions, and acknowledges simultaneous operating realities that reject conformity and ideological convention. It is as an orientation that when operative crosses boundaries in the name of disrupting hierarchies and forging new terms of relation with self and others. Transgression actively undermines manufactured distances and differences. Some of these include "us" and "them," body and mind, girl and womn. As Sharon Bridgforth expressed during a phone conversation, "theatrical jazz aesthetic is about transgression. Transgression of gender, of space, and time," which means transgression is also about unlearning these concepts as we understand them in the normative sense.[63] Discussed in Chapter 1, transgression is queer in orientation. In theatrical jazz aesthetics, "queerness is knowing/living the permeability of reality markers.... Queerness is more about naming sites of possibility than naming a *particular* possibility."[64] Within theatrical jazz aesthetics and Black girlhood, queerness is productive transgression because it establishes terms of conditions rooted in lavishness and uproots norms that rationalize constriction. As guiding attitudes, groove[ing] and transgression pivot away from narrow understandings and toward expansive context-contingent action. As one approach to embodied retooling, transgressngroove is useful toward:

1. Unpacking experiences and stories living and/or festering in the body
2. Exploring limitations and narratives of self that misalign with (w)holistic embodiment
3. Activating bodies
4. Mediating the continuous and cumulative and residual effects of navigating carceral geographies
5. Establishing new meaning of experience
6. (Re)Orienting people to their archives and expanding their repertoire
7. Strengthening vulnerability muscles

Pedagogical Tools

Pedagogies in Black girlhood are liminal, organic performances, and processes that result in the unearthing, upending, and/or discontinuing of a lesson that potentially impales Black girls' spirits. Likewise, pedagogies that impart terrible educations are those that attempt to foreclose wholeness and self-determination or, à la Bambara, "destruct the journey entire."[65] To assist in my journey of excavating less legible pedagogies, I call on memory. Discussed at length by Black feminist thinkers and Black studies scholars, memory and (re)memory are key elements to liberation and connection across difference. Described earlier in "Education of a Storyteller," memory is something that gets lost when terrible educations are awry. Speaking explicitly about the significance of memory to Black womn, forgetting, then, is a symptom of continuous exposure to pedagogies of foreclosure as well as an outcome of terrible educations.[66] In her essay "The Site of Memory," Morrison proposes memory as a means of accessing interiority and unlocking halfknown, partial stories specifically of Blackness, Black culture, and consequently history.[67] Situated in the literary tradition, she considers the relationship between truth and fact as arbitrated by human knowledge and ways of knowing. In speaking about memory as pathway, both Morrison and McKittrick offer memory as place and possibility. To practice (re)memory is to access, as best as possible, those qualities, experiences, and knowledges disposed of and disappeared in previous ways of carving up and seeing the contours of a landscape. (Re)memory becomes a mode of Black healing, a suturing technology and a means of broadening and seeing truth and promise in Black bodies. (Re)memory was used throughout data collection processes and the writing of this book. Here, (re)memory is adopted to complicate what is known about Black girls' encounters with carceral spaces and modes of confinement as well as expand geographic terrain of Black liberation and worldmaking.

While pedagogies of foreclosure induce what Cynthia Dillard describes as the "seduction to forget," pedagogies of transgression are exercises that incite meditation, nurture embodied spirit, and support repair from the former pedagogies. Here, pedagogy denotes processes that produce dead ends (*foreclosure*) and gateways (*transgression*), accompanied by practices that enliven them (see undressing in public in Chapter 2 and body-activation in Chapter 4, as examples). In Black girlhood, pedagogies unveil and alter the teaching/learning of looking and carrying the weight and paradox of Black mattering; pedagogies provide one answer to the question, "In the midst of so much death and the fact of Black life as proximate to death, how do we attend to physical, social, and figurative death and also to the largeness that is Black life?"[68] Black gurl reliable is a pedagogy of transgression and a necessary addition to Black Girlhood studies because it disturbs relational tendencies rooted in hierarchies and justified ways of relating to bodies read as young and youthful, youthful and seasoned, Black and female not inherently cisgender, femme, or feminine.

Who Raised Me and How: A Note on Positionality

Being a Black girlhood scholar is a matter of subject, form, and positionality. Such a responsibility is "no trifling matter."[69] I chose my doctoral program for the opportunity to work explicitly alongside girls and to be guided by a scholar-artist creating spaces and bringing together people invested in working with Black girls under a set of precepts that defied conventional hierarchies and behavioral expectations. SOLHOT introduced me to the paradigm of celebration. Penned in *Black Girlhood Celebration* and rehearsed in this intergenerational praxis, celebration crosses lines of age, ethnicity, sexual orientation, gender, and citizenship status. Celebration entailed the difficult and nonnegotiable work of seeing girls because they are alive. It is through SOLHOT that the idea of reliability took root in me. Prior to graduate school and practicing homegirling in SOLHOT, my familiarity with Black girlhood lay steeped in mentoring and enrichment programs, at-risk discourse, and becoming an expert in knowing when not to look nor sound like y/our inner city with southern roots working-class garden from which I grew. My Black girl self and I weren't friends. Unknowingly but with some calculation, we shared space where our Black womn iteration became spokesperson. Hence, my internal yearning and agreement to study and practice Black girlhood through SOLHOT did not forestall the tension and growing pains I faced.

I entered Black Girlhood studies a Blackgurlwomn through the door of SOLHOT and as a co-conspirator of the feminist project. A multifaceted, multidimensional, global endeavor dedicated to the eradication of domination for the advancement of embodied living and pleasure, the feminist project is concerned with structures, politics, and norms that arrange people's lives and mediate our capacity to know and seek satisfaction. The feminist project attends to how power is configured, how and by whom it's wielded, the ways difference arranges and disrupts bodily value and meaning, the ingredients that fuel domination, and strategies for exercising (w)holeness. Enlarging that project, *Black Gurl Reliable* examines and shines a light on mechanisms of oppression distinctly endured and produced at the nexus of Blackness, youthfulness, and girlhood. It broadens Black feminist thinking to directly contend with and acknowledge theory birthed by Black girls and from the geography of Black girlhood. *Black Gurl Reliable* adds to the toolkit of the feminist project. It introduces language and theory derived from subjectivities and geographies often undermined, neglected, and/or illegible. Lastly, *Black Gurl Reliable* embraces and melts the longstanding tension in the field of Women's Gender and Sexuality studies around what Barbara Christian described as "the race for theory."[70]

While birthing the ideas within this book, the people and places I continue to know helped birth a new iteration of me. In the midst of penning the words here, I packed up and moved several times, co-organized a memorial for my godmother and honored her transcendence, took to the hair shop and got box braids for the first time ever with hot pink ombre blended throughout, took a rough fall that landed me on crutches for six weeks, closed in by grief, and aware of just how deep my love and need for dance goes, and much more. I share these instances to disclose the sentience that lives beneath my words and as Black girl citation of what do you know, how do you know it, and from whom and/or where do you know. At the inaugural Curriculum Inquiry Writing Fellowship in 2017, Eve Tuck gave a workshop titled "Citation Is Political." During this workshop, Tuck discussed citation practice as a political gesturing toward what mattered to us. She explains that citation is an academic tool for making a theory and/or concept matter.[71] This citational understanding apprises my decisions throughout related to language choice and enacting vulnerability with purpose. It is from the gift of practicing Black girlhood along with movements generated from knowing with girls, friends, homegirls, scholars, and creatives that I came to see part of my work to be about vulnerability. And it is with this knowledge that I take seriously Black gurl reliable, an academic-facing term to put it to use by enlivening my body to awake the (w)hole house up so "little Dominique" guides my research on contemporary Black girlhood with a focus on embodiment.

Experiments in Black Feminist Auto/Ethnography, Performance

A study of self in culture, auto/ethnography is invested in illuminating larger phenomena through the scale of the individual; it is never solely about one individual. Related to Black sensibilities like those imparted by Grandma Dorothy to li'l Toni, I am responsible for how I show up to, with, as, and for Black girls. Minimally, this book provides two levels of insights. The first comes out of examining embodiment in relation to dimensions of confinement experienced in Black girlhood, and the second is actively unwinding through my writing and connected to self-unearthing personally and as related to the persistence necessary to do reliability work. As Bridgforth shared in an interview about *dyke/warrior-prayers*, "You can't let what wants to happen happen if you haven't tended to what scares you. . . . There is a kind of release when you do the inner work, the more and more we do it the more we get released, so we can tend, allow, grow, shift, heal, change, offer."[72] Time and determination made it possible that I no longer extract elements of my being in the off chance of appearing more palatable in academia. With this transformation also came an awareness of my particularities as a humanistic social scientist who first learned to speak in dance and then poetry. The best description of a dilemma turned respected complexity is offered by Eve L. Ewing, who wrote, "Where the social scientist uses empirics to gather a descriptive understanding of the social world, and uses theory to render these observations into more broadly applicable, abstract connecting threads among social phenomena, the poet uses imagination to extend the social world from the realm of the observable into the world of the possible."[73] To stage a conversation about Black girls and girlhood that does not oversimplify Blackness, girlness, and bodily experience necessitates imagination, an embrace of the enigmatic, flexibility, and acceptance that accuracy is relative and relational. This book therefore is, and is a product of, experimentation. Experiments refer to persistent and ritualistic rehearsals and reflections related to, in this case, Black gurl reliable.

Auto/ethnography preserves what is seen and becomes known, is informed by bodily experience and interpretation filtered through ideological underpinnings, logics, and culture. Stories, fictive or otherwise, exercise power in determining how culture, social norms, and ailments are acted out upon the body. Often regarded as consequences of body politics in Women's Gender and Sexuality studies, auto/ethnography prioritizes encrusted narration that invokes feeling, incites introspection, and reveals intricacy. Moreover, in auto/ethnography the body is appointed an official interpreter of what is witnessed and draws upon a variety of data. Black feminist auto/ethnography is a means of rewriting history and writing futures that challenge power relations. A form taken up in fields like anthropology, sociology, and even the arts, it is a critique of the god trick or the idea that seeing everything from nowhere is possible.[74] Irma McClaurin explains: "While categories and rhetoric have shifted, power relations in everyday life remain enmeshed in identity politics as constituted within a modernist and essentialist cultural worldview. . . . Identity remains a contested and negotiated arena in which we struggle to fashion transformative strategies. . . . I nonetheless propose that autoethnography is a viable form through which Black feminist anthropologists may theorize and textualize our situated positions and elevate our subjugated discourses."[75]

Black feminist auto/ethnography upholds that power is manipulated by theories of knowledge and ideological hierarchies, and maintains a commitment to bringing forth stories and insights otherwise untouched, overlooked, and inaccessible. As Aisha Durham states, auto/ethnography is "a spiritual act of political self-determination, of reclamation."[76] This methodological approach of interpreting and representing culture supports cultivation of self, alongside living with and amid others; it is a means of treasuring one's living and position in research and relation. Spirit, as described by Rev Angel, is "concerned with the essence of what gives life meaning, what makes it worth living."[77] Black feminist auto/ethnography is a spiritual act because it subverts social de/meaning attributed to Black living.

Relatedly, Performance studies is concerned with the "ongoing redefinition of cultural, social, and educational practices."[78] A call to redefine and imagine through formalized curiosity à la Zora Neale Hurston, the field of Performance studies keeps one curious about quotidian happenings as well as the crafting of staged representations of experience. As event, theory, and method, performance acknowledges the rub between convention/innovation and physical/intellectual. More, "performance is an intimate space to speak Blackness into its own existence, a space to imagine and practice freedom."[79] Performance is a critical modality to marking and maintaining embodiment because as theory and method it compels invention and (w)holistic narration. Jones describes performance ethnography as "how culture is done in the body."[80] Since culture is made by and mapped onto the body, performance ethnography is documentation of the sense made by cultural processes and how these productions are made visible to others.

When coupled with auto/ethnography, performance facilitates a process of examining realities seemingly commonplace that require and archive themselves in the body. Auto/ethnography orchestrated by Black feminists connotes a legacy of politics—of representation and self-definition—guided by ancestral and spiritual connections.[81] An examination of lived experiences usually within multiple and sometimes competing cultures, auto/ethnography is a methodological opportunity to observe self in culture and "intentionally makes room for exploring dialectics between bodies, cultures, histories, and the self."[82] Performance auto/ethnography is concerned with how politics of identity and location, as well as social milieus such as racism, sexism, and heteropatriarchy, inform how one performs, subverts, and devises the self. As performance never ends and continues to live, changes form, and takes flight in spaces different from its origin, the creative writing throughout this book is a performance—a cumulative set of enactments that animate possibilities for living otherwise. *Black Gurl Reliable* sutures textual and non-textual data, including interviews, creative workshops, original archival research, literary analysis, and media, as well as a personal archive.

Embodiment is integral to performance-informed research; it references the experiential and conveys understanding in and through the body. Connecting and locating the body as integral to the research process facilitates the creation of embodied knowledge: "Embodied knowledge is knowledge that is gained by paying close somatic attention to how and what our body feels when interacting with others in contexts. The knowledge is articulated through a performative-I disposition where the researcher critically reflects upon what and where the body *knows*."[83] Throughout data collection and while writing this book I performed somatic workouts. Within various chapters somatic inquiries appear in a variety of forms. They appear as part of experiences with girls, mediative decisions made and written about as reflections, and they appear in creative texts (see Chapters 3 and 5). Neglecting the work done on the body by anti-Black and carceral logics leaves a partial visual of justice work, devalues the body's instrumentation to liberation and self-determination, and disappears what Black girlhood and Black gurl embodiment are already doing in service to creating expansive futures. To provide access into my general methodological movement, I offer an original poem, "rupture." Beyond serving as a summary of data collection processes, "rupture" implicitly communicates how my work is informed by and seeks to extend principles of theatrical jazz aesthetics to the effort of growing repertoires of embodiment.

rupture

Step inside/
paperspoems,
memoriesmusings,
lovesnlosses,
they guide/
look about,
release/
Dance the meaning of/
listen to the quiet
In it,
find your rhythm/
spirit, some call it,
jazz, some named it,
a calling, some felt/

'Til you can hear it
recognize it, Sway
sway anyway
Get inside of,
Dance your way into,
archive/
Let
papersnpoems,
memories
lovesnlosses,
out,
(re)memory yourself
back together/
see them,
help them,
feelseeknow,
seefeelmove/
allow,
invite them in,
to show,
to see,
to listen to,
archive/
direction lives there,
deep inside/
dig for it,
feel it,
ooze out/
breathe.
Step out,
breathe.
look, show, feel, write/
Step in,
breathe.
feel, move, sort, discard/
Step out,

breathe.
sweep up,
shake out,
shimmy,
in to
    touch.

Crossings can resemble war, for instance, and Black gurl embodiment is made through a series of crossroads. Actualizing aims of the feminist project requires removal of dominance and a wielding of power that shores up Black girls as well as a shared quality of life. In the spirit of experiments, this book introduces pedagogical practices or exercises that open up new ways of seeing and being with Black girls, while sharing my journey to unearthing them. To stage a continual grappling with layers of embodiment and the effective uses of transgression in maintaining one's in bodyness and (w)holistic connection to self, *Black Gurl Reliable* includes *transgressn texts*. An element of transgressngroove, transgressn texts are creative productions that fuse data (what happened), analysis (how it got archived), and the possibility that emerges (retooling) of an experience. To create a new present that feels different than what currently is observed as reality, creativity is of necessity. Transgressn texts materialize in a variety of mediums including but not limited to performance scenes, a dance, even a revised course syllabus. Importantly they, like the experience used as their raw data, are context-specific and context-driven. As intuitively generated texts, transgressn texts derive from being *with* and deep listening. They push on and highlight a boundary crossed or imagine into existence a transgression. Transgressn texts are indicators of transgression that in *Black Gurl Reliable* take the form of recipes for retooling, archival documents (re)membering, and worldmaking incantations.

Embodiment is multilayered and speaks to being inside and in relationship with the body. As a verb, it's about taking on the act of expressing, taking on or even performing the look and feel of something. When a state of being, it refers to one's quality of connection to layers of self—intellectual, physical, emotional. It's also an ethos, an essence that speaks to spiritual spaciousness. As essence, embodiment describes spiritual spaciousness. In other words, girls can be in body, alive and disembodied, distant from or maintaining a fragmented self. Similarly, disembodiment is a state of being that arises out of a lack of connection between dimensions of self. Thereby accumulated effects of disembodying experiences can induce stuckness. As a web of curricular and cultural processes that work to align bodies and social structures generally, pedagogies of foreclosure are avenues and proceedings that underwrite confinement. In direct tension with these are pedagogies of transgression or actions, habits of being, and practices that energize and endorse embodment.

Overview of Chapters

Riffing off Gloria Ladner's *Tomorrow's Tomorrow*, Chapter 1, "Sing a Black Girl's Song" provides a tracing of Black Girlhood studies. Organized around the overlapping temporalities of yesterday, today, and tomorrow, it outlines a Black feminist theory of wrongness that orders Black girls' living and embodiment and, I argue, undergirds an impulse to transgress wrongness. The section "Today" discusses the current landscape of the field and its structuring around larger disciplines and presents the metaphor of "corridors" to breach academic conventions of research. The third and final section of the chapter calls for an intentional politics of Black Girlhood studies. Here I propose a set of starting principles and commitments to root interdisciplinary debates, conversations, and lexicon while honoring the multifariousness of Black girlhood.

Chapter 2, "Reverse Osmosis to Awaken Flesh," explores textures of confinement before and after juvenile detention and introduces undressing in public as a practice post forgetting. A personal account of navigating the juvenile legal system, it utilizes court documents, discussions with family, and (re)memory as methods to explore built-in technologies that encourage self-silencing and surveillance. I argue that forgetting is a plausible response but temporary solution to living after a disembodying experience and propose undressing in public as a practice for releasing an event and its debris from the body's archive.

As a case example of present-day Jane Crow oppressions relevant to the corridor "mapping carceral geographies" outlined in

Chapter 1, Chapter 3, "My Hair, My Mirror, My Own," examines formally sanctioned and commonly practiced hair policies experienced by Black girls in schools. Drawing on news coverage and two original interviews with activist and model Vanessa Van Dyke about her survival of bullying and anti-Black antagonism, I present sartorial literacies as a specific form of Black resistance facilitated by Black girls in response to state violence.

Chapter 4, "Willful Touch," presents the practice of body-activation as a resource for retooling the body. Revisiting an arts-based workshop implemented in 2012 through the frame of Black gurl reliable, it presents a curated process of entering the body's archive and exhuming experiences and their lingering emotions. Through the original somatic exercise "feels like," I depict interconnections among one's repertoire, embodiment, and the bodily archive while advancing the practice of body-activation as an erotic pathway and means of foster spirit. The chapter shows how bodies and somatic work offer ways of retooling girls' archives. It extends a discussion of repertoire as related to accessing spirit.

An application of the corridor "practicing Black girlhood," Chapter 5, "Teaching Black Girlhood," reveals accentuating voice and voice as key component in the practice of Black gurl reliable in the college classroom context. Using data collected in 2017 during my first time teaching Black girlhood in a college setting, this chapter offers focused analysis of students' submissions of two assignments: "Assumptions" and "Black Girlhood Statement." As course bookends, they elucidate the productive tension in Black Girlhood studies between external gaze and internal definition. A class comprising Black, queer, Latinx, multiracial, and gender-nonconforming individuals from five different schools through the Five College Consortium in Massachusetts, this chapter details the complexities and necessity of teaching Black girlhood through a diasporic perspective and ethos of celebration.

To end this experiment, the Conclusion, "Gifts of Being with Black Girlhood," pays homage to Black girlhood, Black girls, and related geographies of magnitude. Honoring the Black epistolary tradition, I present four letters that reveal interior moments, key interactions, and necessary ruptures that informed the research, writing, and lessons that appear in this book. As a form of reliability work, these letters reflect on what I've learned (to date) from ridin' with Black girlhood and discloses challenges embraced, as well as unlearning done to inhabit with care the location youthful and seasoned Blackgurlwomn.

Black Gurl Reliable is a transdisciplinary performance about Black girlhood, embodiment, and liberation. As a pledge and practice of Black gurl reliable, it is organized around the idea of experimentation and praxis. Invested in contributing to the contour and futures of Black Girlhood studies, it advances terminology and proposes a set of politics for the field. *Black Gurl Reliable* sews together the fields of Women's Gender and Sexuality studies, Education, and Black studies to craft a widening repertoire around justice work, pedagogy, and Black worldmaking. Broadly, its conversational kin reside within the flourishing field of Black Girlhood studies in these United States, as well as works grappling with contours of confinement, bodily autonomy, and intergenerational work. Grounded in a Blackgurlwomn sensibility, *Black Gurl Reliable* actualizes and introduces concepts and experiments that pivot away from the question "What's 'wrong' with Black girls?" and toward energizing Black Girlhood studies and the practice of Black girlhood as fertile ground for stimulating intimacies across continued boundaries related to bodily difference, authority, and carceral logics. Each chapter features a site that, though architecturally different, unveils modes of confinement beside the effects of their bodily absorption. In *Pedagogies of Crossing*, Alexander urged that the breadth of a pedagogy is in relationship to a teacher's expansion.[84] Building on Alexander, the scope of pedagogy named, detailed, and practiced will reflect varied teachers and the extent to which I show them naked, newly arranged, and textured. The chapters that follow narrate textures of confinement in Black girlhood, disembodying experiences, and introduce pedagogies as well as practices that cultivate deeper connection with and/or a retooling of the body. What lies here is what emerged since saying yes to self-excavation and embracing the tall order of living out the ethic of Black gurl reliable, to wholeheartedly, even if out of key, sing a Black girl's song.

CHAPTER 1

"Sing a Black Girl's Song"
A Code for Black Girlhood Studies

According to the Collins English Dictionary, policy is a "set of ideas or plans that is used as a basis for making decisions, especially in politics, economics, or business."[1] Fittingly, policy is the set of end terms established and the ones used to generate them. To sing a Black girl's song "necessitates a keen ear and a will to be disrespectful to policies that negate their humanity, dignity, and sense of self."[2] Black Girlhood studies is policy and potential site for deciding on what terms Black girls and girlhood are to be engaged as well as what tools best enliven complex living and narration. Black Girlhood studies is rigorous action toward interrogating and interrupting boundaries that forestall (w)hole living, intergenerational worldmaking, and collective fashioning; it is a geographic imaginary where policy is (re)oriented toward celebration.

Ntozake Shange's *For Colored Girls Who Have Considered Suicide / When the Rainbow Is Enuf* is a choreopoem and artistic rendering of Black girlhood that removes sharp beginnings and endings to sets of stories that are simultaneously singular and collective. As a series of poems that draw on music and movement to tell a polyphonic, polyrhythmic story, the choreopoem is a production of theatrical jazz aesthetics. In content, it is a lesson in multiplicity. Equally, it is a guide for portraying Black girlhood in ways that grapple with the material backdrop of Black girl living. Some of the muddy waters of girlhood that Shange addresses are generational tensions, lines between girl and womn, racial-sexual violence and violations, and how living happens anyway. *For Colored Girls* makes clear the interrelation of language, active assumptions, gaze, architecture, and action. The opening poem, "Dark Phrases," details contradictions and trials of being in a body assumed Black and female though not inherently cisgender, femme, or feminine. As a provocation and directive, "sing a Black girl's song" is a call to celebration and recognition before the formal inception of Black Girlhood studies. Imagined at the tail of the Black Arts Movement, Shange envisions a world on stage that centers girlhood and womnhood, bodies marked as Black and female, and told stories that absolutely aired dirty laundry. Shange deemed it fit to establish in the theater world broadly and Black art culture specifically a different set of assumptions. Agreeing with the need for a new set of assumptions about home life between Black men and womn, in particular, Nikki Giovanni, in conversation with James Baldwin, insists, "As long as the assumptions are the same, nothing will change. So we must corner ourselves to make a new assumption."[3] Giovanni's avowal reminds us that rules undergird our actions and inaction and that it is on these premises that life is built, and decisions are made.

I take my cue from Black feminist thinkers of the twentieth century who recognized naming Black Women's studies as a necessity with those who crafted and/or continue to devise art that presents Black aliveness and to counter mass media representations of Black dejection, death, and/or chasing whiteness. In her book-length poem *Who Look at Me*, June Jordan curates a conversation about Blackness, gaze, and reading bodies. Combining image and poetry, this children's book investigated social as well as cultural realities of Blackness while affirming Black life. With no picture to accompany the words, a rarity in the book's structure, the statement, "I am black alive and looking back at you," appears.[4] Black aliveness is an ability to look at, look for, see, or read the world, and choose when and how and if to be seen. Taking a page from *Who Look at Me*, Black Girlhood studies is more than an area of study that looks at Black girls; it is a Black spatial imaginary that crosses borders of region, country, ethnicity, conventions of gender and sexuality. Black Girlhood studies is fertile ground on which to play and practice otherwise ways of living that make possible quality of life and embodiment for all Black girls. This chapter presents one version of the yesterday, today, and tomorrow of Black Girlhood studies. Thinking with Gloria Ladner, specifically her ethnography on Black girlhood, *Tomorrow's Tomorrow*, I present the idea of wrongness as a state and status that organizes constructions of Black femininity irrespective of sexuality, gender expression, and identity. To begin, I distill Black feminist writings and theorization to discuss transgression or wrongness embraced. From there, I discuss the field's current configuration and introduce "corridors" as a metaphor and active transgression useful toward making Black Girlhood studies a politic. Corridors turns attention from fields of study to what the work being done makes possible. To start developing a politics of Black Girlhood studies, I submit three initial (re)orientations that ensure the field *does* things of use for girls living, girls' communities, girls to come, and girls not yet.

Yesterday

To be conferred wrong or wrong-adjacent is a weighty and conceivably freeing condition. The challenge, if accepted, is to hold the material realities of the status with its imagined and unknown consequences while working from a place of knowing otherwise. A long legacy of Black feminism provides contestation to how certain bodies are made "wrong" and forced to endure the rolling ramifications of the designation. As an appraisal, *wrong* describes absence of proper behavior, placement, or value.[5] This particular judgment happens at all levels of society and the human experience. US chattel slavery is one geography of confinement where Black bodies and those read as Black and female are configured in this way. Represented in Sojourner Truth's statement, "I have plowed and reaped and husked and chopped and mowed and can any man do more than that? I have heard much about the sexes being equal; I can carry as much as any man" are conditions and duties specific to individuals designated Black and female in the nineteenth-century United States.[6] Truth's statement reveals the rubric for determining Black girls and womn are wrong—their strength, engagement in "male" responsibilities, and Black skin. These signs of inferiority justify one's wrongness. With a focus on Blackness as a social and psychological experience, Du

Bois, decades later, calls attention to the "color line," a barrier Black feminist thinkers trouble within a network of other systems of power that predetermine what constitutes a womn.[7]

Paying close attention to *what* happens at the nexus of race, gender, class, sexuality, and body politics, Black and womn of color feminists continue to leverage critiques that describe and seek to find ways to improve psychic and physical currents of living with and despite the rank of wrong. These concepts, theories, and applications disturb boundaries between school/community, artistic/academic. Here, however, I focus on literary and cultural work. Wedged between standards of Blackness and "feminine," Black girls and womn are citizens of the other side of sovereignty and humanity. Inner knowing and external projection of Blackness articulated by Du Bois and Truth transpire in twentieth-century works of creatives like June Jordan and Pat Parker through the concepts wrong and bad, as theorized and contested states of Blackness.[8] In "Poem about My Rights," wrong is conceptualized as relational, based on identity markers, cultural norms, ideologies, and institutions that reinforce them. Written in 1980 as a poetic analysis of imperialism and racial capitalism, Jordan wrote:

I have been raped
be-
cause I have been wrong the wrong sex the wrong age
the wrong skin the wrong nose the wrong hair.[9]

Amid a discussion of gender violence and violation, Jordan theorizes how Blackness, across geographies, is appraised as wrong. Further, she documents how the decision to assign Blackness no place and therefore possessable becomes rationale for displacement and even death. For Jordan, these instances display how being named wrong excludes and/or installs a high tax for full humanity, self-expression, and bodily autonomy while endorsing possession in the form of imperialism, gentrification, gendered racial violence, and other forms of domination.

Almost a decade later, Jordan resumes the conversation of wrongness in the essay "Wrong or White." A reflection on the ingredients of war, Jordan contends that "El Salvador, South Africa, Israel—these were categorically different situations of wrong and white. Your nation, your family, your face was neither European nor of European descent. You were wrong."[10] This time, Jordan places attention on the production of whiteness and wrong through white supremacist heteropatriarchy. Her commentary on 1980s imperialism and the shortcomings of democracy provides a metric to wrong seen in Ruthie Gilmore's definition of racism as "the state-sanctioned or extralegal production and exploitation of group-differentiated vulnerability to premature death."[11]

When a person is deemed wrong, they become culpable for their own experiences, including what happens to them. Worse, sometimes things like genocide and bullying never in fact occurred because to be marked wrong is to be declared suspect, unbelievable, and responsible for others' inappropriate and usually heinous behavior. In effect, adultification is one youth-specific exercise of this analytic. During an interview and collective discussion of "Mama's Baby, Papa's Maybe," Spillers described her motivations for writing the essay as a response to the question, "What is it like in the interstitial spaces where you fall between everyone who has a name, a category, a sponsor, an agenda, spokespersons, people looking out for them—but you don't have anybody?"[12] Problems Black girls and womn navigate historically and present day stem from what is seen when people look at us and the ingredients of their gaze. These living legacies convert into how things like protection, bodily autonomy, treatment, and ability to make mistakes are structured by others' seeing of us. Said differently, Jordan contends:

> and whether it's about walking out at night
> or whether it's about the love that I feel
> or whether it's about the sanctity of my vagina
> or the sanctity of my national boundaries.[13]

An antecedent to carceral state studies, a project concerned with "how carceral logic and carceral control expand beyond the prison and . . . [are] in fact the social fabric of the United States," Jordan's theorization of wrongness maps confinement at the site of the body into carceral terrain.[14]

Noting harmful effects of internalizing the idea of being wrong, Audre Lorde's poem "Good Mirrors Are Not Cheap" overviews bad mirrors and their implications. She writes, "and the fault in a mirror slaps back /

becoming / what you think is the shape of your error."[15] Expressed in the title of her poem and documented in Chapter 3 of this book, mirrors are a modality and measure of perspective. So, if "down the street a glassmaker is grinning turning out new mirrors that lie," anything seen through them is skewed.[16] Lorde's imagery reveals the dominance of the botched mirror—because it is built with distortions, it disfigures truths. Lorde's visuality connects to pedagogies of foreclosure and the production of Black as wrong. These pedagogies reinforce systemic and ideological notions distributed through mass production of "cut rate" mirrors that maintain status quo hierarchies of regulation.

An introduction to identity politics and the ways social identities place certain people in closer vicinity to confinement, the Combahee River Collective asserted, "Our politics initially sprang from the shared belief that Black women are inherently valuable, that our liberation is a necessity not as an adjunct to somebody else's but because of our need as human persons for autonomy."[17] Extending labor by feminist conduits like Sojourner Truth, Harriet Tubman, and Maria Stewart, alongside organizations like the National Black Feminist Organization, the collective insisted that Black womn's liberation was intimately tied to racial and sexual discourses. Combahee asserted race, gender, sexuality, and class as interlocked systems that subjugate Black womn. From this assertion they theorized the body as a carceral geography, resulting in people's embodiment being tied to systems of power and the social identities they regulate. Embedded within their manifesto is the assertion that categories of difference are inextricably linked to each other and to systems that create more restrictions for people inhabiting nondominant orientations. For example, for Black people in the United States, Black captivity during chattel slavery is a legacy that persists in its many afterlives and codes bodies read as Black and female wrong for our "not quiteness." McKittrick noted, "The 'not-quite' spaces of black femininity are unacknowledged spaces of sexual violence, violence, stereotype, and sociospatial marginalization; erased, erasable, hidden, resistant geographies and women that are, due to persistent and public forms of objectification, not readily decipherable."[18] McKittrick describes how, for bodies regarded as Black and female though not inherently cisgender, femme, or feminine, carceral logics corroborate society's alibi when people are made into sites of confinement, when stuckness ensues and murder (literal and otherwise) occurs.

In 1966, Civil Rights activist and artist Abbey Lincoln asked, "Who will revere the black woman?" She catalogued discourses that legitimize Black womn's dispossession and dehumanization and situated them as productions of larger ideologies and happenings such as patriarchy, whiteness as rule, and Black men's frustrations. Lincoln connects these ideologies to the treatment and debasement of Black girls and womn stating, "hence, the black mother, housewife, and all-round girl Thursday is called upon to suffer both physically and emotionally every humiliation a woman can suffer and still function."[19] As a popularized figure and everyday human, the Black womn is denied respect, protection, and care, whereas the violence Black womn endure is justified by biology, racialized gender, and racist, sexist logic. Paying close attention to the ways race and gender conjoin, Lincoln's outcry is explication of what Moya Bailey names as *misogynoir*.[20] This analytic brings into plain view the ways androcentrism, misogyny, and anti-Black racism coalesce to order the lives and media depictions of individuals who identify and/or are attributed as femmes, Black and female, Black womn and girls. Furthermore, misogynoir exposes schemes used to project blame and defer responsibility. Through varied modes, including but not limited to vernacular, body, and tone policing, behavioral and dress code policies, and disparate expectations, Black womn and girls are assumed elicit initiates not lured targets.

Wrong becomes an appraisal tag and geography. Those of us assigned this designation are relegated marginal, outside the norm, and subsequently subject to mistreatment. Synchronously, this classification is an indefinite capricious occupation, a place of queering and queer possibility. In "Punks, Bulldaggers, Welfare Queens," Cathy Cohen extends the theorization and labor of Black feminism to argue for a conceptualization of queer that holds the ability to "create a space in opposition to dominant norms, a space where transformational political work can begin."[21] She uses "punks," "bulldaggers," and "welfare queens" to introduce the notion of queered subjects. As examples of conferring wrongness and its material consequences, Cohen argues for a queer politic that centers queered subjects. Paralleling Cohen, Durell Callier wrote in his research on anti-Black and anti-queer antagonisms, "As a project queer theory seeks to unsettle various forms of normativity, thus, its utility is to consider how to unsettle logics, which normalizes the degradation of racialized subjects, gender-nonconforming youth, and those outside of heteronormativity."[22] Queer, within the genealogy of Black feminist theory, is anti-racist and imbued with perspective to upend static and homogenous Blackness and bodies. These framings of queerness identify the imperative of rupturing logics at play in the lives of Black folk as well as in framing Black bodies.

Transgression as Politic

I carry on Black feminism, Black performance, and critical feminist pedagogies to rebel against normative aims of education, social structuring, and order. These disruptions honor detailed critiques of wrongness and underline how Black living and living in general is done still and anyway. As a mode of past-presence, transgression is a yesterday's seed that I carry with me today and wish to bring into the future.[23] My introduction to transgression happened in an undergraduate classroom through bell hooks's *Teaching to Transgress*. In it she writes about love as a non-negotiable element in education and argues that love fosters care within academia to incite critical thinking, connection, and communal learning accountability. With direction from hooks, Troutman and Jimenez introduce Black feminism into high school and teacher-education curricula as a transgressive act.[24] Reflecting on how Black feminist consciousness as a teaching tool enlivened awareness in their students, Troutman and Jimenez deploy transgression as a framework for how they taught and as a vision for their students. Present in both the conceptualization and application of teaching to transgress is the element of love.

In her introduction to *love conjure/blues*, Omi Osun Joni L. Jones presents love and gender expansiveness as mechanisms for transgression.[25] Speaking specifically about the people within this performance novel, Jones charts the ways gender is conceptualized as energy, as something expressed and inhabited but beyond our biology and sartorial choices, "because to achieve gender freedom is to chase desire and transgress convention, if necessary, in doing so."[26] Evident here is that self-determination may or may not resemble notions of gender popularized and commonly used. Further, being on one's own terms is central to determining transgressive acts. Jones described love as "a new world order," and introduces transgression as a mode for social transformation and love as a paradigmatic shift: "Love connects us with the deepest mysteries of the universe, and accessing that love is a spiritual path, a covenant with ancestors, the divine and an unknown tomorrow. Such a love is indeed a transgression, because it flies in the face of the social order that asks us to diminish ourselves, to keep boundaries, to be dreamless for the sake of familiarity and predictability."[27] Through defiance of social agreements around borders of intimacy, gender, spirit, and history, people in *love conjure/blues* clarify themselves and practice worldmaking. In the case of love as transgression, it is a noun and verb, being and doing, existence and production. This love, specifically within this novel, embraces gender fluidity and is molded outside of the "natural" order of social relationships and structures, in "liminal spaces, those betwixt and between locations where our bounded selves can give ways to something new, where the present has primacy over the future."[28] Love in *love conjure/blues* is a means of materializing selves beyond the gender binary, beyond the world's definition of Black people; it is a medium for self-definition.

Transgression, articulated in the preceding examples, engenders (re)orientation. Specifically, it reconfigures students, gender, and people to the world in particular ways. Within these texts transgression is constituted as political, ideological, action-centered, subversive, and potentially recalibrating. Transgression entails deliberate, embodied choices, conscious and unconscious, to cross a known boundary while engrossed in its prospective benefits, irrespective of unrealized consequences. To be labeled wrong is a contextual and layered process. Living while assumed wrong is an arduous and innovation-filled journey. As theory, pedagogy, and orientation, transgression is policy for resistance and being. Black girlhood inherits this work and the aforementioned wisdom of dissent around wrongness.

Yesterday, Black womn and girls rejected the label wrong through bodily dissent, art, and everyday living. Yesterday, or before the institutionalization of Black Girlhood studies into academia, Black womn scholars and creatives alike snubbed conventions within their respective areas to bring Black girls into view. In addition to the work produced by Shange, artists like J. E. Franklin wrote plays while Alice Walker, Paule Marshall, and Toni Morrison, to name a few, created literary works that placed Black girlhood front-and-center. Joyce Ladner's *Tomorrow's Tomorrow* examines the survival savvy and coping strategies generated and enacted by Black girl adolescents.[29] As a counterdiscourse sociological project, Ladner listens to and situates these girls as knowledge creators and strategists. She interrogates replicated tropes of Blackness and Black femininity and how adolescents navigated structural and cultural presets, as well as how they made sense of these realities in relation to their future lives. Around the same time, in 1976, Sara Lawrence Lightfoot put out a call for educational research to include Black girls with a focus on sociocultural realities organizing life in and beyond schools.[30] And although scholars like Rebecca Caroll, Signithia Fordham, Venus Evans Winters, Kyra Gaunt, and Linda Grant started to answer this call in the 1990s and early 2000s, it would not be until 2008 that statistical research on educational achievement accounted for race and gender simultaneously.[31] It was not until around 2010 that a concentrated surge of scholarship on Black girls emerged, largely related to education. Frequently studies, though examining Black girls' educational experiences, spotlight comparisons between them and Black boys or white girls.[32] Despite the use of varying frameworks to demystify the particularities of Black girls' educational experiences, there is room for additional framing to be taken up in Black Girlhood studies. I propose wrongness embraced as an orientation able to make legible and hold paradoxical experiences and insurgent knowledges otherwise undermined, disappeared, flattened, and misrepresented when Black girl specificity was clumped to benefit racial and gender-based concerns. Yesterday contains seeds of today's harvest.

Today

Black Girlhood studies is one answer to the call "Who will revere Black girls?" and makes visible creative, intellectual, and cultural productions of girls denied girlhood. Since Black girlhood's existence is sometimes questioned or reduced to stolen goods, Black Girlhood studies serves as a hub for illuminating and expanding innovation and knowledge crafted amid legacies of anti-Blackness and racialized gender. While documenting systemic and cultural realities that contour Black girlhood, the field examines and re-envisions what it means to be and become, be assumed to be, unbecome, and do Black girl in the many lives and afterlives of slavery, imperialism, settler colonialism, racial capitalism, and global anti-Blackness. Lightfoot's 1976 call within academia and Shange's demand from stage in the twentieth century are heard around the world as reverberating echoes and responses appear in the form of initiatives like Black Girls Rock, Black Girls Run, Black Girl Trek, and Black Girl Magic, to name a few. Parallel to these social projects, that importantly are not about girl as an age-specific experience alone, is the proliferation of scholarship with Black girls as the subject of focus.

Increased intentional documentation of Black girls' lived experiences has occurred in the last fifteen years. This proliferation takes the form of special issues, literacy networks, conferences, monographs, and anthologies, and in the creation of the *Journal of African American Women and Girls in Education*.[33] The uptick in Black girl airtime necessarily makes way for expansion. There is multidisciplinary and transnational documentation of experiences and theories generated from engaging Black girls through various modes in a range of cultural and educational contexts and pretenses. The *Black Girlhood Studies Collection*, for example, explicitly names the need to venerate the varying *hoods* in Black Girlhood studies and offers a critical conversation about borders embraced and Black girlhood beyond the limits assigned to it.[34] As a practice of "seeing the world *with* and for Black girls," historians like LaKisha Simmons, Nazera Sadiq Wright, and Corinne T. Field take to centering Black girls in twentieth-century migration and exhuming Black girls from the backdrop of Black struggle and responsibility to place them center stage in nineteenth-century Black literary works and media as a figure and steward of Black cultural and social advancement.[35] The preceding assembly of references expresses a Black girl moment in the United States that unavoidably transcends ethnic and spatial borders.

Celebration and creativity are fundamental to the study of Black girlhood as a diasporic, time-traveling location because they emphasize complexity. These pillars also permit bodily renderings and effects of the aforementioned systems of oppression to be recalibrated. Challenging the relationship between Black girlhood and hip-hop music, Kyra Gaunt explores the musicality in Black girl games and reveals that gender roles, relationships, and identity are learned, affirmed, and redesigned through games created and played by Black girls. Situating Black girls as knowers, Gaunt insists the musical intellect and innovation expressed in games is a form of bodily knowledge production. Interested in the ways games index histories and culture, she posits these games as translocal, which "refers to the ways in which vernacular practices transcend divisions of geography, and thereby class, age, national origin, and migration. The result is a national sense of Black communal memory and experience (or identity) defined by musical practices that involve key strategies of Black linguistic play and musical movement."[36] Gaunt's argument about Black girl games being translocal can be extended to the whole of Black girlhood. In other words, the process of making, coming to know, and imagine Black girlhood is context-specific but not context-determined, and like games, textures of Black girlhood travel and breach borders marked by the particularities of cultural and ethnic differences, language, and even time.

Social institutions determine access and norms through policy and procedure. To envision, as Brown did, a field that stars Black girls is policy making at its finest. To frame Black girlhood as a political project and discourse is to shift the undergirding ideas about Black girls, the function of academic areas of study, and the understanding of whose knowledge is integral to it. I contribute to this policy development by presenting four complimentary networks that order Black girlhood—charting carceral mechanics, practicing Black girlhood, energizing voice, and locating girlhood. These corridors broadly codify the work to date in the field from a nondisciplinary approach. Together, they affirm the difficulty in stimulating Black girlhood and the corresponding promise of a field that knows Black girlhood to be the result of conscious intention, alchemy, and practice.

Charting Black girlhood and specifically recurring themes and apertures within educational research, Tamara Butler pens the concept "Black girl cartography."[37] As a frame for mapping what happens as Black girls' interface with schools, Butler mounts a landscape comprising two broader categories—"Black girl navigational practices" and "Black girl charting." By creating a framework for "the study of how and where Black girls are physically and sociopolitically mapped in education," she indexes how schools as a carceral geography exclude and are changed by Black girlhood.[38] Significant to this framework are the roles of praxis and embodiment, in particular researchers' interaction with girls as a population and subject beside what is captured about the body in the experiences mapped. Black girl cartography locates geography's significance to girlhood and offers an example of how to call forth understandings of Black girlhood that attend to body politics and how education informs embodiment. Linking Butler's cartography with the metaphor of corridors compels thoughtful investigation into gradations of experience that honor specificity of place, soils on which Black girls navigate alongside the landscapes, and ecologies in which girls grow without squelching nuance or congruence.

To pay homage to yesterday and explicitly propose interdisciplinarity as foundational to how Black Girlhood studies is organized and discussed today, Owens, Callier, Garner, and Robinson present an "undisciplined" annotated bibliography. Designed around the concepts, "tools," and "generative works," they sought to destabilize disciplinary and other contrived divides such as that between art/intellectual and scholar/practitioner. Tools are fundamental texts created in a variety of mediums that paved the road for the field, and generative works offer a list of texts "that focus on Black girls or are related to Black girlhood."[39] I recommend that, like the undisciplined bibliographic approach Owens et al. designed, those working in the name of Black girlhood embrace the field as one that intentionally leaks and stretches across geographic and disciplinary boarders. What if, as expressed in this book's introduction, Black is inherently diasporic, where the processes of Blackening are varied and multiple? As an initial attempt at applying a similar mapping to Black Girlhood studies, what follows is an undisciplined curation of work on Black girlhood. Using the corridors metaphor, I intend to incite a dialogue about politicizing Black Girlhood studies. Specifically, I endeavor to position it as a playground for imagining Black Girlhood studies as a dream in the making, a dance cipher, a language. My offering is not intended to be exhaustive nor provide a comprehensive overview of Black girlhood scholarship in a particular context, discipline, or other arrangement rooted in organizing logics presumed appropriate within academia. If immersed in the field, it is likely that while reading, a text or person not mentioned will come to mind. This nonexhaustive offering is one instance of charting out potential corridors or hallways within Black Girlhood studies, together with what portraits and visions arise from them. I am most invested in bringing forth a curation that decenters academic fields and disciplines and pivots in the direction of recurring questions, themes, and terrain as related to academic study and everyday traversing of life. Finally, the idea of corridors invites those attaching their work to Black Girlhood studies to become architects of conceiving and birthing a vision malleable and voluminous enough to hold who and what is now, is coming, is shifting, and is not yet.

Charting Carceral Mechanics

Carceral mechanics refer to schemes that confiscate Black embodiment. As a corridor, it maps varied contexts and processes where attempted seizure happen. Due to body politics and discourses of race, gender, and sexuality, a body (minimally) marked Black, youthful, and female is a carceral geography where hypersurveillance occurs. Akin to the Combahee River Collective's articulation of the ways Black women's confinement is bodily, cultural, and systemic, Black girls also experience constriction. Turning an eye toward Black girls' school experiences, policies and practices within education render the body itself a carceral geography. Specifically, research amassed primarily between 2007 and 2019 capture Black girls standing trial with their bodies as evidence for defining educative potential, success, or expense. In 2015, the African American Policy Forum published *Black Girls Matter*, a US national report examining educational policies and their ramifications on the lives and educational journeys of Black girls and other girls of color. The report reveals that sociocultural factors, including but not limited to familial responsibilities and gender-associated violence, mediate in-school experiences.[40] Further, this research found that Black girls are six times more likely to be suspended in comparison to their white counterparts with respective expulsion rates at 90 percent and 63 percent in New York City and Boston where no white girls are expelled.[41]

Spotlighting conditions surrounding Black girls' pushout of schools in California, New York, Illinois, and Louisiana, Morris finds zero-tolerance policies and particular practices involving corresponding surveillance, such as body policing and infractions for "bad" attitudes, as leading factors that sculpt journeys through schools inside and outside of juvenile detention.[42] The lens of adultification defends overrepresentation of encounters with the juvenile legal system and school discipline. Consequently, dubious infractions like determining the look of disobedience and defiance serve as basis for punishment.[43] There is also a legacy of placement in detention centers and reform schools in the twentieth and twenty-first centuries for behavior that when enacted by individuals perceived to be Black girls and womn is read as criminal. Discussing the ways girls are violated and victimized while traversing the juvenile legal system, Cook asserts that Black girls enter the legal system primarily under status offenses and leave with no guaranteed resources to support everyday living.[44] The history of gender-based reformatory schools reveal how race, gender, and sexuality conjoin to establish the delinquent subject.[45] Made criminals and removed from their communities, these girls were routinely mistreated, violated, and rendered wrong.[46] To honor Black girls' humanity and dissent, scholars like Stacey Ault, Saidiya Hartman, and Maisha Winn employ methods and tools that center creative refusal, imagination, the creative, sensing, and other affective-based methodologies.[47] Through gazes, past and present, that deduce actions to pathology and disruption, Black gurl comportment and sartorial choices presents as having a need (with perhaps no perceived ability) for reformation.

While Black girls disproportionately experience overt violence in school, some of their less-examined injuries involve the policing of their embodiment and self-fashioning practices. Some of the carceral mechanics used include policing of hair and punishment for sartorial choices. Carceral logics live beyond physical cells and national borders and inform representations of Black girls, notions of empowerment, defiance, and marginality. These logics scaffold nuanced forms of injustice for Black girls and womn. Dissection of their details, as Lindsey writes, "acknowledges the roles that ideology and the internalization of injurious ideas can stay in instilling hopelessness among Black women and girls."[48] A cousin to stuckness, hopelessness is a giving up on the prospect of movement; it is a standstill of the spirit. And while context specificity makes some factors more noticeable than others, all humans and geographies are subject to the global productions of anti-Blackness, ethnocentrism, and heteropatriarchy. Sometimes, girls are assumed under subcategories that emphasize otherness and induce self-defining and strategy.[49] In contexts chiseled by US imperialism and economic disparities, girls not necessarily marked by Blackness in their homelands become Black girls. Like Jordan's theorization in "Poem about my rights," these productions reveal textures of wrong as well as how girls practice dissent. When anti-Black logics cross national borders, Black girls are required to deploy strategies for self-recognition, reverence, and celebration. An example of this is when Afro-Brazilian girls resist confinement at the level of the body, precisely through hair stylization and embracing their Black features.[50] Through cultural practices like Candomblé and festivals, as well as religious/spiritual offerings, racism is redressed through music and self-fashioning.

The disappearance of Black girls into discourses of gender or race in education alongside those that reduce girls to a commonly accepted preoccupation (i.e., schoolgirls) and the legitimation of Black girl joy becoming a just cause for strip searches, for instance, make clear the potential outcomes of being tied to the category "wrong."[51] In addition, the many suspensions and denied rites of passage and rituals, like yearbook photos, prom, and graduation ceremonies, for hair volume and aesthetics corroborate that anti-Blackness and racialized gender order the lives of Black girls irrespective of place. These infractions are accompanied by psychic and physical enmity as well as nuanced forms of violence endured by those read and/or are identified as Black girls. Additionally, once criminalized and removed from our homes and communities, mistreatment, violation, and denial of autonomy become quotidian.

Practicing Black Girlhood

Practicing Black girlhood is an active space-making project aimed at creating a container for Black girl being; expanding repertoires of those who identify as Black girls and those read as Black female, femme, and/

or feminine-expecting; and keeping sacred the knowing derived from Black girlhood. Practice also commands understanding that womnhood and girlhood in Black life need not be linear progressions; that the latter need not be engulfed by the former; that Black girlhood instead is where intergenerational covenants, undressing (discussed in Chapter 2), and allowing the process of being with Black girls occurs. While dancing, breathing, eating together, new relational essentials between individuals weighted by and weighing in on Black girlhood becomes more achievable. When girls get rushed to take responsibility for the world's lens, prescription to be a girl is to arrive at a pit stop to somewhere else, perhaps on the way to being important and finding safety. Lorde asserts, "Raising Black children—female and male—in the mouth of a racist, sexist, suicidal dragon is perilous and chancy. If they cannot love and resist at the same time, they will probably not survive."[52] And what kind of love shown to and practiced by Black children produces respect for Black girls and girlhood? To practice Black girlhood is to recognize the veracity of Lorde's words, the big smallness of language, and to say yes to the labor of seeing and materializing Black girlhood in the name of humanity and indivisible freedom.

Sometimes, as articulated in Jillian Hernandez's work on embodiment in Black and Latina girlhood, this love troubles "the dehumanizing formations of race, gender, class, and sexuality operative in the twenty-first-century United States as criminalized populations express their subjectivities and power through them."[53] To practice Black girlhood, then, also entails warping conventional relations of power. When building Black girlhood in real time, power is exercised in nuanced ways and "demands creativity, love, accountability, and reflexivity to always ask questions, to show up and give your gifts, and to do the work to be well."[54] Art and the creative as literacy tools assist the practice of Black girlhood despite confinement at state, societal, and cultural levels. Maisha Winn examines the experiences of girls in juvenile detention who participate in Girl Time, an artistic program created to help girls unpack, make new meaning of their experiences, and imagine possibilities for their lives through art. Winn's study revealed the multiplicative nature of confinement in Black girlhood and the carceral notions that transcend physical confinement.

To make intercultural work more visible, The BlackLight Project, "through movement and text-based performances, workshops, classes and street theater events, reimagine[s] the possibilities for living in under-resourced urban environments."[55] Originally an ethnographic initiative created by Aimee Cox designed to vivify the stories of navigating social and cultural realities of city living, The BlackLight Project expanded in 2009 to organize performance productions. To interrogate Blackness, place, gender, and beauty, Cox created a dance/movement workshop with Rutgers University graduate students. In this intergenerational performance space, participants grappled with the complexities of Black girlhood without being required to take on particular gendered identities.

To meld process and production in Black girlhood, Sheri Lewis introduces melt methodology, a creative process of engaging material culture through constructing magazines with Black girls in Chicago.[56] Furthering approaches to practicing Black girlhood that reconfigure power and identity, Sears explores the negotiation of power and identity within the Girls Empowerment Project (GEP) located in a low-income area in California. In Chicago, A Long Walk Home cultivates youth voices through arts practices toward the goal of eradicating violence against womn and girls.[57] Mindful of how girls and youth receive perpetual communication about "acceptable" comportment and presentation, these projects facilitate intergenerational work between Black girls and womn that engenders imagining Black femininity expansively. To practice Black girlhood is to make it visible. As a mode of recognition, it surfaces ingenious labor in the face of adultification and other schemes that ensnare individuals to turn away from reducing girl to things naïve, play-filled, or inconsequential.

In *Home Girls: A Black Feminist Anthology*, Barbara Smith discusses the intentional naming process and its connection to being a queered subject—Black feminist lesbian—and the incumbency of taking a stake in Blackness regardless of her attribution from others: "Home Girls. The girls from the neighborhood and from the block, the girls we grew up with. I knew I was onto something, particularly when I considered that so many Black people are threatened by feminism have argued that being a Black feminist (particularly if you are also a lesbian) you have left the race, are no longer part of the Black community, in short no longer have a home."[58] An extension of the refusal embedded in Smith's conceptualization, the work of "homegirling" is only possible through the continual labor of retooling the body, the self. As Brown asserts, "to homegirl is to commit to a very sincere practice of remembering Black girlhood as a way to honor oneself and to practice the selflessness necessary to recognize someone else, remembered whole."[59] An orientation and responsibility in SOLHOT, homegirls prepare and hold space for girls/li'l homies. In that process, we stand face to face with hurts, fears, misunderstandings, assumptions, and dreams for ourselves all young and youthful in some context, mostly Black and usually queer in some way. We also stand toe-to-toe with beliefs, pains, confusion, and contradictions in our individual selves, each other, and our collective while choosing to care, make art, and devise new ways of relating to/through Black girlhood. To homegirl is a practice of Black girlhood that demands a level of unlearning; it mandates that adults not hide behind mentorship and/or *I'm grown* rhetoric to name and tend to our wounds. To homegirl necessitates that the time shared with girls is not about self-aggrandizement but is filled with time travel. To practice Black girlhood as a homegirl is to surrender, allow, and make way for how womnhood might sound if girlhood was not relegated to a bound moment in time but was a practice where disarming and collective care occurs.

Energizing Voice

The nurturance and development of voice are indispensable literacy to Black liberation. It is a practice of self-determination wherein Black people develop a sensibility for expressing purpose, our needs, and dreams, and doing so in a way that is in right relationship with our spirits. The work of energizing voice is varied and multifaceted because voice is connected to vernacular and more plausible when those present commit to being Black gurl reliable. Some taken-for-granted modes through which girls theorize include but are not limited to storytelling, dancing, singing, gaming, signifying, hand games, Double Dutch, and poetry cyphers. Discussed at length in Chapter 5, voice in Black girlhood is an aesthetic. This assertion does not preclude voice from being so in other demographics. Here, however, it will be discussed explicitly in the context of Black girlhood to stress its layers, variety, and significance. So much of the sociocultural experience of being in a body rendered Black and female though not inherently cisgender, femme, or feminine is attached to voice. Connected to the carceral geography of schools, and discussed in Chapter 3, girls are tone policed and penalized for sartorial choice. Current dress code policy and zero tolerance lead to high-rate suspensions and sometimes even pushout. Thereby, voice is another element of embodiment and a barometer of the presence and vigor of celebration.

Essential to energizing voice in Black girlhood is the embrace of paradox with respect to so-called femininity. Rejection of surveillance as justification for compliance that goes against the self, Savannah Shange advances "Black girl ordinary." This vernacular marks action and aesthetics to hold in tandem how Black girls do and the raised eyebrows that sometimes follow. Shange describes, "Black girl ordinary is that which signifies on (but does not conform to) normative notions of gender through a performative [B]lackness shaped by hip hop, social media, and conspicuous consumption."[60] Fitting within the rubric of hooks's radical Black subjectivity, a mode of queer(ed) disidentification, and a technology of transgression, Black girl ordinary elucidates the contextual register of Black girlhood. Further, Shange spotlights how the calculation of a girl's legibility as aberrant is contingent upon normative behavior patterns. In the digital sphere, Black girls' usage of particular aesthetics offer departures from and allegiance to tropes mapped onto Black girls and womn. Discussing "Soft Black Girl Aesthetics" and "Cottagecore," two trends on TikTok popularized during the pandemic, Nashid describes distinct ways Black girls practice radical Black subjectivity and enact self-definition through social media.[61] Attending to posts and their captions, as well as the comments made beneath them, she argues that Black girls' and womn's participation in Cottagecore through the subthemes of Soft Black Girl Aesthetics results in a "claiming [of] a certain display of femininity out of which they are often raced."[62] Yet, the insistence by Black girls and womn in embracing softness was not without critique and misogynoiristic comments. Energizing voice, then, is not without stakes, and still, it is incumbent to the embodiment project.

Compulsory surveillance infringes on expression and potentially restrains comportment and other elements of one's embodiment. Thereby, nurturing spirit is an essential facet of energizing voice. To document the interconnectedness of spirit-work and voice, Porshé Garner shares Black girl spirituality and the "sounded-word aesthetic."[63] An outgrowth of Black feminist praxis and womanism, she declares that the sound of Black girlhood is (w)holy, that spirituality lives in and is seeded in the practice and production of music, and that Black girlhood is spiritual work. From working with Black girls and theorizing Black girlhood through music production, Garner notes spirit and spirituality as elemental components in and productions of Black girlhood.

Spirit also lives in breath and breathwork. In *Breath Better Spent*, DaMaris Hill presents a poetic manifesto and incantation for breathing Black girlhood into the future. "Girl" in *Breath better spent* is not relegated to child status nor age bound. As spell, mantra even, the statement "breath better spent" is a reminder to Black girls, young and youthful, youthful and seasoned, and not yet, that our breath is best spent on our living and that our lives needn't be extraordinary to be celebrated. In her documentation of mundane happenings, like the sensory experience of having a period in summer heat, Hill directs her breath to breathing life into girlhood itself.[64]

In the dance performance *Black Girl: Linguistic Play*, Camille Brown stories Black girlhood using sound, visual-scapes, movement, and play. As a witness to its run at Jacob's Pillow in August 2017, I was called by *Black Girl: Linguistic Play* to jump in the rope and be with Black girlhood. I went on a journey and got found somewhere in dancers' movements, stomping feet, and sounds created through chant and slaps onto body parts. The performance returned me to multiple moments. In no order, I went to the field at the corner of my street, to step rehearsal as a member of the junior sorority Kappa Lambda Gamma Incorporated, to dancing barefoot in a Juneteenth parade, and to feeling the summer heat while getting my hair braided on the porch. I mouthed lyrics and cried during the mother/daughter scene. The language of play staged in such a white context exemplified transgression. It was call and response to me, and whether or not all of me wanted to answer, my body took care of our response.

To recognize *Black Girl: Linguistic Play* as performance and pedagogy, Johnson introduced "a politics of tenderness." Johnson studied challenges Brown navigated including what Black girl would be represented and what audiences would want to see of her. Brown crafted a production that celebrated vastness of Black gurl vernacular while crafting a style of process that defied the need to deny vulnerability. Johnson wrote, "The production evidences wonder as an accomplishment, one achieved through rehearsals that attempted to strip away the heft of racial and gendered injury in order to make room for an exploration of a Black girlhood 'before the world defined me.'"[65] Expanding the lexicon of Black girlhood and contributing to multiple corridors, Johnson's politics of tenderness and Brown's *Black Girl: Linguistic Play* indexed Black girlhood as a site of (re)memory and modality for honoring Black bodily knowledge and Black girls.

The work of energizing voice and locating Black girlhood often occurs at the nexus of contradiction and cultural norms. In "Coming of R(age)," Daley, through literature and film, explores tensions between social meanings of coming of age and Black girlhood. Documenting the cultural specificity of Black girlhood through glimpses where boundaries muddle and the seeing of girlhood requires a different set of frames, Daley writes: "Even when prevented from wearing black clothing, it is her black skin that continuously propels her toward her womanhood, despite still being a child. She lives in the liminal space between her black skin and her ensuing black clothing—between her Black girlhood and her ensuing Black womanhood. Her black skin is her Black womanhood long before she is old enough to make it a clothing choice."[66] The above statement makes clear the careful navigation Black girls must engage. Equally, it offers a window into the value of distinguishing childhood from girlhood from womnhood.

Locating Girlhood

Locating is recovery work. It entails appearing girls and girlhood in places and narratives that disappear them from plain view. Locating assists in the establishment of precision about where girlhood is happening, how it operates there, and forecasts Black girls and girlhood futures.

Such aims involve, though not exclusively, (re)memorying, imagining, conjuring, and time travel. To locate girlhood, scholars utilize methods that heighten affect and connection. In conjunction with the usage of the aforementioned methods, there's a legacy of scholars deploying language and syntax as a means to note, subvert, and alter language and conventional discourses that mitigate meaning made and experiences of Black girlhood.[67] Recently, Brown, Daley, and Hunt wrote, "Black/. We strategically write 'Black forward slash Girlhood' to signal both an abstract configuration and a lived embodied experience of Black girlness that is in dialogue with global imaginings.... Black/Girlhood Imaginary is the copy without an original—reconstructing sources of rupture into repair for the Black girl whose image then becomes her own."[68] To locate girlhood in a Black context requires methods that build creative muscles toward generative practices that build imagination rigor. In *Black Girl Magic: Beyond the Hashtag*, Julia S. Jordan-Zachery and Duchess Harris name "speculative freedom" as a tool for bringing the self into view. Related to the expansiveness of Black girlhood, they write "Speculation, a critique of justice unserved, helps connect the past with the present to fulfill a future hindered but not stolen."[69] Presented as a resource within Black girl magic praxis, Black girls, womn, femmes, and those read as these utilize this tool to imagine these labels, their corresponding experiences, and the world around us differently. Through auto/ethnography and the tool of (re)memory, various Black feminist scholars locate Black girlhood and its accompanying lessons that build futures of Black feminist epistemology.[70] As one example, Smith-Purviance et al. revisit personal narratives to document anti-Black and gendered violence endured as young girls.[71] Positioning Black girls as conduits of hip-hop, Kyra Gaunt declares, "African American girls embody the ideals of [B]lack music-making in the games they play," positioning girls as knowers of musicality and sensibility.[72]

The act of tracing here refers to identifying specificity of the *how* and *where* of seeing Black girlhood without creating fixed place or meaning to it. Returning to Gaunt's offering of translocality, like sound and aesthetics, ideologies also travel. Black as a racial category and Blackness as an experience assume multiple simultaneous meanings that map onto bodies. A relevant cautionary from E. Patrick Johnson includes "If the history of the term 'black' has taught us anything, it is that racialized symbols—those that are disparaging and those that are affirming—never quite fade from sight or consciousness but constantly evolve alongside the people who create them. Race alone cannot describe any person's full experience of life."[73] The concept of Black alone proves insufficient when discussing Black girlhood, especially as it concerns inter- and intraracial differences rooted in culture, ethnic identity, and citizenship status. Of equal imperative is the need to mind how politics, media, and racial discourse amplify and construct difference as a tool for manufacturing hierarchies. It is necessary to attend to contextual nuances in Black girlhood without overdetermining the when and where of distinction. As an example, Maima Chea Simmons uses personal narrative to clarify complexities around intercultural dissimilarities and her particular experiences growing up Liberian-American as a jumping off point for thinking about literacy practices of African immigrant girls.[74] Simmons acknowledges the lack of education in schools afforded to all Black people with respect to contributions made by African ascending people and discusses the value additive of learning Black US history in college. One point of contention she raises is around the figurative cultural phrase "African booty scratcher." It is critical to be mindful of this phrase thrown around in childhood and to note how such phrases exceed real and contested edges of the Black African immigrant, Black American, and African American. Such a term that may signify a certain kind of Blackness in the lives of girls does not neatly map onto experience (see Chapters 4 and 5).

Throughout history, girls have been the meaning of Black hope, advancement, and prospective progress.[75] There is a slippery slope to mind when locating Black girlhood outside of the context in which it was lived. Scholars seeking to exhume Black girls from archives find it particularly challenging, as decisions of cataloging life generally and Black life particularly are disparate.[76] Moreover, to collapse girlhood inside childhood may reduce its optimization and scope. Owens recognizes the weight of theory, stating, "Black women's theories of American childhood are more than reflections, they are challenges to the social construction of childhood and the child in American history."[77]

She reminds that theory derives from lived experience and provides (re)orientation to childhood studies through Black womn locating girlhood through memory and (re)memory while challenging the terms on which childhood is commonly defined.

To journey back in time to Harriet Jacob's *Incidents in the Life of a Slave Girl* and bring her story into the contemporary framing of Black girlhood presents an opportunity to bridge a conversation about wrongness taking place across temporal boundaries. Further, it illustrates how Black girlhood functions as a site to thwart mirrors built in the interest of societal order and aims. Jacobs's story is oft regarded as an antislavery narrative, a communication of slavery's atrocities to compel others to fight for its abolition. When placed within Black Girlhood studies, this narrative is a testament of Black girlhood being something that survives state-sanctioned violence, something made amid huge responsibility, and something that can be felt while not materially seen. Jacobs presents the concept of "prematurely knowing" to describe her early exposure to sexual behavior set forth by her enslaver.[78] While Jacobs uses certain moments to crystallize shifts in treatment, awareness, and in turn proximity to varying levels of harm and injury, I ponder the need to firm up these moments into developmental stages that map neatly onto age. Instead, and discussed further in the next section, I encourage a reconfiguration of the concept of innocence in Black girlhood and overall caution the potential reification of normative geographies of girlhood and the tethering of girlhood to a particular time and body. No doubt, girls theorize and do so while drawing upon different mediums. To build on "prematurely knowing" as put forth by Harriet Jacobs is to understand the contemporary concept of adultification. Where the latter emphasizes gaze (or how Black girls are watched through the eyes of others), the former pays respect to what knowledge is forced upon girls and when. With attention to the social critique and inner dialogue disclosed, it makes for a cultural autobiography—an autoethnographic account of traversing carceral terrain and a critique of US culture in the South. Akin to the work of Black feminist thinkers like Toni Cade Bambara and Toni Morrison who featured Black girls as protagonists, critics, and rule breakers of social norms and conditions, *Incidents* is a social critique of wrongness and how it unfolds in the lives of Black girls at the inception of racial capitalism in the US. Enlarging Nazera Sadiq Wright's discussion of "Black girl interiority" within Bambara's *Gorilla, My Love, Incidents* is also a display of "Black girls' political and economic insight into racial violence that is embedded into the rhythm of their everyday lives."[79] The project of locating and in cahoots with the concept corridors is about materializing Black girls and Black girlhood in spaces they are otherwise overlooked and/or given no credit.

Tomorrow

Black girlhood is fertile ground calling for intentional tending and Black Girlhood studies is a viable toolkit for nurturing and envisioning Black girlhood. As new tomorrows unfold in the world and Black life, it's critical to think purposefully about the field, its aims, and scale. To do so I recommend welcoming and revisiting the wisdom of initiates of Black Women's studies and begetting a collective attitude toward Black girlhood. In *Visionary Feminism*, hooks shares a repeat misunderstanding about the work of feminism, noting, "one of the difficulties we faced spreading the word about feminism is that anything having to do with the female gender is seen as covering feminist ground, even if it does not contain a feminist perspective."[80] Her statement draws attention to the inaccuracy and danger of conflating identity with politics. Relatedly, June Jordan perfectly summarizes politics, asserting, "I will call you my brother, I will call you my sister, on the basis of what you do for justice, what you do for equality, what you do for freedom, and not on the basis of who you are."[81] Politics, as articulated in Jordan's statement, hinges on action, and action is dependent on belief. June Jordan and bell hooks are Black feminist thinkers who support my knowing and movement in this world. In their footsteps, I initiate a politics of Black Girlhood studies and instate three (re)orientations useful to ensuring the field flourishes. Each of the following assertions are rooted in transgression and reconfigure limits imposed on Black girlhood and/or Black girls. These attitudes and precepts institute new policy and can be applied irrespective of discipline and/or methodological approach. It is my hope that, with the support of other Black girlhood scholars, these (re)orientations offer some mutual ground on which to work, expand in usage and dimension, and grow into an ethos for Black Girlhood studies.

In 1905, Fannie Barrier Williams wrote "The Colored Girl," an essay that appeared in *The Voice of the Negro* monthly magazine. An Atlanta based press, this periodical kept a pulse on Black education, religion, and labor. An educator, activist, and cultural worker born in Brockport, New York, Barrier Williams indexed the ways race and gender conjoin to form the category and sculpt the living of individuals marked as "colored girls." Thus, the colored girl, like Hortense Spillers says eight decades later, must be invented. Furthermore, "the colored girl is a cause as well as an effect. We cannot comprehend the term American womanhood without including the colored girl."[82] The architecture built in Barrier Williams' statement recognizes the colored girl as an allocated status and an adopted politic. While detailing the ways "the colored girl" is made a category of analysis and site of impossibility, Barrier Williams makes clear the ways individuals assigned to this category defy social norms and expectations in the name of collective social advancement. Without the explicit usage of the term *patriarchy*, she describes how it functions as an ideology to set in motion the creation of and meaning assigned to the category "colored girl." Colored girls were in effect participants of transgression because: "[their] positions so won and held were never intended for them; to seek them was considered an impertinence, and to hope for them was an absurdity. Nothing daunted these women, conscious of their own deserving, would not admit or act upon the presumption that they were not as good and capable as other girls who were not really superior to them."[83] First is the important noting that colored girls were also womn. Secondly, these womn's colored girl status marked dissent as an embrace of attributive wrongness. Akin to Aimee Cox's *Shapeshifters* and Saidiya Hartman's *Wayward Lives*, to be a colored girl meant defying the status quo and pursuing things based on erotic desire and internal directive. Similarly, such actions did not neatly map onto a particular age range nor did the term *girl* exist absent or entirely separate from womn. To trace Black Girlhood studies back into the yesterday is to build on the work of earlier Black feminist conduits like that of Barrier Williams and enlist Black girl and thereby Black girlhood as transcendent of age, referent of action while attendant to its prescribed broader social meanings.

I continue this lineage by expanding Black girlhood geography in three ways. Number one, childhood and girlhood be kin but not interchangeable. Akin to key debates within feminism and Black feminist epistemology that liken differences as shades of purple, girlhood and childhood should not be used as synonyms.[84] To accept the asymmetry between girl and child is also to highlight "the vastness of Blackness in the face of abjection and focuses on what becomes possible when childhood is embraced as a failed project."[85] This tactic accomplishes minimally two critical things. First, it positions Black girlhood as its own lane and not beholden to aims, theorizations, or rubrics that assign it doormat status, and second, it produces the possibility of atonement for childhoods snatched. To position girl and child in relation but not interchangeable increases the possibility of recognizing the value of lamentation while placing focus on Black girlhood as a global community. Commingling childhood and girlhood is to name a girl history where "empowered girls have been configured in relation to their at-risk Others," whereas untwining childhood and girlhood, as seen in the corridor practicing Black girlhood, engenders Black girlhood worldmaking that is intergenerational and attuned to cultural wholeness.[86]

The second maneuver is the redefining of innocent from a quality that describes one's entitled naivety to a practice of dissent. The child in the US imaginary is naïve, rightfully irresponsible, deserving of protection, and by these metrics, white. According to Merriam Webster, innocent means to be "free from legal guilt or fault," "free from guilt or sin especially through lack of knowledge of evil," as in a blameless (or innocent) child, "harmless in effect or intention," as well as "lacking or reflecting a lack of sophistication, guile, or self-consciousness."[87] In *Stolen Childhood*, Wilma King documents the ways enslaved children were expected to participate in labor similar to their parents, unexcused from routine enactments of violence, and robbed of childhood.[88] King ultimately reveals, at least as it pertains to duties in the ecology of slavery, Blackness colors the meaning and status of a child like the ways Spillers discusses the agendering of Blackness in slavery. Black people and bodies are subject to discourses of violence. The possibility of innocence is oft rejected or assigned rank and the "prematurely knowing" or exposure that happens all too often in such a position. Given that one's life depends on understanding the way things work, to rehearse innocence is a commitment taken toward one's body and presence in the world in spite of one's status.

Early exposure to how life is ordered may preclude childhood amenities in the conventional white middle-class cultural sense. But as illustrated in literary texts like *The Bluest Eye* and *The Color Purple*, racialized childhood need not govern the presence nor practice of Black girlhood. Sparked by an embodied social justice certificate program, Shamell Bell—co-conspirator for Black liberation—and I discussed inner-child work in relation to Black girlhood.[89] During this conversation in the summer 2021, I verbally penned thoughts on a nuance I'd experienced when innocence is understood as resistance. Innocence, I propose, becomes (and is) a decision and transgressive ingredient of Black gurl embodiment and Black embodiment broadly.

Adultification is the active theft of Black childhood innocence; it is what happens when such robbery is normalized. "Prematurely knowing," as Jacobs asserts, is Black girls' early contact with adult matters, an awareness that is forced. Innocence, for Black girls particularly and for Black people broadly, is a form of protest. Innocence is coming to know how the world works, whenever that happens, and choosing not to play the part/s that the world insists. As such, if innocence is stolen, there is social and personal responsibility involved because innocence is no longer something simply banned from Blackness. Rather, innocence is a practice with internal and external properties. In her discussion of Black girlhood, literature, and dreaming as a worldmaking tool, Janaka Bowman Lewis maps a pathway away from stuckness, directing, "We get to brilliant Black girl futures through dreams, through spaces to move and perform, through creating literary and even fugitive life spaces for Black girls to believe that they are, have, and can be whatever they need."[90] The rehearsal of innocence evades "stuckness."

The third and final maneuver I propose here is the affirmation of Black girlhood as a queer and formative geography. Drawing from Carbado, McBride, and Weise in their framing of contributors to the *Black Like Us* anthology, "queer in terms of how they defined and embodied their racial identity, queer in terms of their conception and performance of their gender, queer in how they articulated and practiced politics, as well as queer in their intimate relationships and sense of sexual identity."[91] Queer on these terms is a political commitment to capaciousness, complexity, even contradiction. Likewise, queer exercised is transgression or persistent actions toward right relationship with one's inner knowing, yearnings, curiosity, and self-definition. In theatrical jazz aesthetics Jones notes, "queer as a permeable and multi-determinant suggest an experiential relationship with liminality which need not be conceptualized solely as 'not this and not that' but, more fruitfully, 'this and that.'"[92] Black girlhood is a portal into the future. To practice Black girlhood mandates a constant tilling of its soil so that when folks show up ready, hurt, yearning for, and/or in search of, space is already cleared for them.

As a scholar who enters Black girlhood through practice and applied theory, I know the concepts Black girls and Black girlhood to be engineers and holders of expansive ideas, especially as related to gender, sexuality, and age. Though this book does not explicitly focus on the complexities of gender nonconformity in Black girlhood (stay tuned), it is birthed from practicing Black girlhood in communal and classroom spaces where queerness and gender fluidity contoured the work. I've learned, for instance, that the most important and sometimes the only pronoun necessary is one's name. In addition, I am mindful that by entering Black girlhood through practice that a homegirl is a Black gurl reliable origin and is sustained by individuals who self-identify as Black men, womn loving womn, gender nonconforming, and others. From this orientation, girls are not always children (in the confined age sense), girls are not always girls (as in gender identity), girls are not always girls in the biological sense; and girl is a noun, verb, and punctuation. In the practice of Black girlhood, trans girls conceive of a girlhood that ensures a proper toolkit for a right relationship with self, now and in the future. Black Girlhood studies is hefty and voluminous enough to house multiple and paradoxical stories, experiences, becomings, and ruptures. To uphold queer as an orientation within the field also means that Black girlhood is not a pit stop to womnhood. Further, queer holds that girls need not become womn. Finally, adopting a queer orientation to Black Girlhood studies insists that the celebration is not contingent upon a certain performativity or achievement.

Black Girlhood studies, like Black Women's studies, is audacious because the act of naming is political and calls forth existence. Black Girlhood studies in name declares Black girlhood a thing, even if it is unfounded or untenable to some, mourned by some, and/or known and desired. The long memory of being marked Black and female affords an attribution of queer, or what McKittrick describes as "not quite."[93] Whether imagining, practicing, teaching, or living, Black girlhood entails constant dialogue with and between the self, society, and others who self-identify and/or are read as belonging to this culture and knowledge base. The preceding orientations magnify the celebration paradigm, reconfigure language applied to Black girlhood, and make room for internal measures of girlhood and being a girl. They also speak to what becomes possible when meaning is unhinged from whiteness, heteropatriarchy, conservatism, and other conventional logics of hierarchy.

Conclusion

To sing a Black girl's song requires attunement to modalities and scales of speech. To sing a Black girl's song calls for seeing Black girlhood as a collective wherein girls live as "indisputably single" with local and translocal qualities.[94] To sing a Black girl's song is to be a participant and witness of celebration. For Black girlhood to flourish, Black gurl reliable must be in play. Changing the quality of Black girls' livelihoods necessitates attendance to and recalibration of gazes employed to see Black girls. Built into the preceding mapping of the field is lineage. Black Girlhood studies is identity-attentive not identity-bound. Through the paradigm of celebration, Black Girlhood studies seeks to decenter "woman" as aspiration, and the adult (possibly curbed) voice to make way for Black girlhood and the theory engendered from locating, dreaming, and practicing it. Within this configuration is the critical nature of intergenerational relationships to what Black girls see as freedom possibilities and the care Black girls receive. Etched into a celebration paradigm with transgression as a guiding frame is the requisite willingness to resist hand-me-downs of femininity, Blackness, Black girlhood, and even sisterhood. Black girlhood is a spiritual collective pedagogical project and a keeper of innocence for posterity. In observance that "the ritual of call and response makes room and worlds [and] this worldmaking has been a collective means of maintaining doorways and connections to ancestors," I invite you to undress with me.[95]

CHAPTER 2

Reverse Osmosis to Awaken Flesh

An Experiment in Undressing

> I do not know
> when my lessons began
>
> I have no memory,
>   of a teacher,
>   or books.
>
> osmosis—perhaps
> the lessons slip
> into my brain,
> my cells—silently
>
>   —Pat Parker, "Group"

Theory in and accepted: A busy schedule and formal education keep inner city Black youth away from trouble, out of handcuffs, and away from harm. *Theory in action and complex*: Education acquired by a Black girl is an access card, not a bulletproof shield; injury is unavoidable. While my family insisted I go to school, get an education, and keep busy, this routine curtailed trouble, but it did not protect me. My involvement in extracurricular activities, youth church, honors classes, and enrichment programs, alongside my college aspirations, did not stop me from getting ahold of the world after it took hold of me. In 1997, when I ran away from home and entered the juvenile legal system, it would take thirteen years, the same number of sun orbits I'd experienced prior to running away, before processing with my entire being that I, Dominique, served time in juvie. When instructed by my advisor and dissertation chair to go back to how *I knew* Black girls' bodies mattered to their movement through the world, how *I knew* the body to be a key ingredient to Black girlhood, the memory of juvie almost instantly surfaced.

This chapter is an experiment in *undressing in public*. As a transgressive practice, undressing in public lives under the umbrella of enthusiastic embodied vulnerability and is used to eliminate boundaries between layers of the self and/or others. Examining memories and artifacts from my time in juvenile detention, I utilize (re)memory as a method to examine kinships between forgetting and disembodied living. Buoyed by the courage and honesty of Elaine E. Richardson in *PHD to Ph.D.*, I utilize my experience navigating the juvenile legal system after running away as a case to illuminate how the body archives disembodying experiences.[1] Through this case, I examine the following questions: What does (re)memory recover and uncover? What about the self becomes accessible that was otherwise tucked away, suppressed, locked within a past iteration or echo of an event? What textures are made and unmade by repeatedly returning to a site of injury à la Katherine McKittrick?

Through the structure of three echoes of my time in juvenile detention, I argue that moments experienced as potentially murderous of one's spirit make clear the tenuousness of Black survival and forgetting becomes a tactic, enacted intentionally or subconsciously, to boost one's assessment of possibility. Forgetting functions, in this case, as an ad hoc solution to injuries incurred from disembodying experiences. Each recitation contains vestiges of my encounter with the state through the juvenile legal system. To mirror on the page a process of dehumanization, I begin with court documents. Sterile and laden with accusation, these documents mark my entry and exit from juvie from the vantage point of the law. Alongside the other impressions, they offer stark contrast and capture the disembodiment I experienced once I entered the system. The second echo, a story turned monologue, presents lessons learned about the body while in juvie.[2] The third and final echo is a dialogue with myself that divulges what got lost through forgetting, the lessons unknowingly learned and adopted (osmosis), and what becomes possible following a decision to (re)member.

Forgetting and Embodiment

Busy work provides distraction; it's movement without progress. There are a myriad of reasons for busy work, but here I focus on keeping busy as a symptom of violence and explore busy's usefulness in burying, not terminating violence. As a child, I stayed busy. The village of womn who raised me believed that idle time invited trouble and perpetually kept me in the future. Maybe they knew and just didn't tell me, but busy work also aids in forgetting. Keeping busy leaves little space for sitting with things like feelings. A seemingly harmless intention of theirs—to keep me busy and out of trouble—became my way of surviving. Whether they knew then or now, I learned this strategy from them in overt and inconspicuous ways. For example, since I was a young child, whenever my mom felt (or now feels) frustrated and/or hurt from being overlooked or unheard, or is simply annoyed at something, she hums and subtly bobs her head. Perhaps it takes her away from the scene of the problem, or I once thought the literal hum moves her mind elsewhere. Embodiment and somatic training later alerted me that my mother's hum calmed her nervous system. Before this knowing and still, I catch myself humming in times of high frustration.

In *Learning to (Re)member the Things We've Learned to Forget*, Cynthia Dillard describes forgetting as a temptress and argues for (re)memory as an endarkened means of bridging cultural connection in people of African ascendance. She strives to reconcile the compartmentalization of body, mind, and spirit as it pertains to research describing the seduction of theory and its allegiance to patriarchy, racism, and other hierarchies of dominance.[3] Dillard insists that careful attention must be paid to what and who is forgotten and who it benefits. Who benefits when scholars ascending from African roots forget cultural ways of knowing? Stated differently, in the epigraph of this chapter "osmosis" is offered as a metaphor for the ways "bad" gets inscribed onto Black children's skin and bodily memory. Moreover, it is through

Black idioms in the form of chants, playground bullying, and advice from adults like *stay out of the sun, it'll make you darker* that Black children come to forget other meanings of Blackness, their beauty, and even their vastness.

To forget, as an African ascendant person, Dillard argues, is to cover up our culture, identity, our knowledge until the concealment becomes unconscious and default—a façade. And busy work is the diversion that incites forgetting and at the very least, suppression. Keeping busy keeps us from addressing our ailments at a core level. Initially it helps to allay unwanted feelings and difficulty. Given its strangely attractive quality, time passes, feelings reduce, and so does connection—the thing that maintains internal and relational footing. In *Living a Feminist Life*, Sara Ahmed articulates the sensation of knot binding and violation, expressing, "I remember each of these occasions not only as an experience of being violated, but as a sensory event that was too overwhelming to process at the time . . . you are left with an impression that is not clear or distinct."[4] Forgetting, then, is not abrupt nor a magical disappearance. Rather, forgetting is a potent event plateaued into numbness, a "not there, always there" reality. For bodies, forgetting does not engender excretion of these events, their aftermath, nor their consequences. As a form of terminal anti-Black brutality, muting anesthetizes; its pervasiveness becomes banal but always impactful. Dillard declares, "learning to (re)member is about recognizing and examining our seductions. Those irresistible moments when we have been enticed away from ourselves led away from our duties."[5] Seduction pulls us into an orbit created by and comfortable for others.

When bodies continuously engage in behaviors deemed proper or in line with convention without introspection, a self is being produced without the active agentic engagement of the person being made.[6] Self-making, then becomes a disembodying in-body experience. I often felt this way growing up attending church, where I built a religious routine with no deliberate connection to Jesus. My full self consisted of my body as a multidimensional entity but I unplugged connector pieces between its components. I did not divulge this detachment nor work to shift it. I learned it was better to look like I knew Jesus than to vigorously form a relationship. Each time I kept parts of me concealed, presuming it was safer to compartmentalize, I widened the welcome to being blotted out, unknown to myself—a body with no spirit, flesh asleep. Unintentionally, I formed a disjointed self—a disembodied embodiment of myself. Pieces of me but not (w)holy me. As a scheme, muting obstructs holistic and conscious living and instead enlists a pedagogy of foreclosure wherein one's embodiment is almost frozen in time and therefore prepared first and foremost for external consumption and use. Christina Sharpe contemplates: "If museums and memorials materialize a kind of reparation (repair) and enact their own pedagogies as they position visitors to have a particular experience or set of experiences about an event that is seen to be past, how does one memorialize chattel slavery and its afterlives, which are unfolding still? How do we memorialize an event that is still ongoing?"[7] Sharpe's line of questioning raises important realities about the project of spirit-murdering, its connection to time, and its roots in anti-Black racism and Black abnegation. In troubling the idea of memorial as commemoration of a past event, it highlights the fragility of time, and asserts that memorial is death unfinished. Connecting the dots between forgetting, memorial, and bodies, disremembering—a "not there, always there" reality—maintains order. This collaboration forges the "abstracted and imagined figure [that] shadows or doubles the real one," that then becomes part of popular social memory and delivers incessant exposure to ruses that subdue calls for retooling, unraveling, and unbecoming.[8] To disrupt its business-as-usual flow or its cultivation of what I describe as "dead and breathing happenings," a new orientation toward confinement and how it occurs is necessary. To (re)member entails contact with sentience and involves admittance, exhumation, disclosure, and touch (see Chapter 4).[9] To access deeper understanding requires returning—physically and emotionally—to the site of injury.

Asserting memory as a type of geography and clarifying its nuance in Black women's lives, McKittrick argues: "Reconstructing what has been erased, or is being erased, requires confronting the rationalization of human and spatial domination; reconstruction requires 'seeing' and 'sighting' that which is both expunged and 'rightfully' erasable.

What you cannot see, and cannot remember, is part of a broader geographic project that thrives on forgetting and displacing blackness."[10] (Re)memory is archiving on repeat, remixed, again, and never quite the same. More, repetition is spiritual, sacred, a leaving from and returning to, and it is holy because it consecrates memory and offers continual recognition of the possibility for rewriting the body. During a podcast interview with David Naimon, poet Nikky Finney narrated her father's commitment to civil rights, fighting injustice in the legal system and the execution of fourteen-year-old George J. Stinney Jr., a Black boy accused and instantly convicted of killing two white girls in Sumter, South Carolina. Finney details how her stylistic choices in the poem "Black Boy with Cow: A Still Life" built on these histories: "Repetition is holy, and so the repetition of maroon eyes happens in the poem quite a bit, because I want to deposit in the reader's mind how the state of South Carolina saw George Stinney Jr. at fourteen. Not as a boy, not as a boy who loved to draw, not as a boy who had a future, but really as a monster—and he was anything but that."[11] The performance of the police depiction of George, "negro hair with maroon eyes," memorializes the event. Her decision around repetition criticizes the state's reliability and restructures the meaning of having maroon eyes. In the poem, she offers, "Johnny is twice George's age, / with Negro hair and maroon eyes, and no bowl to his name."[12] Johnny was George's cellmate, his kin, his steward for the time as he awaited his murder. Later in the poem, Finney affirms:

> Being seen as fear and trouble is the brick and pebble of each story. The perception of being a person of trouble, aimed for trouble, because of what we always come in the door wearing. Negro hair and maroon eyes.[13]

Repetition raises rigor. To have maroon eyes is to be Black, to be made criminal, to be deemed disposable. "Black Boy with Cow: A Still Life" is itself an event of (re)memory and disclosure. The intentional employment of repetition builds new possibilities, muscles, new memories.

In 1997, the year youth incarceration peaked in the United States, I ran away.[14] My decision forced my mother's hand to report me missing. On February 11, 1997, the state declared me "A Person in Need of Supervision" and issued a P.I.N.S warrant. After a mutual decision and a judge's allowance, I entered the Erie County Detention Home, whose street name was Ferry. At that time, I would rather be anywhere than under my mother (and stepfather's) roof. While many of my peers sat awaiting trial or their seventeenth birthday to be tried as an adult for murder, I sat waiting for someone to ask what happened that incited me to run away. Instead, if anyone asked anything at all, they rhetorically scolded me or called attention to my actions and how they poorly impacted our family's reputation. After a little under two months in Ferry, I left the system under false pretenses and never returned. The echoes to come are sites of memory that contain and disclose a piece of my time in the juvenile legal system. Taking direction from Dillard and McKittrick, I go back to East Ferry Detention Center.

Back to the many cells of the juvenile legal system.
Back to lessons handed out but named much later.
Back to my enrichment program teacher seeing me whole and possible.
Back to juvie and vital lessons gained about the world and my supposed place in it.
Back
Back to what formal education offered but could *not* prevent.
Back to undo something I did not know happened—

Back because (re)memory is a means of accessing my young and youthful girlhood. Back because, being Black gurl reliable as a youthful and seasoned Black girl is a practice of how I treat us, myself included. Back because within this happening is a set of performances and processes that crystallized the body as a site of confinement wherein pedagogies of foreclosure, inclusive of accumulated exposure to regulation, surveillance, and harm, heightens violence and the prospect of stuckness.

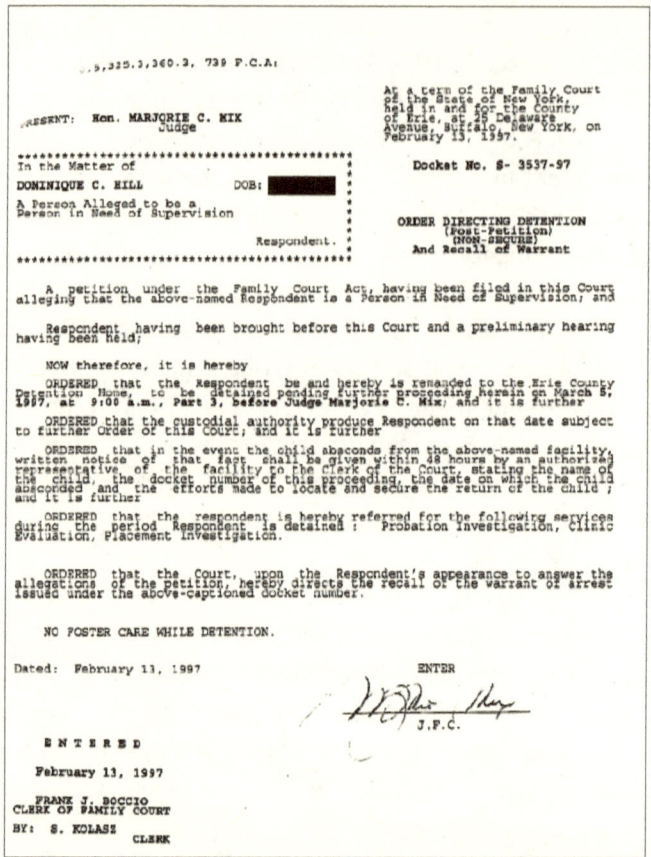

FIGURE 2.1. The first image is documentation of my first court proceeding on February 13, where I informed the judge that I did not want to return home and my mother expressed disinterest in the matter. It orders that I am to be held at the Erie County detention home and was to remain there until my next court date, March 5. Further, it offers protocol should I run away. Lastly, it documents the "services" I will receive during my time in the detention home, which included a look into the need for probation, a health exam that included a pregnancy test and my first and unnecessary pap exam, as well as consideration of group home placement, which I was later denied. On this day, I became a "Respondent," the warrant for my arrest was repealed, and Ferry—an actor of the state—became my temporary guardian and surveillant.

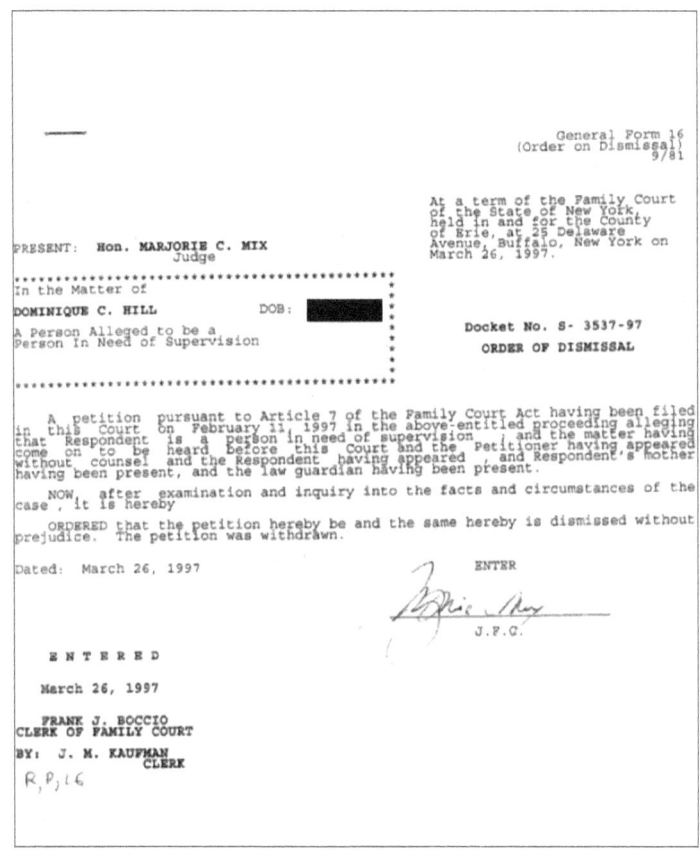

FIGURE 2.2. This second document records that on March 26, in the presence of myself, my mother (also the petitioner), and my required legal representation as part of family court, the label Person in Need of Supervision was withdrawn from record. Yet the supervision continued. When I started this project and sought to access the paper trail documenting this event, I was instructed by the county clerk records at City Hall that these documents capturing a moment of my life could only be accessed by my mother. At the initial point of request, it had been sixteen years since I was released from Ferry; I could (re)member but could not retain formal artifacts attached to it.

Echo One: Marked and Detained

Echo Two: A Monologue On a Black Girl's Navigation of Body Politics

Four days before my fourteenth birthday, I pleaded with the judge to be released from juvenile detention and into my mother's custody.
LIES.
I was going to live with my teacher.
I longed for escape.
Done with my mother, and tired of pretending I was not hurt.
Mom said I had run away. Bullshit.
I called it temporary escape.
Emulating my family,
> I turned my sadness into a party.
> Ran away, drank. Skipped school, drank. Smoked weed, drank. No sleep, drank.
> I partied alllllll the way to juvie.
> Persuaded, there, by family members, that my presence in juvie affected them more than it did me.

LIES.
My family had a name, a reputation to uphold.
The shame.
"What will they think of my granddaughter being locked up like this, Domi?"

Silent Lesson: My body is not my own.

Hurt. Staring past her, cuz
she seemed more invested in returning everything, me included, to its proper place.
I yearned, she never asked.
She never asked.
She never asked!

She never asked if anyone touched or tried to touch me in an unwanted way. Maybe, out of fear, she did not want to know.

Silent Lesson: What happens to my body is mine to deal with.
Strip. Apply. Massage. Rinse. Shower.
Her eyes never left my skin.
Assault (mostly mental).
"If you were so smart you wouldn't be here."
Then, he'd look at my breasts.
"If you were just a little older,"
he'd suggest. I'm thirteen!
A pap. What the fuck is that?!

Note: Being incarcerated, Black, female, and youthful are probable causes of STDs, pregnancy, and promiscuity, right?!

LIES.

Lying there in cold.
On the table lay three sizes of an awkwardly shaped something,
to go inside me?
I ask for the smallest,
nurse opts for the medium-sized one.
I scream, no pause.

Silent Lesson: Disposable property; my body is worthy of no breaks.

honor roll
top two percent of my eighth-grade class,
student athlete
leader
no merit.

Instead, I received a strict daily regimen of remedial coursework; blame and shame; sexual solicitations in exchange for food from the "outside;" and having my feelings disregarded almost daily—

I silently accepted what they wanted me to know about my body.
I get it.
My body has no value.

Echo Three: Watching Me Forget, Watching Me (Re)member Myself Together

Setting: Sitting on the floor in front of a mirror, allowing revelations to unfold while listening to Jill Scott's "Watching Me" and talking to myself, looking at the window to the right.[15] *A dialogue unfolds between* DOM *in this moment and* DOM, *a rendering of previous iterations.*

Damn Dom, it only took you seventeen years, two degrees, and explicit instruction that you (re)membered, we been to juvie. Girl, not to be funny but how?! Was it because no one brought it up? Hadta be about your focus on a winning ticket straight outta Blo. [laughs] Seriously though, you never thought about it? At all? Oh right, you forgot. Bet yo azz wonderin' why you decided to (re)member that day. Unlocking one memory opens to other doors. [takes a swig of kombucha and smirks] Might as well keep going, but we gotta go back to go forward.

                      I was good at doing school. Young Black girl growing up in the inner city on the east side of Ruff Buff with big dreams of leaving the state altogether, becoming a poet, and opening my own school, I took my education seriously, ya know. It was my ticket out and a sure way to make my family and community proud. I drank the Kool-Aid about formal education and each year did what I thought it took to move closer to my dreams becoming reality. For my dreams, it was no big deal to spend eight hours Monday through Friday at Buffalo Prep in what we called "good" summer school. The reward—admission and financial support to attend a private high school—well worth it. No biggie to attend an all-girls Catholic high school, purchase uniforms, and catch a train and two buses to school, sometimes three when going to Buffalo Prep for class after school or extended study. Each day, each program, each adversity endured, meant a step closer to manifesting my life vision.

So, it was the "keeping busy" schedule your momma put you on that made you forget?

Nah, I won't say that. I guess, with each opportunity, I got new tools, new reasons, and new language for making myself visible. I didn't know and wasn't checkin' for the pieces of me falling away. Can't say I noticed how many pieces I tucked away. I returned from Ferry and it was like it never happened. I returned back to school, still on the honor roll, still in Buffalo Prep, still focused on my next right move. I never talked about it and nobody asked. Maybe I was ashamed. Granny's words cut deep: "What will they think of my granddaughter all locked up like that Domi?" The judge released me into the care of my mother. I went to live with my teacher and eventual godmother and never looked back.

First and foremost, I believe you, know that. I'm stumped about y/our ability to go all this time with no smell, person, place sending you back to juvie. Was the experience unmemorable?

I legit get y/our suspicion. I'm with you, smirking,

> rollin' my eyes, the whole nine. Truth is, I'm still shocked at the witchery of that moment when Lighthouse instructed me to write the story of how I know the body matters to Black girlhood. The flood of images and events shocked my nervous system and returned me to fist pounding on doors to wake us, my door with that tiny film of dirt and the tasteless food served. I instantly (re)membered how they watched us. They offered no privacy. They watched us eat and shower. During nurse visits they watched and sometimes whispered. They watched our bodies as they talked to each other in our presence.

That's wild AF and also high key gross.

> Wild indeed. But the more outlandish thing about it was my response.

Say more.

> I became skilled at burying my thoughts and feelings deep in my poetry, deep in my yearning for school, deep in my imagined nighttime chitchats with BJ, my great grandma. I put my feelings into places inaccessible to others including myself. You could say I retreated 'cept I devoted my time to learning the game of pretend. While becoming hyperaware of the process of being watched, I developed skill and a space to store my feelings. I learned to give from the depths without assigning much to what it meant.[16] I learned, if I handed over what they wanted, there would be fewer, if any, problems. If I gave them what they wanted without them asking, I might be "rewarded." When staff brought in pizza and wings or a legend-

ary steak sub from Rick's steakhouse, I watched girls turn on or up their sexuality in exchange for a piece of pizza and sometimes a wing. Often an unwanted target of sexual solicitation, I played up my "of service" capacity and wiped down tables, swept the floor after all meals, and always asked staff how else I could help. Such actions produced a "reward" in the tender of wings, pizza, other "outside" food; an extra call home that week; and/or inclusion in detention gossip like who is confined to their cell, what happened earlier that day, and what activities they have planned for us. If a cunning smile, a peep of sexuality in my walk, or a held, quiet tongue earned reward, so be it, I thought.

Whoa.

To receive as many breaks as possible, I appeared tamed, accommodating even. In there, they saw me as a problem and I saw my body as both my problem and a tool. I became versed at reducing the meaning I attached to otherwise overly compliant and degrading behavior. I made it all a game of manipulation to deliver what others wanted to see in me.

Whoa. Say less.

You asked, so I'm keeping it a buck. That's how we heal, right?! Quietly, beneath the surface, perhaps in the spirit plane, I left pieces of me inaccessible. They watched me and showed me the how of surveillance. Unconsciously, I started watching myself to make sure I didn't get out of pocket "in front of company." I did not realize I was watching me. Watching myself became policing, became correcting, became trying to exist as something "presentable," "legible," "appropriate." Though my initial interest was about "looking" the part, the constant watching and my added self-monitoring shifted beyond presentation to my embodiment. I became what they wanted me to know about my body. I became my body. Captive and configured as "wrong," unheard, unrecognized when in and out of order, denied personhood and benefit of the doubt. In juvie, I became who they told me I was, and I remorsefully accepted that. I fought to conceal those pieces of me that didn't match the conventionally oriented eye to what success and promise looked like on Blackness, on bodies marked femme or feminine-expecting. I suppressed my call to dance and shake and feel—the very things that justified the surveillance of my body.

I see. You, shid we, got railroaded, tricked into forgetting. Seems like it was much easier to forget. Almost like there was little choice or benefit to (re)membering. Is that what you're saying? How does it feel to (re)member now? Is it worth (re)membering?

Despite the extra treats, occasional allowance of phone time, and the loving "get it together" pep talks, I was not safe. Those "privileges" are cherished in juvie, I cherished them. They should not be dismissed as trivial. But they did not protect me from violence of any kind, R. Kelly–light interactions, or spirit rupture. The other part I tripped about, especially on court days, was the race reality of this carceral performance. White folk walked the halls in professional attire. Had me wondering "where they send the 'bad' white youth?" [laughs]

I saw the racism, classism, androcentrism, adultification, not by those names of course, but could not see the relationship unfolding between my physical body and self. I wonder if mom, Granny, and teachers noticed my acquiescence after juvie. I wonder if they saw my bodily comportment as a sign of repair, progress, a return to the "old me"? Or did I disappear from their view altogether? If I were to think solely from the level of my family, these womn watched because they're nosey and want to be of help. More, they want to guide and take pride in me. From a cultural angle, they watched to assess my comprehension of good Black commonsense. Even bigger is the weight of ideologies and structural realities that keep Black folk watching out. From this position, my family watched me through a lens not entirely of their own making.

Now that's tough titties, as BJ would say.

Without hesitation, I pressed onward with an amplified understanding of surveillance and confinement. Desensitized but not completely numb, I collected pain and used it like ammunition, turned it into a poem or a dance. These days, I embrace but don't expect pain. I am certainly no longer collecting pain pennies. Moving toward freedom involves looking back and looking inward to examine what happened, what got missed, and what is worth salvaging. Now, I know that bars, chains, and having someone approve your every move are carceral mechanics. They are procedures that generate stiff and stale energy. It took studying Black girlhood alongside practicing it in SOLHOT and while teaching mostly Black and Brown girls in an enrichment program to (re)member, return to, and own being marked P.I.N.S. My time in juvie revealed seeds and insights around my leanings toward critical education and my hunger for creative opportunities and art, as well as the evolution of the key agents in my scholarship: embodiment, Black girlhood, healing, and practices that engender imagining and nourishing full presence.

There was also no way to know all of this that moment. You, we, were thirteen and some change. Looking back though, what do you make of your forgetting? What, if anything, did it gift you/us? What value exists in forgetting?

    I survived.

I forgot.

    We survived.

We survived.

[*In unison*] I hit play on my goals and the rest was irrelevant until it wasn't. Until I (re)membered and went on a spree of tracing my actions and bodily comportment in relation to that event. Forgetting permitted physical survival. With little effort needed, it authorized me to live outside of what happened to me. (Re)membering pieced me—past, present, future—back together.

"Undressing" to Unlock the Cage

This chapter and the exercise of (re)memory are trial and error moments and reflections on undressing in public. As if waiting to be plucked from the depths of me, I mouthed *juvie* and my body grew cold, my chest seized, and my mind's eye opened to my tiny cell with the window that required use of my tiptoes. These physiological reactions surfaced accompanied by flashing images of the Black womn with a Toucan Sam nose and freckles who processed me into Ferry, invasively searched my body, and watched me bathe before putting on a Level One uniform—an itchy off-white cotton sweat suit with dollar-store taupe slides. My tongue itched with the memory of the tasteless food and then watered when I thought about the occasional spoonful of collards, pieces of a steak sandwich, pizza, or the occasional wing received when certain staff worked.

Once I decided to (re)member, the rest of me awakened to the (re)memory. The shame, anger, and ache between my legs returned as if I just survived another forced pap smear test with a speculum appropriate for someone with a dilated cervix or who had previously given birth. I managed to maintain my belief that education afforded escape. Truth is, I rarely felt safe, not in juvie, in my mother's house, nor in schools. Being in juvie increased my proximity to disposability and exploitation. Our youthful bodies, locked away, were excusably unguarded. In juvie, my body signaled varying things and, in each instance, differentially assumed me in need of external management. My underage status, being an early developed girl, runaway, Black girl, and a respondent of the state, determined me incapable of knowing my needs, a body to be exploited, and a voice to be omitted, unless it corroborated with a story shared by an authority figure.

As a facilitator of forgetting, disembodying experiences act as dead and breathing happening—a memorial. Under the rubric of body politics and hegemony, bodies get reduced to service, often to things and people outside of and in opposition to self. Over time one's touch with spirit is weakened. To strengthen and rebuild contact, Alexander insists, "the work of rewiring the senses is neither a single nor individual event. Practitioners . . . must show up, in other words, for this appointment, to the ceremonies that rehearse over and over again the meaning of Sacred accompaniment."[17] The perpetual violence of spirit-murdering delivers constant reminders and reinforcement of hierarchical oppression. More than putting people in their allotted place, spirit-murdering memorializes by keeping people and bodies in a holding cycle and cements their prescribed position. Through physical and psychic maneuvers, pedagogies of foreclosure diminish and potentially inhibit sensation.[18] In juvie, someone else observed and determined every move we made. We were not able to refuse "resources" they identified as required, because they claimed to know more about our needs than we did. To add insult to assault, when I screamed out of pain, the nurse continued without batting an eye. Subconsciously, these lessons tattooed me. In (re)membering though, I made contact with the "more intense" and actively disrupted stagnation.[19] Akin to the vocabulary attributed to Black womn and Black people through education, to cut the present participle, *-ing*, offers the possibility of shifting moments of disembodiment from *dead and breathing happenings* to events with provisional endings.[20]

My guidance counselor, a white woman with wrinkled, tanned skin, brought me my homework weekly and collected my completed assignments. I cannot recall what made her start coming. Conceivably it was my complaining to my granny about the basic worksheets or maybe that was the one thing my mother heard during our phone calls. What I know for certain is that I didn't ask her to come but am grateful she did. Despite my attitude, and "waywardness," I knew support when I felt it and allowed it in (though not without suspicion).[21] Support looked like my granny bringing me clothes when I advanced to Level 3 and was able to wear my own clothing. Support looked like my history and geography enrichment program teacher (whom I lived with and later became my godmother) investigating my whereabouts and showing up to my court hearing. Support felt like, *I gotchu*. Not all Black girls are held when detained and confined. When researching encounters with the juvenile system, I found no specific documentation of youth choosing to be detained nor the sociocultural circumstances that inform and/or encourage our eventual placement in detention. This does not mean that no such stories exist, nor does it mean one narrative is valuable and another is forgettable.

If, however, a stellar student's report of violence in the home is not credible enough for serious investigation, what hope do Black girls routinely visiting juvie have? If, while under the care of the legal system, a thirteen year old is "softly" solicited for sex, what is the likelihood that something sexually deplorable did not or will not happen? If a Black girl from a "respectable" family, on the honor roll, and part of an enrichment program is met with disbelief about instances of violence and considered a problem by many of the adults in her life, what possibility is left for those without intelligible accolades or accomplishments?[22] What I endured is part of but not the whole story. Pedagogies of foreclosure, memory, and education are entanglements, and perhaps because of their interlaced realities, (re)memory and violence are in relationship. What conditions make surrender to these advances plausible? Although I remain uncertain, I wonder what might engender (re)memory to be felt as a violent process. Honestly, I quarrel with the nature of the bond between violence and healing. Does healing carry violence in tow? If trauma is a form of violence and (re)memory of a traumatic experience is also trauma, then might healing come only through violence? I am unsure. Today, I have only questions. I sense, however, there is something traumatic but not tragic about my (re)memory of juvie. What I know is that my going back to feel and recalibrate the event poses prospects that outweigh the potential sensational trauma.

(Re)memory is a tool for countering muting processes like hypersurveillance and "prematurely knowing" and their impacts. (Re)memory provides growth opportunities and can take place anywhere. Around the same time of my initial exhumation of this incident, I was working with Black and Brown girls through a Trio program in Baltimore, Maryland. I was teaching in girls-only classrooms after receiving approval from the administration to design and teach culturally grounded college-readiness courses. Simultaneously, I was collecting dissertation data exploring the usefulness of artistic practice and communal space for encouraging self-reflection and examination of Black girlhood. Through different modes—mini performances, anecdotal stories, and journal feedback—I shared pieces of my life, educational experiences, and evolving identity with the students. In both the research setting and all-girl college-readiness courses I taught between 2012 and 2017, students expressed the value of learning about my life. They shared how it tore down walls and spawned ideas about who they could be despite and perhaps because of their familial backgrounds and life challenges. Undressing in public, a practice of vulnerability, emerged from the ongoing feedback I received from my girls, combined with the longings verbalized by girls and womn in my dissertation research related to spaces where they could be and process their lives as a conduit for cultivating intimate and potentially rupturing experiences. This practice is effective alone and in front of company. The public in undressing gestures toward intention, is less about numbers of people, and is geared at least to one of three primary aims: a) to dispel myths, b) to establish raw self-recognition, and c) to subvert unproductive barriers.

Undress in public to obliterate myths. By never recalling, speaking, or naming juvie, I distanced myself from the experience. Unintentionally, forgetting also facilitated a distancing of myself from other girls locked up or detained, or who did not escape the juvenile system. My family colluded with me. It was not until I started my journey of (re)memory and shared my sense-making of it through performance that they inquired into my experiences in juvie or shared what they imagined about my time there. Compartmentalizing who I was from who I saw myself becoming worked for the world I was making for myself as a budding scholar, until it didn't. Around the time of my adviser's firm suggestion that I excavate the story driving my research, the girls I taught wrote in their journals about feelings of inadequacy, family abuse, racist teachers, and more while expressing their assumptions that I had it all together and kept it real. Although I had talked about my bad attitude, as well as my mother/daughter relationship struggles, I had not yet divulged running away nor time in a detention center. These salient moments of call out with girls' binary thinking that you are or aren't put together, you make or don't make it, and you do well or you let people down, compelled me to undress.

When invited to locate the lesson that prompted my knowing that the body matters deeply to girls' educational experiences, I heard my then–dissertation chair's invitation to be: Undress to see yourself wholly and (w)holy. Elizabeth Alexander discusses Black interiority and art making, proposing the creative as a space not void of white and external imaginings but where Blackness is not bound by them.²³ A will to be and be seen (w)hole is required. Sometimes too, my clouded vision offered no refuge. Unknowingly, I showed up personally fragmented while engaging scholarship that implored that Black girls be seen in their fullness. I divided myself along neat superficial lines that deflected attention away from my coarseness. My writing revealed me to myself and clarified for me the façade I had constructed and how I learned of its prominence. Cloaking allowed me to escape the image of myself that I'd concocted at the conscious level to counter and complicate the all too common but effectively circulated narrative about inner city girls who do drugs, run away, come from single parent households run by womn, and land themselves in juvie.

    The practice of undressing is multifaceted. Here, it happened through a dialogue occurring between my academic studies, poetry, and body. Through this mirror conversation, I saw more clearly that all my parts were not coming along, *and* I had a part in that. I had not yet located a next level theorization about the why and under what circumstances could all my parts not come, but I knew and accepted that one of the reasons they did not come was because I was taught and had acquiesced to the idea that they had no "proper" place. In my acceptance of this teaching, I denied myself innocence. Undressing proved essential to self-recognition and my work with girls, as well as how I chose, still choose to show up in the world after this reckoning moment. No doubt, undressing is a vulnerable act that comes with costs. Black lesbian poet Pat Parker explains, "The day all the different parts of me can come along, we would have what I would call a revolution."²⁴ Undressing in public, no matter the size of the audience, forces a coming to terms with self, events, my/our part in the happening, and its footprint in our future. After my initial enactment of (re)memory and turning it into a monologue, Pat Parker's words sat differently in my body. I pondered, Who determines what parts of me come along?

    To exercise (re)memory is to transgress borders between past and present with a goal of bridging and forging new possibilities. Through it, I located and documented the story of what happened in juvie and how it informed my comportment and show up in the world. Repeating the happening multiple times, I learned that it is a choice to wait for someone to sanction bringing your whole self to living and the spaces you visit. Undressing in public intentionally muddles barriers and materializes opportunities for deeper, emmeshed connection and intimacy. I undressed before my girls to erase imaginary distinctions between me and them. My purposeful vulnerability aimed to impart information that folk learn after auntie is on a third shot or after Granny transitions—raw inconvenient truths intentionally kept sacred until they were called forth and/or needed. I practice undressing here to name the compartments I used to make between Dominique the A-student and the runaway; Dominique the scholar and the juvie girl; the presentation of me and the parts of me that constitute this presentation. Undressing in public creates the conditions for body-activation and touch (see Chapter 4). Undressing in public (re)orients the entire self.

Conclusion

To undress in public is to unlock the cage from the inside. Through reengagement with stories and things I denied and/or forgot, (re)tooling happened. Additionally, it is a form of (re)memory work that "connects time, space, matter, and histories, including creating memories of the future."[25] To participate in undressing is to employ transgression and peel away veneer and external standards. The deployment of (re)memory occurs in many ways and when repeated furnishes new understandings of an event while reconfiguring the meaning of its presence. Undressing affords the opportunity to recalibrate relationships between the site of injury and the self. Moreover, the act of (re)memory and undressing is necessary "wake work" for reducing disembodiment and dismemberment.[26] (Re)memory is an inversion of forgetting that Alexander describes as "never having known or never having learned something, the difference between staying in tune with the source of our own wisdom and relying on borrowed substitutes."[27] To (re)member makes reliance on internal measures and guides possible and requires wrongness to be embraced within the body and its many layers. Such work is disruptive, likely unpleasant, reorienting even.[28]

Going back revealed lessons once unavailable to me. My encounter with the juvenile system was not the first nor the last time my body stood trial as its own witness. Confinement, as revealed in the preceding echoes, happened before, during, and after my voluntary entrance into the system. Still, Black girls and "Black people everywhere and anywhere we are, still produced in, into, and through the wake an insistence on existing: we insist Black being into wake."[29] Our existence as young and youthful, youthful and seasoned girls, our doing of knowing and creativity amid hypersurveillance, oppressive environments, possession, and death—literal and figurative—demand we do more than critique such violence and injustice. Girls come with volume that resounds in the physical body, sartorial choices, thinking and theory, and adornment. It is at the level of the body—its psychic, emotional, spiritual, physicality—that schemes to tame and distort one's internal mirror get employed. Black girls and stakeholders of Black girlhood must undress, take inventory of what's been buried, and even locate new mirrors that support a (re)membering of magnitude and mattering. *Theory out and applied.*

CHAPTER 3

my Hair, my Mirror, my Own
A Lesson in (Self) Recognition

> And I feel like that's really mind boggling to me how I was such a good student but at the same time my hair took over that perception of me being that good student.
>
> Vanessa Van Dyke

In November 2013, Faith Christian Academy in Orlando, Florida, proffered twelve-year-old Vanessa Van Dyke the ultimatum of altering her 'fro—cutting or shaping it—or being expelled. Vanessa's hair embodied what the school policy sought to temper when it stated, "Hair must be a natural color and must not be a distraction."[1] Enrolled there since the third grade, Vanessa was a community member of Faith Christian and yet, as echoed in her statement in the epigraph, her tenure at Faith Christian Academy and her academic success held no merit. According to Vanessa, the bullying, initiated by her "mostly white and Hispanic" classmates, followed the change in the volume and texture of her hair. When asked about the policy before and after her initial leaving, Vanessa shared, "I remember after I officially left the school they changed their student handbook to hair couldn't be a distraction, three inches out from the head—oh, and no accessories. I remember I wore a flower on the side of my hair. They said that right after I left, and I said that sounds really similar to how I used to wear my hair."[2] Bullied by peers and configured to be wrong, a distraction, Vanessa faced anti-Blackness as a logic that remained in circulation and undetectable. Making Vanessa into an archetype by the revised hair policy, even temporarily, reinforced the school's misguided concern even at the risk of causing harm. Vanessa, like Jordan, knew, "I am not wrong: Wrong is not my name." This knowing led

my Hair, my Mirror, my Own · 99

FIGURE 3.1. Essence in Bloom. Sabrina Kent ©2013. This image is a self-selected image of Vanessa Van Dyke that she felt captured her essence in 2013. Taken before her experience of surviving attempted spirit murder and before being given an ultimatum by her school principal, Vanessa provided this image in response to the prompt "share an image from 2013 that you feel captures your essence before you started actively freedom fighting." Vanessa approved the title via Instagram chat, March 27, 2024.

to her decision to stand up for herself, which then landed her in the principal's office facing expulsion.[3]

This chapter interrogates violence that occurs at the site of the Black girl body. It examines actions at the nexus of body politics, school dress-code policies, de facto practices of school authority, and hair stylization. I illustrate how de facto and de jure school policies related to hair and sartorial choices function as a contemporary form of Jane Crow oppressions. Carried out through state violence, these oppressions facilitate deaths but instead become hauntings. Drawing on two interviews with Vanessa Van Dyke, this chapter establishes sartorial literacies as sites of underrecognized justice work and violence in Black girlhood unambiguously. To offset their spirit-murdering effects, I introduce mirror theory as a valuable counterdiscourse and highlight what reliability work could look like as it relates to affirming Black girls' crowns.

When Black hair adornment as done by girls in particular becomes an unexceptional component of lived experience generally and the school day specifically, the barometer on Black mattering will have moved in the affirmative direction. While narrow configurations of justice circulate within media and primary agendas within movements, embodiment is an underrecognized measure of it. From zero-tolerance to dress codes, school policies serve as quotidian devices for advancing the carceral state and supporting anti-Black racism. Infused with anti-Black and racialized gender logics, these codes mark a particular moment within the afterlives of slavery and broaden the range of Jane Crow oppressions by configuring gender differently when attached to Blackness. These policies reproduce hierarchies by echoing social expectations and norms around bodies read as Black and female, though not inherently cisgender, femme, or feminine. In these settings, distraction is enacted through conditioning strategies meant to break the spirit and pivot Black girls away from becoming on their own terms.

Schools as Body Battlegrounds

Black girls are molded by the gazes applied to seeing them. Also, "the gaze from people with dominant identities onto those with non-dominant ones creates narratives that evolve into definitive and state constructions."[4] Youthfulness, race, and gender, minimally, coalesce to produce unequivocal consequences for Black girls that are not contingent on the social identities those looking upon girls inhabit. On one hand, girls are often relegated to the margins in educational inequality and equity discourse, denied opportunities to advance in honors and gifted education, discounted for their academic faculties based on behavioral assessments, and left to fall between the cracks.[5] On another, these realities potentially mean becoming "prematurely knowing" and required to receive "the talk" to prepare Black girls to dodge and handle encounters with sexual violence by teaching Black girls how to perform "lady."[6] The act of imparting lady politics, a category once denied Black womn and designated a quality of white femininity only, onto Black girls is one strategy to protect girls. It is also evidence that Black girls "prematurely knowing," as articulated by Harriet Jacobs, not only occurs in the presence of white men, specifically those who abduct and abuse Black bodies in the interest of profit, but that it is incited by men's lewd and predatory actions. Equally, Gonzalez's study on Black parents' approaches to protecting their Black youth illustrate that there are some overlapping ideas that govern the appraisal and interpretation of Black youth bodies and others that are contingent on meaning made of one's gender. "The talk" and its specific content also illustrate that Black girls' and boys' combatting of violence will likely look different.

Black girls' navigation of predatory figures and bodily harm happens everywhere, including on the way to and while in school. Irrespective of location, Black girls' bodies are read against racial, feminine, and sexual codes, which cannot be partitioned, explained, nor traversed in isolation. Rather, as Deborah King stresses, "the modifier 'multiple' refers not only to several, simultaneous oppressions but to the multiplicative relationships among them as well. In other words, the equivalent formulation is racism multiplied by sexism multiplied by classism."[7] The conjoining of race and gender logics then justify punitive measures for defiance, which lead to the criminalization of Black girls for "breaking" arbitrarily enforced dress codes.[8] Culturally, these same firm decisions—to ask a clarifying question, for instance—signify commonsense Black resistance and/or sheer curiosity. The heightened connotation of Black bodies generally leaks into school policy where "acting up" by Black students is nebulous but supports school administrators passing off disciplinary responsibilities to on-site police officers and the state.[9] Increased attention to Black girls' in-school experiences is important work to addressing social injustice, improving Black life and living, and more. Its contents, however, confirm a significant and overlooked reality regarding the interdependence of bodies. As Wanda Pillow notes, "at the same time and likely precisely because 'bodies are dangerous' policies are all about bodies—controlling, regulating, shaping and (re)producing bodies."[10] Illuminated in Pillow's study of education policy generally and teenage mothers specifically, this quote underscores the co-constitutive relationship between policies and bodies. Beliefs used to structure society also order bodies. They assign meaning, value, and capacity depending on social identities embodied and their geographic location. Policy is a set of ideas imposed on bodies and people. Within a given context, bodies become policy—a principal reason that a set of regulations are imposed.

Something distinct happens at the nexus of Blackness, gender, bodies, and policy. More than adultification or implicit bias, the infractions imposed that sometimes result in loss of instruction time due to in-school suspension, reduced support from school adult authority, and/or what Monique Morris frames as "pushout," should be understood as Black youthful inheritances of slavery and its many afterlives. Increased exploration of the experiences of girls in school is of necessity, and alone insufficient. Contact with high-stakes policies and school discipline reveals new, distinct qualities that expand popularized notions of carceral geographies and modalities. Accordingly, it is imperative to surpass context and attend to discursive outputs of criminalization in schools, because "to know how the boundary between inside or outside is constituted, policed and transgressed, we must approach specific cases empirically."[11] Examining disparities of punishment in Denver Public Schools, Annamma et al. observed that 52 percent of Black girls referred to the principal's office were suspended from school and were then more likely to be expelled altogether.[12] The top three reasons for referral include "detrimental behavior, disobedience and defiance, and third-degree assault," and involve subjective assessment from authority figures and witnesses.[13]

In examining rates of suspension, expulsion, and referrals through quantitative comparisons across race, gender, and their compounded realities, Black girls, irrespective of region, school locale, and academic performance, are disproportionately represented in disciplinary and punitive practices. Further, when penalized, it is more frequently for reasons that require personal determination rather than fact. Black girls' voices are largely muted, scarcely solicited, and/or presumed immaterial.[14] Zero-tolerance policies make future suspensions and even pushout likely, spotlighting conditions surrounding Black girls' in-school run-ins with punishment. Morris finds that zero-tolerance policies, body policing, and infractions for "bad" attitudes are leading factors in Black girl pushout. Her work identifies policies and practices and exposes attitudes (read: consciousness) that cultivate hyper(in)visibility, disregard sociocultural realities impeding success, and sanction Black girl criminalization in schools in California, New York, Illinois, and Louisiana.[15] There are covert ways, revealed through girls' theorization, that behavior, body adornment, and Black femininity scripts creep into policy. In places like California, zero tolerance is paired with "willful defiance suspensions" that allow dubious arbitration.[16] Wun's examination of girls at a California high school surfaces the disproportionate punishment for nonviolent and arbitrary violations such as disruption and defiance. She argues that formal and informal punitive practices bolster social ordering and are permeated by anti-Black sentiment.[17]

Black girls are made the targets of sanctions that can be racially and culturally coded to ideas of Black signifying incivility and tie both the categories Black and girl to a need for saving.[18] The body—how it is adorned by material and discursive elements—stands in as a barometer for Black girls' identity and worth, particularly as it relates to educational attainment. It is not surprising then that Black girls fall through the cracks—the cracks of Black mattering, where they go unnoticed for their distinct and indispensable contributions to fashion, style, art, and music; the cracks of society where they literally go missing without a trace; and the cracks of care practices because they are stationed as caregivers. Ricks warns, "asking Black girls to privilege their identities places them at risk for falling through the cracks" of education, and she proposes frameworks and models that acknowledge more dimensions of personhood.[19] Ricks's notable urge for theoretical perspectives and strategies for working with Black girls is vital but does little for the potentiality of falling through the cracks of structural gaze and bodily mistreatment. Equally important to this metaphor are the questions, When Black girls fall through the cracks, what happens to their bodies? How do bodies fill cracks and what might Black girls fill those cracks with instead, if they felt free and whole?

Sometimes, Black girls are subjected to anti-Black policy that forces school absence and disinvitation from educative rites of passage experiences.[20] Dress-code policies are one such that also double as a form of confinement. Moreover, these policies rationalize the denial of Black girls' self-fashioning by categorizing self-expression as a form of defiance and thereby criminalizing girls and their actions.[21] Whether in or beyond school walls, Black girls' bodies invoke a shift in the deployment of policy and sometimes prompt other policy.[22] The cumulative effects produced through and heightened by discourses of difference result in casting the "Black girl" as a prototype of wrong. Exploration of school discipline in an urban school district in the Midwest uncovers that Black girls are overrepresented in restrictive disciplinary measures for largely arbitrary offenses. Twice as likely to have in- and out-of-school suspension as their white or Latinx counterparts and four times more likely to experience in-school suspension than white girls, Black girls' actions are judged as criminal.[23] While mandated suspension for white girls (truancy) and Latinx girls (truancy and tardiness) are legal matters of the court, Black girls' primary offenses (defiance, improper dress, and fighting with another student) are social expectations of classed conduct.

Unfair treatment does not always occur in the form of penalty disparities; it also manifests in gatekeeping practices wherein alternative rubrics are applied. For example, Black girls' behavior corroborates one's potential success or failure.[24] These lower expectations were then justified by the need to frequently address "behavioral" issues. Counselors framed students' "behavioral" concerns as cultural deficits assumed to be a result of a lack of active parental presence.[25] Beneath counselors' assessment of girls' capacity for learning live ideological investments, myths, and essentialist renderings about performances of Blackness and femininity.

Going back in time, Linda Grant's 1994 examination of first-grade classrooms and the roles assigned to Black girls unearthed informal expectations in the classroom that encouraged the adoption of specific roles: "helper, enforcer, or go-between."[26] Both Black and white teachers placed more emphasis on girls' comportment, commenting on and rewarding girls for particular behavioral practices. Studies like Grant's and later those of West and Olatunji, for instance, exhibit interconnections between Black womn tropes and hyper-assessment and conflation of Black girls' mannerisms with their assumed academic performance. Equally, the roles surfaced in Grant's study all correspond to service, lodging Black girls' currency in the capacity to be of use to others. Another foundational education study on Black girls is Signithia Fordham's examination of in-school gendered experiences at a magnet school in Washington, DC. Fordham finds that Black girls who fared best in school—good grades, high test scores, and support from teachers, aligned with the established hierarchy between Black boys and girls.[27] "Loud Black girls," however, tended to have good grades but lower test scores and less teacher support. No documentation existed that the latter group received referrals or punishment for their behavior. They were, however, ostracized for not performing acceptable femininity. This study reveals the gravity of the body generally to reading and determining Black girls' merit in school particularly. Continuing with a critique of Black girls' volume, Edward Morris's "'Ladies' or 'Loudies'" study identified the coding of loudness as Black and non-normative (code for inappropriate) in-school behavior.[28] Related to the rendering of certain qualities as distractions, Morris and Perry reveal how, by default, certain Black girl expressions interrupt conventional narratives of race and gender.

To investigate Black girls' encounters with school discipline, Morris and Perry used an "intersectional framework" to examine data from grades six through twelve from the Kentucky School Discipline Study. They found Black girls three times more likely to be referred to the principal's office for less serious and more ambiguous misconduct, such as "disruptive behavior, dress code violations, and aggressive behavior."[29]

Aware of the power wielded through frames as an initial point of impact, Black feminist, womanist, and critical race scholars took to applying conceptual models to educational research. Through a critical race framework, Neal-Jackson examines qualitative studies conducted in school spaces that speak directly to circumstances girls navigate, finding that most studies are absent of first-person accounts.[30] She determined that school administrators and authority figures unfairly substituted girls' behavior and performances of femininity as a stand in for measuring academic potential and success. As evidence of frames' influence, the study illuminated the rub between sartorial choices, politics of identity, and school authorities' perceptions of Black girls. Working with the frames of critical race feminism and figured worlds, Hines-Datiri and Andrews explore relationships between Black girls' bodies and zero-tolerance policies, arguing that Black girls' invisibility and debasement are reinforced through policies that maintain whiteness and white femininity as measures of normalcy. Hines-Datiri and Andrews purport that policies and practices built into the larger zero-tolerance umbrella "not only affect the racial and gender identity development of Black girls but perpetuate anti-Black discipline and represent behavioral responses to White femininity."[31] As a figured world, schools assist in the making of gender as well as the girl and set Black girls up to acquiesce to its order or suffer the consequences. Further, because schools are steeped in social histories and binary discourse, Black girls' potential and self-definition in this figured world are informed by historical hauntings and pathological frames.[32] Connected to historical ideologies and their omnipresence, Apugo, Castro, and Doughtery apply Patricia Hill Collins's specific framework of "domains of power" to analyze the ways power is wielded in school settings. They found that schools operate as a carceral geography and constrict Black girls through de facto and de jure policies, repeat messaging about normative behavior, and school culture.[33]

The above review is in no way exhaustive. Instead, I painted a picture of the body's significance to formal education, in school handling, and exposure to punishment. Further, this review reveals indictments of the Black girl body in United States schools primarily published between 2000 and 2022. Additionally, it exemplifies Foucault's description of how the "juvenile delinquent" is made through the conflation of social wrongdoings and legal violations. What were once disciplinary issues to be handled in-house by school administrators are now "crimes."[34] Outcomes of girls' contact with disciplinary measures, the juvenile legal system, and school authority are contingent upon external reads of their bodies and the frames built into people's looking. While some studies employed alternative race-centered and feminist frames for seeing Black girls, there remains a continued need to consider what frames best capture the fullness of Black girls' experience. Heightened consequences for noncriminal offenses become mechanics of confinement and expose the ways adultification and what Hines and Wilmot describe as anti-Black aggressions conjoin to ordain Black girl problems.[35]

Schools, as part of the social institution of education, participate in the maintenance of social order and convention. They parrot society's assessment that Black girls are wrong. Policies proliferate that are context-contingent while supporting original policies that label Black girls as problematic. For instance, to legitimize "preventive detention," a policy that excludes students from school for their perceived potential danger is to confirm policy to be a stakeholder in geographies and assumes Black girls a likely academic disturbance. Such logics connect to mapping carceral geographies and energizing voice as discussed in

Chapter 1, in that school as a carceral geography impacts how Black girls exercise, define, and utilize voice. At the junction of bodies and policy, Black girls must scrutinize the mirrors used upon us and those we use to see ourselves.[36]

Mirror Theory

An outgrowth of Black feminist and womanist theorizing is guidance and critique around the work of gaze and perspective taking. Black feminists, through poetry, music, and literature, launch conversations about mirrors in relation to self-definition and politics. In this section, I introduce mirror theory. Mirror theory encapsulates a set of ideas about why mirrors matter, how to assess perspectives imposed upon Black bodies, and consequences of believing faulty mirrors. To live and embody a Black feminist and womanist ethos requires (re)orientation to the world. For such a shift, a reliable reference is needed and demands recalibration of one's relationship to one's body, the world, popular narratives offered about them, and one's interrelation. Through distinct and interdependent tools practiced with an aim of ushering in a more livable, loving world, these credible sources, or mirrors, direct our attention away from mirrors that stifle flight. For perspective and vision, womanist Layli Maparyan introduces LUXOCRACY as an alternative governing system. Its premise is that education, not schools, and health are key ingredients to the cultivation of Inner Light and spiritual connection. Through these pillars, embodiment, or one's deliberate relationship with bodyspiritself, grows and enlivens the ability to make decisions that foreground collective advancement.[37] Releasing the misnomer of culture as race, a defining marker of community, hierarchical placement, and boundaries of responsibility, LUXOCRACY and womanist ideas advance a planetary identity where "it is not a decision between adopting global culture / planetary identity or maintaining one's ancestry / culture of origin. Rather, it is about recognizing that one can simultaneously maintain a connection to one's roots, adopt a planetary identity with its identification with global transculture, and incorporate aspects of other cultures with which one feels spiritual affinity."[38] Organized around spirituality and the notion of adopting a planetary identity, womanism associates our societal condition as symptomatic of the governing systems under which we live and their complementary values—dominance is natural and difference should be separated. As more people nurture their Inner Light, we as a society and planet move closer toward the aim of commonweal, or "a state of collective well-being and a modality of collective thought/action that does not compromise individual well-being or freedom."[39] Further, Inner Light generates interdependence between and across humans and nonhumans. Womanism promotes the enrichment of one's Inner Light so the external and the self can be reliable and healthy mirrors of each other.

Related, Black feminism crafts and intuits intellectual, creative, cultural, material, and ephemeral expressions that critique forms of domination and oppression and animate practices and theories attendant to change. A knowledge paradigm committed to enlivening self-definition, acceptance, and being, Black feminist thinking is concerned with building narratives and that reflect dimensionality, survival, and genius as linked to systems of power and practices of exclusion. In the poem, "Good Mirrors Are Not Cheap," Lorde theorizes the danger of relying on mass produced mirrors "that lie / selling us new clowns / at cut rate," insisting that such mirrors deceive and steward improper self-indictment. Infused with systemically induced blemishes or "slight enough to pass / unnoticed," these mirrors, when unchecked, incite self-doubt and judgment.[40] Built into Lorde's illustration is the weight of continuous encounters with cheap mirrors. Lorde contends that mirrors can engineer misplaced trust until "the fault in a mirror slaps back / becoming / what you think is the shape of your error."[41] Assumed flawless, the mirror, if ever, is the last place of suspicion. When a mirror, literal or figurative, exposes a problem, the person standing before it is determined to be what needs fixing.

Lorde's "Good Mirrors Are Not Cheap" bares necessary consideration of the materials of frames used during mirror construction. Since these mirrors are created in high volume and sold for cheap, their value is in their ability to manipulate what masses of people see in themselves through them. These mirrors contribute to internalized sentiments of feeling wrong and forge a systematized output. Like bombs set to detonate under appropriate heat, when these mirrors arrive in the homes and hands of Black girls and womn, they have potentially damning effects. Lorde begins with the insistence, "it is a waste of time hating a mirror / or its reflection / instead of stopping the hand / that makes glass with distortions."[42] This statement offers caution to a surface level critique and redress of gaze. Without confronting the makers of such mirrors and stopping their work, shifty mirrors will continue to be accumulated. If viewers remain unaware, another faulty mirror rises as reference point or "another blindness."[43] Crystallized here are layers of mirror theory and the imperative of reliability work where Black girls and womn can take inventory of the mirrors on which we rely and the messages we receive from them. The mirrors Lorde references were deliberately flawed. Black girls and womn deserve reliable mirrors, ones that facilitate seeing what is and what's infinitely possible. A projected image through a rigged technology can only offer inaccurate depictions and worse, potentially inspire self-injury.

In Lucille Clifton's poem "What the Mirror Said," ideas communicated by the mirror talk back to anti-Blackness and conservative images of Black womn that perpetuate stereotypes and inferiority. The mirror's speech is both reminder and reframe. Repeated within the poem is the word "listen"—a call to remember. An homage to a Black womn landscape and a form of counterdiscourse, Clifton proclaims, "listen, you a wonder. / you a city."[44] A memory jogger followed by a variety of truisms, "you got a geography / of your own," the mirror demands that whoever stands before it owns one's magnitude.[45] Acknowledging the potential messages communicated about being illegible and wrong, Clifton exclaims, "somebody need a map / to understand you."[46] In contrast to the mirrors Lorde describes, Clifton's animate aims and ensure that each womn and girl who stands before it knows:

> you not a noplace
> Anonymous
> girl;
> mister with his hands on you
> he got his hands on
> some
> damn
> body![47]

The preceding assertion is (re)orientation and reinterprets meaning potentially circulated on repeat about one's bodily value—past and present. Clifton's usage of the phrase *some damn body* emphasizes both the material dimensions of the body and in Black vernacular references being someone who matters. This affirmation brings forward body violation and nonconsensual touch, both of which can occur physically, psychically, and spiritually while certain mirrors designed by Clifton are a different brand.

Describing a necessary practice in Black life and self-actualization, E. Frances White offers an example of counterdiscourse and its usefulness. Recounting her girlhood in Wilmington, Delaware, and the contradictions between homeplace education about Blackness and school conceptualizations of Blackness, she writes, "My paternal family's political and moral beliefs created an important foundation that helped me make my way through public school without being completely damaged."[48] Subjected to a form of racism that remains, one that translated and infused segregation into school standards of tracking and discipline in the form of punishment only, the counterdiscourse circulating in her family provided an opportunity to acquire personal understanding of Black culture and Blackness. And because, as Moten states, "Blackness bears the history of the epidermalization of the alternative," Clifton's poem facilitates practice with tools forged by a different grammar of Blackness, one that spotlights Black possibility.[49] In the lives of Black girls, mirrors formed from Black density discard one dimensionality.

Black counterdiscourse and its gravity as a reliable mirror is represented in the song and children's book *No Mirrors in My Nana's House* written by Ysaye M. Barnwell and sung by the group Sweet Honey in the Rock. With no glass mirrors in the home, "the chil'" in the story grows up immersed in personal and familial meanings of life and living.[50] Unaware of social configurations of Blackness, the chil' asserts, "I never knew that my skin was too black. / I never knew that my nose was too flat."[51] Seeing her face through Nana's eyes without judgment or comparison fostered a strong sense of self and a curiosity for things deemed ugly and inappropriate outside of Nana's house. The story continues, "I was intrigued by the cracks in the walls."[52] In the world, trash is semiotics of poverty. The absence of mirrors in the house made by the world allowed chil' to maintain wonder and internally derived meaning. Nana, an elder, becomes a steward of healthy perceptions of Blackness, self-watered chil' imagination, and inadvertently, chil' critical analysis. Nana displayed a wherewithal about the power created from the act of looking and the need to then mind through whose eyes Black youth see themselves.

Words operate as mirrors. Mirrors are also made from language. Nana, through eye communication and verbal offering, taught chil' about the world in a way that did not diminish self nor naively describe the world. These messages delivered by Nana fed chil's spirit. *No Mirrors in My Nana's House* uses Black cultural intentions of storytelling to educate youthful persons about mirrors as sites from where terrible educations occur. As Bambara recounts in "Education of a Storyteller," she learned from her Grandma Dorothy a story "should be informed by an emancipatory impulse ... a story should contain mimetic devices so that the tale is memorable, shareable, that a story should be grounded in cultural specificity."[53] The rhyme and repetition in *No Mirrors*, alongside visual images of a neighborhood and building poorly cared for by those who owned it but loved and tended to by those who lived there, crystallized the relation between so-called reality and gaze. Stated differently by June Jordan: "is that how we look to you / a partial nothing clearly real?"[54]

In another children's book made in the form of a book-length poem with accompanying mixed-form images, June Jordan's *Who Look at Me* interrogates gaze and probes social interpretation of Blackness and its effects on Black life and living. Entrenched in Jordan's questions, "WHO LOOK AT ME / WHO SEE?"[55] is a knowing that looking is political and that seeing is not something predetermined. While Nana ensures chil' is primary author of themself, Lorde showed the necessity to exercise caution when choosing a co-signer or co-author of one's humanity. In "Poem about My Rights," Jordan continues mirror theory by detailing costs associated with fixed mirrors programmed for domination. To convey detail about how mirrors support regulation, Jordan recounts, "I can't do what I want / to do with my own body because I am the wrong / sex the wrong age the wrong skin." Jordan describes the liabilities attached to lying mirrors built in opposition to one's existence.[56]

"Poem about My Rights" chronicles the ways wrong become a demographic of people actively making daily decisions about life and survival while becoming marked a "thing," no longer someone, criminal, and a threat to society's business-as-usual proceedings. As theory for understanding how people are made collateral damage, the poem codifies the process and product of what it means to *be* policy. Said differently by Jordan:

> I am very
> familiar with the problems because the problems
> turn out to be
> me.[57]

Despite acknowledgment of the ways wrong is compounded by Blackness alongside body politics, Jordan refutes the mirror's prognosis. Jordan's pronouncement that her name is her own snubs the perversion created by a gaze that reduces her and others like her to a problem. The "I" here, therefore, is both deliberately personal and a signifier of a subject position otherwise dismissed and objectified. In addition, her exhortation is followed by a warning: "my simple and daily and nightly self-determination" is unwavering.[58] The preceding proclamation applies to Black girlhood and embodiment work as it pertains to Black girl hair deliberations. As a language, hair is a geography of self-definition, freedom-fighting, and sartorial literacy. What a Black girl decides to do with their hair, particularly in the face of legislated inspection and consequence, is informed by the mirrors available and most believed.

Body Policing Through Hair

Mirror work is tantamount to Black girlhood. In November 2013, faced with the school mandate to warp her 'fro or be expelled, then-twelve-year-old Vanessa Van Dyke used internal sensibilities alongside the support of her mother, Sabrina Kent, to refuse the ultimatum and declare her hair to be her own. When meeting Vanessa Van Dyke on Zoom December 13, 2021, for the second time, our "heyyyy girl" check-in quickly blossomed into me sharing a moment of discarding cheap mirrors. What started as me reacquainting myself after a big chop turned, looking back, into a moment of recalibrating my mirror's reading of my beauty, body, and capacity. Without having hit record and roughly seven minutes into our time together, we were using my body and journey as a site of analysis to theorize connections between gaze, mirrors, and self-understanding. As Vanessa shares, "I think a big part of it was me realizing that what other people had said didn't necessarily have to be true."[59] As I candidly discussed my practice of selfie taking to shift *what* and *how* I saw myself in the mirror, unknowingly mirrors and mirror theory emerged as a useful theme and metaphor for further explicating discourses of hair and which frames are useful to Black girls. What follows is reliability work to narrate Vanessa's survival of attempted spiritmurder situated in the paradigm of celebration.

During an interview with HuffPost, Vanessa shared the significance she attached to her hair: "It says that I'm unique. First of all, it's puffy and I like it that way. I know people will tease me about it because it's not straight. I don't fit in."[60] The school administrator's initial decision was supported by the school's student handbook, which insisted, "hair must be a natural color and must not be a distraction."[61] Akin to wrongness, Vanessa's hair, specifically its volume, must have caused distraction. Based on the language, distraction is an offense to the learning environment and process. Reflecting on the hurt experienced and circumstances she was forced to navigate, even in the face of her once favorite teacher, Vanessa recalls:

VANESSA: He was like, "I agree with you, but I don't think you should've gone to the news about it."

DOMINIQUE: "But you agreed with me, so what would you suggest?"

VANESSA: Right, what would you suggest here?[62]

Gaslit and unsupported, Vanessa Van Dyke became policy—both object and subject. A composite of ideas grounded in a mother's love and desire to learn, Vanessa showed up to school daily sporting "puffy," how-she-likes-it hair and a will all her own.[63] Recounting the details of her meeting with the school's principal and the blame she directed at her, Vanessa describes her as saying, "Well um. I think the bullying is because of your hair, you know, you might need to cut it, straighten it. Whatever you need to for you not to be bullied anymore."[64] Far from being innocuous, the principal's determination that Vanessa was the problem to be fixed made her an active target of spiritmurder.

The stealth anti-Blackness boiling beneath the surface of students' reactions to her hair and Vanessa becoming a scapegoat for unaddressed harm falls in line with what Hines and Wilmot coined as "anti-Black aggressions."[65] Defined as "conscious and subconscious forms of anti-Blackness and anti-Black racism that are expressed through verbal, nonverbal, interpersonal, and environmental violence directed at Black individuals," the designation of Vanessa's and countless others girls' hair as "distracting" is anti-Black aggression at work.[66] Central to this model is the body and its function as a pedagogical tool. This model articulates how such aggressions operate interpersonally, institutionally, and ideologically to shape anti-Black in-school violence against girls. Policy retitled Vanessa's bullies to "distracted students." Vanessa was discredited and her disrespected body and being were used as proof of the need to "fix" her hair. Vanessa's Blackness and youthfulness made her an unbelievable subject and unworthy of protection.

Enrolled at Faith Christian in Orlando since the third grade, Vanessa was an established member of the school community. Vanessa's multiple-year attendance, active class participation, and A-student status qualified her for school backing. Yet, the principal's ultimatum aligns with politics of racialization in the United States and contemporary school policies where Black bodies endure harsher punishment for dress code violations and other noncriminal offenses.[67] Neither behavior nor grades should dictate treatment. While a rubric based upon exceptionalism is antithetical to the paradigm of celebration, special modifications arise for certain people and bodies. Vanessa's clean disciplinary record and stellar academic performance should have cued a different set of logics. However, her body engendered a different response. Vanessa experienced restriction on multiple accounts. Peers' bullying prompted Vanessa to move her seat to further back in the class. Her choice, on a particular day, to clap back at a classmate's browbeating and antagonism landed her in a meeting with the principal. The particular frames used by her principal to see and determine the problem, resulted in her further assault. Distinguishing between harassment and bullying, Meyer explains that bullying involves, "repeatedly and over time intentionally inflicting injury on another individual."[68] Whether in the classroom or bathroom, Vanessa was Othered and therefore relegated wrong.

When asked to describe the culprits and instances of bullying she remembered, Vanessa describes a moment of hypersurveillance that took place in the bathroom:

> Specifically, this girl. I remember her so, so clear . . . one time I remember that I was in the bathroom, and I had, I would always bring my pick with me to school cause I would like to, you know, for volume. I mean, who doesn't, who doesn't do that?! . . . So she came in the bathroom and she caught me picking out my hair and she said, "I got you!" She said, "You're picking out your hair. I knew that you picked out your hair and that your hair wasn't naturally like this." . . . She literally jumped over the stall just to catch me picking out my hair. What?! Who does that?![69]

Recall, Vanessa is not new to this small private academy, and her bullies were longstanding classmates. (Re)member that her hair had recently changed in texture. Vanessa's classmate's oversimplified analysis missed that her use of the pick is confirmation of her faculties in stylization, and the labor required to take care of her new 'fro. In this (re)memory are Vanessa's word choices, which signal the invasive nature of the bullying. Significant and absent in other articulations of her story are the ways such happenings sit in the body as well as how she carried this incessant scrutiny. Embedded in Vanessa's language, "she caught me," is a sense that her actions were construed as deceptive. Spied upon through a bathroom stall, this classmate set out to shame Vanessa and find some "unnatural" explanation for Vanessa's hair.

Vanessa is also a survivor of harassment. Described by Meyer as "biased behaviors, intentional or unintentional, targeted at an individual or no specific targets," the criminalization of the 'fro made Vanessa a target of her peers and school administrators.[70] Expanding the prison nation, carceral services, and offices that "replicate the control, surveillance, and punishment of the Prison Nation, and thus, punitive and social services become indistinguishable," schools operate as "carceral services" and share in the responsibility of criminalizing certain bodies, even as "resources" are distributed.[71] While there were a few other Black girls at the school, Vanessa made sure to note that "you did see Black classmates of course, but their hair was either in braids or straightened."[72] In the context of the state of Florida and a private Christian academy, there seems to be something particularly pointed and disruptive about the 'fro.

After months of being bullied, a turn in hair texture, and pervasive taunting, Vanessa decided, enough. A peer's insistence that her hair looked like "a cactus" and "squirrel" tipped the scale, and Vanessa proceeded to clap back. Overheard by a teacher, Vanessa landed in the principal's office. I wonder, What did that teacher hear before Vanessa's voice entered the battle? When asked to describe the context, the day, and other things remembered about meeting with the principal, Vanessa recounts:

> I finally said to my principal, "I'm being bullied by my peers for this ongoing amount of time." Um, I thought like she was going to be on my side. You know thinking as a principal in a Christian school, you'd think, okay well, she's gonna side with the victim, of course. So that was not the case at all. And, you know, after that it just really affected me because I knew that the principal was not on my side, the pastor was not on my side, he agreed with the principal wholeheartedly.[73]

Initially, Vanessa kept silent and "didn't say anything to the teachers or the principal about the bullying because [she] was like, 'Eh, you know, it's gonna blow over. I'll be okay.'"[74] In that room, twelve-year-old Vanessa, after doing her best to wait it out, chose to release with the principal the weight she'd been carrying. Figuratively and quite literally, Vanessa read the room. In the presence of a primary authority figure of a Christian school espousing Christian values, Vanessa spoke her truth with an expectation that explicit support and redress would follow the meeting. The decision to divulge the particulars of her suffering offered the principal an opportunity to be a thoughtful Black girl stakeholder and affirm Vanessa's self-development. Instead, the principal attempted to mute Vanessa and extinguish any hint that injustice was afoot. Vanessa's actions, expectations, and even possible trust in the principal were not met with a dependable mirror. Being reliable to Black girls demands practice.

Vanessa's peers and principal made her the meaning of wrongful distraction. Appointed the cause of her own bullying, Vanessa's truth proved inconsequential. Worse, the persistent judgement from peers at a critical moment of personal change and dismissal from school authority relegated her a scapegoat and promising candidate for experiencing spirit-murder. Adultification raids Black youth of consolation and fortification. As a process it shores up the responsibilities others expect Black youth to manage for their actions as well as those taken in their presence. After moving her seat to the back of the class to avoid unsolicited scrutiny and mistreatment, and after teachers took no concern in Vanessa's decrease in participation, she turned the volume knob to the right and spoke her truth. To underscore the bounded relationship between the body and power, Lorde asserts, "that invisibility which makes us most vulnerable is that which also is the source of our greatest strength. Because the machine will try to grind you to dust anyway, whether or not we speak."[75] There are many kinds of instruments and procedures that conspire to mute Black girls that result in one's exile and/or punishment.

Faith Christian Academy rebuffed Vanessa, a twelve-year-old learning to manage her new hair texture and the meaning it assigned to her body. In the place of duty and accountability flowed blame and onus for her suffering and injury. To boot, school authorities blamed Vanessa for her peer's actions and discomfort. Vanessa's (hair) volume and her mother's refusal to concede to the school's threats breeched a likely unspoken norm operating at the school: if you are different, don't make it too obvious. Furthermore, Vanessa's critique of the school and insistence on continuing to rock her hair boldly defied the child/adult hierarchy.

Vanessa left Faith Christian, hair intact, with other parts of her body bruised and atrophying. She survived bullying and attempted spirit murder, and I remained increasingly curious about how Vanessa's body made sense of this happening. I wanted to know how Vanessa's body digested the violence and sought to name and honor the wholeness of her living before and after being violated. Knowing how she processed the event and within her body was pertinent. I inquired about "how you were feeling or just making sense of your body, of your hair," and immediately she shared, "Hmmm, I don't really remember a whole bunch."[76] Similar to my episode of forgetting detailed in Chapter 2 and worth noting here are the multiple and justifiable reasons to forget: to get on with the show, to avoid shame, to escape, and to have less weight to carry, for instance. Vanessa could not recall how her body processed the experience. Her mom, off screen, heard my question and asked Vanessa if she could speak. Though off screen, Sabrina Kent's emotion was palpable. She releases, "I was scared for you. I was really scared for your mental health. That's, that's how bad it was."[77] The shake of her voice, deep gulps as if trying to swallow something thick, and repeat of the word "scared" conveyed the toll of the event. I sensed a collective loss experienced by them along with the long road taken for Vanessa to return to herself again. The resonance and affect communicated by Sabrina exemplified the magnitude of Vanessa's endurance and the degree of violence enacted at Faith Christian. In speaking with Vanessa and Sabrina, I learned of the intangible effects of the incident that initially captured me while writing my dissertation. The endorsed denial of self-definition and expression in school is an example of Bambara's "terrible educations" because it communicates to students that their knowledge is undependable.

Spirit-murdering seeps into different layers of society and takes on an assortment of styles. At twelve, Vanessa's body was indicted by authority figures at Faith Christian and used to substantiate her peers' uneasiness. Further, her body served as justification for the torment of peers. Conversation with the principal resulted in clear instruction that Vanessa alter her hair or be expelled from school. Although the school quickly recanted its position, possibly a result of the backlash received, harm happened and continued to unfold. Girls' hair stylization is a form of self-definition, identity, and unbecoming. In Black life and expression, it is also a cultural marker and rite of passage. Vanessa's refusal to change her hair or distort her being kept her present in and to her body. Such dissent aligns with historic practices of resistance and liberation. Hair policies that plague the educational journeys of Black girls and force a choice between receiving formal education or maintaining self-concept initiate spirit-murdering. Girls' deliberations about their bodies unnecessarily become politicized action. As with the hypersurveillance of girls' comportment and the sanctions imposed on them when authorities label them as "defiant," Black girls receive retribution for being "distracting."[78] Black girls learn at a young age that their hair affects their movement through school, and eventually reach an impasse: my crown or your comfort.[79] As schools criminalize hairstyles rendered "Black" and use hair policies to deny girls access to sports or entry to prom, or require their partaking of in-school suspension, they engender the forced and farcical choice between culture and academic success.[80] When told that their hair "could distract from the respectful and serious atmosphere [the school] strives for," girls arrive at a crossing. Within this crossing is a grappling with being designated wrong and from there, Black girls must decide which mirror is most reliable.[81]

The opportunity to speak with Vanessa and indirectly her mom, Sabrina Kent, revealed multiple, layered dynamics that in different ways informed Vanessa's embodiment. As theory, method, and event, performance is a happening, a frame for seeing the multiple and many of what *is*, and a mode of capturing a phenomenon as is and as imagined. Further, because it creates "intimate space to speak Blackness into its own existence, a space to imagine and practice freedom, a space for unbridled pleasures," performance affords a simultaneity of truth-telling and recognition of the sacred nature of embodied listening, disclosure, and undressing.[82] Performance is also a liberatory tool in that it makes spacious and complex meaning of events by capturing what happened, what didn't happen, what could've happened, and how the event lives on and from different angles.

Below I present a transgressn text in the form of two scenes that add contour to popular information about Vanessa's case. Scene 1 contains movement and a performance with no written dialogue. Relying only on movement, sounds, and what you as witness envision, this scene is a tender experiment in intergenerational holding. The second is an imagined clap back where Vanessa invites the principal to see the violence she experienced through her body. These scenes emphasize seemingly banal actions that supported and/or boosted Vanessa's volume while creatively reconfiguring harmful acts Vanessa endured. The texts below seek to give visuality to the process of excreting disembodying experiences and demonstrate lasting effects pedagogies of foreclosure have on students' physical movement, self-expression, psychic affect, and sentiment. It is my aspiration that Sabrina and Vanessa and other Black mothers and daughters especially look on these scenes and see care, my appreciation and commitment to sharing Black girlhood in technicolor. When Black girls endure disembodying experiences, a process of retooling is one way of restoring spirit. Vanessa is a survivor of spirit murdering. Sabrina fought to ensure Vanessa's realignment with self.

SCENE 1: SUMMONING A STORM, A BEGINNING AGAIN

> On a beach with Black sand and rolling, cyan waves, two silhouettes—IN THE MAKING and SEASONED—are seen having conversations of the body, no words spoken. IN THE MAKING embodies storm elements. She rubs her arms as if grating cheese. Convulsing around on the sand. She cowers. This movement sequence repeats. As observer and caretaker, SEASONED takes note of her daughter's movement. Afraid, committed to holding IN THE MAKING, and aware that her daughter's spirit is mangled and afraid, she plans this trip and allows the process to take hold. She knows the water, wind, and wonder of the sand will speak to her daughter. SEASONED's hair stands at attention while IN THE MAKING's droops as if bowing to the ocean or embracing defeat. After sustained time drooping, IN THE MAKING hears something and draws near the sand to hear better.
>
> SEASONED – Arms open then wrap around but do not swallow IN THE MAKING. A tear falls onto IN THE MAKING's curly slumping 'fro.
>
> IN THE MAKING's curly 'fro softens, as does her neck that goes limp.
>
> SEASONED – Softly rocking, breathing, her gut fills—empties—howls, her tears pour into IN THE MAKING's 'fro. Feet push further into the sand. A side-to-side rock accompanies a firm embrace to the spot beneath IN THE MAKING's rib cage, her daughter's powerhouse.
>
> IN THE MAKING – Right arm swings out and sweeps across her front side on a diagonal until it covers her eyes. She tenses. This motion repeats.

SEASONED *senses* IN THE MAKING's *spirit pulsating and decides to give her daughter more room while keeping a watchful eye.*

IN THE MAKING – *Arms flail and feet submerge in the sand. Slowly, she makes her way to a crawling position. Eyes close then abruptly open. She looks beyond the ocean in front of her and then behind her. Repeat.*

SEASONED, *maintaining a watchful eye, gathers materials as if to build something.*

IN THE MAKING – *Right arm reaches out to the waves and behind her to* SEASONED, *as if calling out and toward. Left arm pats and poofs her hair until the right hand grabs a portion of hair and pulls it to show what shrinkage is and does. Repeat. A shaky attempt to stand becomes a face-to-face meeting with the sand. Off balance, her right palm presses into the sand. Left palm follows. Head lifts, then neck, she spots the sun, collapses. Repeat.*

SEASONED *watches through soaked eyelids.*

IN THE MAKING – *Claws at the sand and carefully watches the water. Arms swing out and sweep across her front side. Unable to embrace herself, she tenses. Tenses. Repeat.*

Spotlight on SEASONED.

SEASONED – *Arms swing open from the heart space, soften, and then squeeze inward, as if taking another into her arms for a hug. Repeat. Right arm swings open. Hold. Right leg lifts. Right knee bends. A step forward is taken. Repeat. Left arm swings open. Hold. Left leg lifts. Left knee bends. A step forward is taken. Repeat sequence of movements.*

IN THE MAKING *is sweeping her arms across her front side. On the third time, she catches hold of herself, tenses, and thunder roars.* SEASONED *is seen observing* IN THE MAKING *and when her daughter successfully grabs hold of herself, her face relaxes as does her neck.* SEASONED *tilts her head back until the water from her eyes and from the sky meet each other.*

SEASONED – *Slow inhalation through the nose as the belly fills and eyes close. Slow exhalation through the nose. Head quickly tilts back to sky, left toward the storm approaching, then right toward her daughter and ocean. Surrendered to the storm coming, arms writhe in the wind, heart opens, her hair reaches for the place where the elements and she meet, feet take root.*

The wind increases as does the rain and IN THE MAKING *undulates and stomps until there is only water beneath her feet. As if she knows this location, she stops and begins slow, deep breathing through the nose, prompting her eyes to close.*

IN THE MAKING – *Slow exhalation through the nose. Head quickly tilts with sky in view, then upright to face her wound, then left to her mirror, her mother. Breath quickening, hands brushing her skin as if to get something off that doesn't belong. Abruptly, body cradles as if being taken in, held. Breathe. Repeat. Right arm swings open. Right leg lifts. Right knee bends. A step forward is taken. Left arm swings open. Left leg lifts. Left knee bends. A step forward is taken. Surrendered, the storm disappears from view. Arms writhe in the wind. Heart opens. Hair starts to stand and reach for the stars hiding behind the lingering grey sky. Feet take root.*

From the soles of IN THE MAKING*'s feet, her roots descend and float in the water until feeling a magnetic pull.*

SEASONED *and* IN THE MAKING – *Three-count breath inhalation through the nose.*

IN THE MAKING – *Drops into the ocean's entry beneath her feet and eventually emerges in the ocean's center.*

SEASONED *stands at the shoreline, arms at her sides then up and out toward* IN THE MAKING *with palms up to the sky.* IN THE MAKING *takes inventory of her location, the waning rain, the distance from the shore and the new closeness felt to herself and decides to walk atop the water.*

SEASONED – *Three-count breath inhalation through the nose. Five-count exhalation through the nose. Repeat.*

SEASONED *stands at the shoreline repeating the three-five breathing sequence until* IN THE MAKING *stands face-to-face with her and places a hair pick made of bone and shell in her mother's hands.*

SEASONED *and* IN THE MAKING – *Arms swing open from heart space and close around the other, squeeze inward.*

Their silhouettes are seen collecting things as if to build something new.

The wind now imitates the motion of their hair. They are seen occasionally looking into each other, swinging arms open and then closing them around themselves. Their conversation rhythmic now, mutual now, no watchful eye present.

Nina Simon's "Here Comes the Sun" plays.[83]

SCENE 2: ATTEMPTED ABDUCTION OF ESSENCE

"Don't Touch My Hair" by Solange plays low in the background.[84]

Over an intercom, a nasally voice announces: "Slight change in plans, the new rules are as follows: hair accessories are not allowed, and hair must not be three inches from the head. Have a great day and remember . . ."

Solange continues and lowers in volume to a whisper.

VANESSA	PRINCIPAL
	There was a problem. I was just doing my job, Vanessa.
Your job?	
	Yes, to address the concerns brought to me by your teacher. She said you made a scene in class and students got distracted.
Was there mention of my being bullied by Ms. Halfheardthestory?	
	Bullied? No. She mentioned your classmates found it difficult to focus in your presence and after your outburst. Your hair is a distraction. I'm sure you're aware of this Vanessa.[85]
Did they just say no afros allowed? No Black girl jewelry. What about barrettes? Flowers?[86]	
	Well, there are always options. You can still cut and shape your hair.

Make it manageable?

                Less a problem.

Ah, less different?

                I'm not following Vanessa.

Less me? Would that work?

                It's just hair, Vanessa. You don't seem like yourself. Is something troubling you?

And yet it can only be "three inches from the head" and contain no accessories. [Pauses, leaning forward, hands on desk.] Whose hair fits this equation? Respectfully, can someone tell me how the school arrives at that math and where I can find this documentation in writing?

                You are inappropriately comparing a school policy to hair.

School policy. Hair policing. Policy is policy. My hair is my own and this is official notice that you didn't snatch my essence. You can't take my mirror.

> VANESSA *calmly stands up from the desk, pulls out her pick, slides it into her 'fro at the base of her scalp, and fluffs hair. She repeats until her 'fro fills the room.*

Unearthing Dimensions of Confinement

Conversation with Vanessa and occasionally Sabrina, her mom off camera, prompted new policy. The textures of her bullying, apparent anti-Black terrain, alongside the politics operating in her mom's instincts to contact the news and support her daughter's choice to maintain her 'fro, pivoted me toward the understanding that Vanessa and Sabrina were creating counter-policy. While writing this chapter, I felt the process of confidence snatched, felt the crack in Sabrina's voice, the intimacy Sabrina and Vanessa shared, the violence Vanessa experienced, and the distortions that followed. These are all mechanics of confinement that instigate disembodied living. I returned to thinking about the potential set of ideas percolating beneath the school's initial and revised policy. While the school kept busy with assembling policy to maintain what they regarded as order and decency, Vanessa lived fastened to another set of de facto policies about Blackness and its significations. She explains: "And usually, the perception is, mixed girls are supposed to have ringlets, they're not supposed to have an afro cause that's just like weird. Like, if she's half white, she's not supposed to have an afro. No, um, actually that can happen sometimes, um, turns out I do have an afro . . ."[87] Policy transgression was at play because Vanessa's hair exceeded common perceptions of "mixed girl hair." Her hair's shift from "wavy" to "look[ing] like my mom's hair, which is very kinky," became a disturbance to those around her. Although Vanessa was never hiding anything about herself, the evolution of her hair outed her to be a viable subject of wrongness.

The preceding transgressn texts illuminate the costs of being the object of policy. At Faith Christian Academy, the students consigned difference to being problematic, something to get rid of and/or reduce. Yet, Vanessa and Sabrina operated from another set of ideas about distinction. With the support and advocacy of her mother, Vanessa, despite the long and arduous journey, maintained ownership of her hair and spirit. "Summoning a Storm, A Beginning Again" and "Attempted Abduction of Essence" are portrayals of Vanessa's encounter with spirit murder from the position of Vanessa's body. These scenes bring into focus the psychic and physiological changes in Vanessa alongside the soot and residual debris left on her skin and spirit.

Black Girls Made Policy

Hair policies that plague girls' educational journeys and pressure a choice between their schooling or their essence are pedagogies of foreclosure. I use this word in a context similar to home foreclosures, to accentuate the legal nature of pedagogies that hijack Black living and wholeness. In the interest of the state and its complicit actors, such as schools, procedures are created to prevent youth from trusting their inner voice. More than punishments that in different ways inconvenience students, dress code policies, as one example, prevent Black girls from achieving embodiment optimization. To be penalized or in closer proximity to penalty for speaking one's truth through hair is an act of deprival. Whether unending or a single instance, such intensity penetrates the skin and seeps into other parts of the body, increasing the possibility of stuckness or "the sense of not seeing a future, which leads to a sense of stuckness that may linger."[88]

A year before the official launch of the #SayHerName project, Vanessa Van Dyke survived state inflicted violence through hair policies, a form of spirit-murdering rampant in the lives of Black girls. Despite the school's almost immediate recant, the harm was in motion. Therefore, Sabrina Kent's knowing that "no, no, no, no, this is wrong," and her decision to go to the news, importantly halted asphyxiation.[89] The school's ultimate decision to allow Vanessa back into school without altering her hair does not change the fact that without Vanessa's consent she became the prototype for the school's new hair policy—"hair accessories are not allowed, and hair must not be three inches from the head."[90] Their dismissal of Vanessa's faculties to fashion herself and building policy around her adornment displays mockery of Black aesthetics and misplaced priorities. For some, Faith Christian's predominantly white demographic student and staff body coupled with its religious affiliation could explain their emphasis on obedience. Notwithstanding this possibility, the coding of Black hair worn at its natural volume as a distraction is an example of policy around wrongness. Policies about hair rob students of their learning and force Black youth into activism and organized resistance.

In 2016, students at the Pretoria High School for Girls in South Africa scorned the school's code of conduct that banned particular hair formations including wide cornrows and dreadlocks.[91] Within these rules (no longer accessible on the internet) were diameter specifics of braids and clear indication that the school also policed how much Blackness could enter the school. This wall also applied to one's native language.[92] Although news coverage stated that there was no explicit reference to afros, the school required that hair "should be conservative, neat and in keeping with the school uniform."[93] Parallel to Faith Christian's use of the word "distraction" and other cases where girls are punished for Black hair cultural expression, certain hair ornamentation was criminalized and marked in opposition to schools' views of the proper student and the image of well-kept.[94]

Until 1990, Pretoria High School for Girls was a white-serving institution. Admission to Black South Africans began in 1994, the same year apartheid was abolished by law. Those who attend Pretoria High School for Girls remain under the haunting gaze of apartheid, a racial capitalist system that denied Black South Africans citizenship, restricted movement throughout the country, and used extreme violence to ensure Black poverty and servitude. On August 28, 2016, a student of Pretoria High School for Girls wrote, "At school we learn our names are complicated, nose-ugly, hair-untidy, skin-dirty! We learn 2be at war with our bodies. #StopRacismInSchools."[95] Saturated in a distinct form of anti-Blackness based on apartheid's differently racialized violence, this tweet reveals the ways Blackness is punishable and tendered as antithetical to the educational project. Although, like Faith Christian's recant, this school eventually suspended their code, it could not erase the damage. The erasure of the harm is so egregious it even extends to internet sites where links no longer work and no redirection is provided. Criminalization of Black aesthetics in schools is happening in and beyond the United States. These geographies have exacting meanings associated with Blackness that must be considered during analysis and redress. Yet, regardless of nuances, anti-Blackness and misogynoir are pervasive textured schemes that transcend national borders and affect Black youth. Furthermore, these policies and the activism that follows solidify the reality that state policy makers use policy to tame students, and Black girls' self-determination necessarily disturbs that system.

As educational researchers attend to inequities within educational policy, it is necessary to complicate the narrative by exploring the fabric of carcerality and its form in varying contexts. In her book *Hair Matters*, Banks discusses the political nature of hair and the many meanings it holds for Black girls and womn.[96] From debates about "good" and "bad" hair, to the proper diction used to describe the texture and look of Black hair, to "going natural" and buying bundles, these choices are also elements of voice. Whether Black girls are pushed out of school or required to navigate the politics of school spaces, their navigation of the carceral is heightened by readings of bodies, hair, and comportment.

When Blackness is regarded as a precondition of criminality, Black girls' bodily decisions operate as dissent. Vanessa and other Black girls' noncompliance around socially accepted hair standards are "Black girl ordinary" in practice. As practiced steadfastness on personhood, Black girl ordinary "improvises on social and aesthetic choreographies to disrupt the inherited rhythms of captivity, progressive or otherwise."[97] Embodying clear-cut Black girl iconography, Vanessa's embodiment became carceral services' business. In a world where Black girls are invisible, hypervisible, and interpreted through misogynoiristic and pathological frames, hair is made unnecessarily political.

Black hair has and continues to be a point of contention and struggle, with national policy headway made officially in 2019 with the CROWN Act. Ironically, the need for this bill points to racial injustice and body politics. Specifically, the bill prohibits discrimination against those participating in federally assisted programs, housing programs, public accommodations, and employment.[98] Proposed in California, to date the CROWN Act has since been approved by twenty-seven states.[99] The act was voted down by eighteen with the recent rejection of the Act by West Virginia in March of 2024. Despite its passage in some states, additional provisions are necessary to ensure administrators can't rely on loopholes that result in students foregoing school to ensure their self-determination.[100] Moreover, within the list of those states that did not pass the act is Florida, the same state where Vanessa Van Dyke retooled her body and began her journey as an activist.

In "Poem about My Rights," Jordan breaks down the process and formation of wrong as a social category:

> I have been the meaning of rape
> I have been the problem everyone seeks to

eliminate by forced
Penetration with or without the evidence of slime.[101]

When designated at best a quality or at worst the nature of a person, one's body, sartorial choices, comportment, and hair operate as testimony of one's wrongness. Written into Title Seven as an addendum to the Civil Rights Act of 1964 is language to prevent hair discrimination on the basis of afros. Within this essential legislation is consensus that hair and race have a symbiotic relationship. Passed during the Black Power Movement, spearheaded by the Black Panther Party, Black liberation steered the primary ship of social change. The afro was an aesthetic and symbol of freedom-fighting during this era. With the proliferation of Black bodies in all Black attire and 'fros, Black people got dress coded on the grounds of sartorial style and perceived to be a point of distress. Significantly, Title Seven declared hair is indeed political. Though physical death did not necessarily follow donning a 'fro, this legislation underscores stakes associated with Blackness, resistance, and Black hair ways. Whether for fashion, a freedom-fighting uniform, armor, all or none of these purposes, costs accompany Black hair worn in ways that accentuate and/or are assessed as embodying Black boldness.

In 2014, one year after Vanessa left Faith Christian Academy, Sabrina Kent created Vanessa's Essence, a hair line for girls with curls that stand up and out. The mission of Vanessa's Essence is to "to promote natural beauty in all young girls and raise awareness of bullying and other types of demeaning acts that girls may be exposed to. We want to inspire young girls all over the nation to embrace their natural hair and love themselves as they are."[102] Moved by the intimacies shared with Vanessa, this hair care line aims to express, "baby your hair is beautiful . . . this is for you. To let you know your hair is beautiful and that legacy will live on."[103] Similarly, Vanessa's Essence assists in holistic care of girls' crowns during changing social and hair textures. While speaking with Vanessa, Sabrina conveyed the alarm and insight from being a trustworthy mirror for her daughter stating, "You know it wasn't just about her natural hair being discriminated against. It was also about her mental health. What it did to her mental health. . . . And people don't realize when you try to change someone's being, who they are, it's detrimental."[104] Her statement encourages the need for a more holistic approach to thinking about embodiment, self-definition, and sanctioned harm as well as layers of the body. Sabrina's declaration exemplifies an awareness of mattering as something accomplished and exuded through action. Sabrina's trust in Vanessa's decisions about her hair, confronting school authority, and tending to Vanessa's spirit as she recalibrated and healed from assault are examples of reliability work. The elimination of self-determination, or "when you try to change someone's being," has unaccounted-for consequences that connect to issues of embodiment, racialized gender, Black living and survival, and more.[105] At the origin of her actions lies a commitment to guaranteeing Vanessa's volume remain intact and decided by her daughter.

Conclusion

When Tiana Parker, an elementary school girl, decides to transfer because the school insisted that one's hair "could distract from the respectful and serious nature [the school] strives for," celebration of self-expression is in order.[106] #STILLGOTVOLUME. When a teacher invites Lamya Cammon, a Black girl, to the front of the room and sends her back in tears with her braid cut off, naming the violence and seizing the assailant's teaching rights is in order.[107] #STILLGOTVOLUME. When Marian Scott excitedly dresses and shows up in red afro puffs and is denied the opportunity to take yearbook photos, redress is in order.[108] #STILLGOTVOLUME. When, after four games of a softball tournament, Nicole Pyles's beaded braids are deemed an obstruction and she is forced to sit out of the fifth game or remove the beads, respect for whatever decision she makes is in order.[109] #STILLGOTVOLUME. When Mya and Deanna Cook, two sisters, receive more than fifteen hours of detention in a month's time and are banned from playing sports or attending prom for wearing 1b box braids, curiosity about the impetus behind their braids is in order. #STILLGOTVOLUME. In the face of state attacks on Black girls, a recognition of the overt and subtle violations is necessary. #SAYHERNAME was envisioned by Kimberle' Crenshaw as a way to "bring awareness to the invisible names and stories of Black women and girls who have been victimized by racist police violence and provides support to their families."[110] I present #STILLGOTVOLUME as a companion of #SAYHERNAME to continue the work of identifying key state actors in the affliction and violence of Black girls in particular and Black people in general. Equally, this hashtag honors lives likely temporarily muted while noting, in the words of June Jordan, "some of us did not die." Within the rubric of celebration, #STILLGOTVOLUME allocates precedent to the maintenance of Black crowns. In each of the above instances, girls took issue with policy and made decisions that reflected inner knowing and the mirrors through which they looked. This affirmation and hashtag connect volume of hair and of voice. Finally, though it emanates from a case study about effects of hair discrimination on Black gurl embodiment, it can carry the truth that it is not only girls missing class time, being bullied by state actors, and strained by school hair policies.

Black youth are subjected to anti-Black metrics that create consequences for inhabiting Black bodies. And when it comes to hair policy, it is Black youth and Black womn who are made into archetypes as policy breakers. In February 2024, a Texas judge ruled in favor of a school's grooming policy that justified in-school suspension for Darryl George, an eighteen-year-old high school student who wears pinned up locs to school.[111] While the school filed a declaratory judgment lawsuit to determine whether or not Barber Hill Independent School district was in breach of the CROWN Act, in effect in Texas, George entered a federal civil rights lawsuit to protest the unjust action of the school. Arguing that the CROWN Act does not include length within its policy, the court determined that Barber Hill Independent School District was justified in its bullying of George, providing evidence that the passing of policy and legislation is necessary but insufficient for the immobilization of anti-Blackness.

These acts of violence are demonstrations of foreclosure. They are occurrences where society's regard for Black aesthetic is clarified, and where Black girls, though not solely, come to know that hair is an artifact and translation of one's spirit to the world, a channel connected to the inner self. As quotidian tactics in school spaces, processes of foreclosure create often undetectable cracks capable of altogether shattering. Each of the above students and their encounters with anti-Black aggressions occurred in states that have not yet filed the CROWN Act or, in the cases of Tiana Parker and Vanessa Van Dyke, where it was filed but did not pass. And in Durham, North Carolina, where the CROWN Act is law, it did not prevent Pyles from having to decide on the fly, "I was gonna remove my beads and I was gonna play my game."[112] Furthermore, the implementation of policy requires that people read and interpret it.

Black girls' encounters with the state vis-à-vis formalized and practiced policies show apertures in justice initiatives as they pertain to gender, race, and schools. They highlight faulty outcomes in the absence of intersectional examinations of what injustice continues to look like regarding race and gender in particular. When #BlackLivesMatter is evidenced at the site of an injured Black body, justice may be nearby. Justice must include redress for filmed murders, botched raids, and lives physically snatched at the hands of police violence, the prison industrial complex, and other forms of institutionalized injustice. Equally, justice must account for everyday forms of violence that contribute to the denial of Black mattering.[113]

While it can be argued that the world is better served by Zulaika Patel, Vanessa Van Dyke, and countless other students, known and unknown, moving to organize against injustice, such action need not come from repeated muting and mishandling. Deliberate defiance by Black girls across the globe toward the coding of Black as trouble is certification Black girls know the difference between "cut rate" and reliable mirrors. Black girls are resolved to more just and (w)holistic reads of their bodies. These willful acts are also in decrees that Black girls' quality of life will not be contingent nor gauged in proximity to others. Finally, Black mattering, in action, must happen at the site of Black aliveness.

Black girls be policy. Within a Black Girlhood studies ethos, so-called defiance is deliberateness. When Black girls assert, "my hair, my mirror, my own," the practices of reliability and bodily reverence are in play. The world makes premature mandates of Black girls, and to live beyond the scope of being of these roles and requirements, Black girls develop toolkits, sometimes with the assistance of others and sometimes in

FIGURE 3.2. She Knows Her Essence. Carlos Velez ©2023, @carlosvelezstudios. This image is a self-selected image of Vanessa Van Dyke taken in 2023. Asked to share "one image that captures the core of who you see yourself to be now," Vanessa decided to offer this image in place of the initial one provided, stating, "I'll be glad to attach some updated ones for you that really captures the true essence of me!" Personal communication, email, March 26, 2024. Vanessa approved the title via Instagram chat, March 27, 2024.

isolation, for deciphering mirrors and their corresponding shadows. At times, Black girls are met with bags of tricks that seduce, mute, and contort, and when unchecked, lead to distrust and worse, disembodiment.

Black girls need not be forced to respond to invasion in particular ways. Paramount, however, is the availability of time and space for undressing and (re)orienting our archives.

CHAPTER 4

Willful Touch

An Experiment in Body-Activation

> We are involved in a struggle for liberation . . . liberation from the constrictive norms of "mainstream" culture, from the synthetic myths that encourage us to fashion ourselves rashly from without (reaction) rather than from within (creation).
>
> Toni Cade Bambara, The Black Woman

When Black girls come together unarmed, something transformative happens. Attendant to embodiment as a foundational gauge of mattering manifested and justice achieved, this chapter is about what is seen and felt anew from Black girls agreeing to touch. Expanding Audre Lorde's theorization of the erotic, I introduce it here as a useful element for discussing and expanding personal repertoire. Parallel to this framing, I put forward body-activation, another practice within the broader rubric of embodied vulnerability. Guided by the orientation and sensibility of groove[ing], I activate Black gurl reliable using the facet of "tracing" (refer to Chapter 1). Together, these help create the necessary conditions for archive exhumation and *touch*. To illustrate inciting bodily animation and excavation of stories stowed in our bodies and archives, I describe the exercise "Feels Like," a multifaceted practice composed of a set of three interdependent movements that could be done in sequence or in isolation. From the exercises, a discussion of repertoire as related to accessing spirit unfolds. The content that follows elucidates how girls live through injurious happenings and how reflective somatic work offers ways of retooling girls' archives. Before sharing the exercises and what they I unearthed, I trace my evolving understanding of this workshop.

Flashback, Flashforward

I woke up to love on a Saturday morning in 2012, nervous, excited, and flooded with ideas about the day but mainly about the workshop I'd facilitate in a few hours. Eagerly, I packed my props—old report cards, markers, pictures of my dad, paper, and recording devices. I showered, dressed, and gave love a peck. Focused and too anxious to eat, I used my eighteen-minute drive to make mental notes of the activities I imagined doing, and in imagining how the girls might respond, recalled exercises and rehearsed pivots I might take depending on what came up. I wanted to be ready. As part of my dissertation, this workshop was to collect data on bodily experiences of Black girlhood. The workshop format made room for the roundness of story, for data to be moved about and collected through multiple modes. The activities, I aspired, would discern different layers of the body in relation to Black girls' lived experiences. I wanted to know more about the ways the body mitigated Black girls' educational experiences in and outside of schools, what I could learn, and what we could make together by accessing and storying bodily experiences of life through art.

I arrived motivated to explore the following: What stories do Black girls hold in their bodies? Where in the body do stories dwell? I perceived that my ask for us to go on a journey together of exploring our bodies could be refused, invited, questioned, mocked even. I took comfort in my sensibility and trust in Audre Lorde's insistence, then and always, that I had to make the invitation "even at the risk of having it bruised or misunderstood."[1] During room set up, I took deep breaths until the first Black girl arrived.

Steeped in doing the "right" things, mentally reciting feminist ethics and cautions discussed in qualitative research texts and by faculty, I found it difficult initially to be fully present to the session. It took me performing excerpts about my young and youthful Black girl life and hearing girls' responses to background research protocol questions to center the gift of being with five self-identified Black girls and a few Black womn program staff also of varying ethnicities and backgrounds coming in and out of our session. These womn always participated when in the room. While I immediately felt the beauty of what happened that morning in 2012 and received direct receipts from the girls' mouths, it took me four years after graduating with a PhD to arrive at Black gurl reliable—a principle capable of being a container for reliability work in Black girlhood. I first penned this idea in publication form in 2018, two years after the concept of reliability generally landed on my lap from poet and homegirl Nikky Finney during a Black Girl Genius Week Master Teacher session. It wouldn't be until 2021 that I made connections between the idea of reliability work to the workshop I facilitated in 2012 and the data gathered there. The girls and the happenings in that 2012 workshop called to me often. I, therefore, revisited them through participant-observation notes, interviews, video recordings, and written texts. I did so at least twice annually, not including my studying of data to write my dissertation. These data offered answers to my initial guiding question—What stories do Black girls hold in their bodies? Equally interested in processing and building engagements that might spark new meanings of the experience, I returned to the workshop repeatedly. Each time I returned, another layer of connection surfaced. Today, I know, we agreed to look, feel, and be touched in each other's presence that day.

Tools Utilized

As the facilitator, I brought all of me—healing human, seasoned youthful girl, and un/becoming Black womn, wanderer, dancerpoet—all had a stake in this moment. As part of my preparation for the somatic components of the workshops, I facilitated for dissertation data collection, I attended Urban Bush Women's Summer Leadership Institute (SLI), a ten-day intensive dedicated to bringing together artists, community activists, and students invested in arts for social change.[2] Founded by Jawole Willa Jo Zollar, a dancer named within the genealogy of theatrical jazz aesthetics, I put to practice the work of breath to create space, pause, and anticipation. It was also there that I honed my practice of listening to my body while near other bodies. Through Urban Bush Women's methodology of "Entering, Building, and Exiting" communities, I observed and honed my skill of building an impactful container in a short amount of time. Coming to Nia dance classes initially for personal pleasure, mindfulness, and health, I increased my weekly class attendance during my dissertation data collection phase after learning of its somatic awareness intention. In 2013, while writing my dissertation, I earned my white belt certification. Nia provided that space and invited me to think about the interconnection between power, grace, and internal rhythm. These techniques, paired with my Black feminist education and Black girl praxis, urged me toward thinking about curricula of the body. Nia, SLI, SOLHOT, and Black feminist thinking, as documented in the poem "Cultivating a Measure" in the introduction to this book, became doulas to me birthing groove[ing].

Groove[ing] as a Key to Unlocking Ourselves

Can I craft an experience that makes a way for us to show ourselves or let go altogether? Could we lighten our loads in some way? These questions sat at the pit of my stomach as I guided us that Saturday morning in 2012 to go inside, explore, feel, bring up and bring out lingering debris and living stories that corset us from the inside. An amorphic technique, groove[ing] demands a will to use the full self without overprescribing or requiring an exact outcome. Jones advises, "you don't let the training eclipse the spontaneity of the instinct in the moment."[3] Groove[ing] poses a challenge of accepting the many repertoires within the body but endorsing those movements that keep us most honest, most free, most useful in any given moment. Alongside personal responsibility for the space, I made room for what happened in the workshops to be directed and moved by those there, by what they expressed they wanted and/or were interested in, and the pieces of me that came forward.

I started with my performance to be vulnerable and step first into the agreement of being seen. This time and reflection allowed girls to decide how and if they wanted to be seen. They could also determine what if anything about my life resonated with them. Groove[ing] is a mood and commitment to being in and with the moment, the now, and to making decisions in an organic way. Listening closely to girls' reactions to my performance, groove[ing] guided my choice to utilize the exercise "feels like." Specifically, it was participants' disclosure of certain experiences that prompted me to begin the exercise "Feels Like" and to do so in the specific arrangement enacted that morning. While "Feels Like" lay stashed away in my body-activation resource chest, the discussion and girls' reactions to my performance is what prompted me to use that particular exercise next. I did not have a turn-by-turn protocol. My decision to foreground groove[ing] in the process of facilitating meant my plans were always suggestions. I listened to body language and words and used them to determine the next best move. It is also thanks to groove[ing] that I organically remixed the conditioning activity to implement the exercise "Body Affirmations" at the end of the chapter.

The Erotic as Pathway to Touch

In *Uses of the Erotic*, Audre Lorde refutes popular connotations of the erotic and conceptualizes it as an underutilized resource situated within the feminine plane of spirit. Lorde describes the erotic as a process of working from and with feeling, as emotional intellect that emerges from the nonrational (the gut), one's intuition house.[4] Importantly, this domain, Lorde argues, lives in all humans and is therefore accessible to us all but instead skewed to concoct sexual inferiority as well as to regulate bodies read as femme and feminine-expecting. Infused with feeling and spirit, the erotic becomes a resource for rousing intimacy with ourselves and others.

As a power source and tool for living open-hearted, honest lives, and in healthy and deep reverence of ourselves and the world around us, the erotic is a sensibility and a cultivated measure of "how acutely and fully we can feel in [our] doing."[5] To commit to conjuring the erotic is to pledge to create the most effective space to grow potential. The workshop, for instance, entailed slowing down enough to truly touch. This slowing took the form of rehearsing movements, practicing different paces and orders of events, asking lots of questions, assuming connection existed and that our primary charge was to locate it. Touch is an ingredient of the erotic, as it consents excavation of what lives inside, exhuming, and designating space to rehearse more of what feels good. Connected to the method and (re)orientation of "undressing in public" discussed in Chapter 3, touch is a technology for rousing rupture. Within the rubric of the erotic, "to share the power of each other's feelings," the activation of our bodies magnified and created a path toward retooling.[6] Touch requires permission and necessitates visitation of our archives to see, sort, and shift its contents.

Practicing Touch

Despite the world's propensity to mishandle, gawk, and mistakenly deem Black girls' bodies everyone's business, these actions—even when physical hands are wrongly placed on girls' bodies—is not touch. Before a Black girl, youthful and/or young, agrees to be touched, reading for the substance of one's mirror is recommended. Gaze is power laden. To gaze is a move loaded with muscle and politics. Calling into question anti-Blackness circulating in gazes used in educational settings and advocating for accountability in the act of looking, Callier and Hill contend, "to gaze is a communicative process between the gazer and the object [the focal point] in view, steeped in history and culture."[7] In many ways, gaze is the result of what our pre-existing frameworks orient us to see, how we *do* seeing, and what room, if any, we make to read and do in order to see breadth within a given moment. What is seen when Black gurl reliable is built into gaze? Reliability is paramount to gaze; it is the mirepoix of a story because within it are ideological and experiential trails.

Tracing is a form of citational practice about how an idea or concept grows in one's care and mapping the who and how it entered one's cipher. It, like genealogy, is a means for honoring an idea, its conduit/s, one's coming to this idea, and the relationship between these. Tracing as a means of practicing reliability takes seriously who is gifted access to an insight, an idea, a pedagogy, and serves as a means of creating a thoughtful, sometimes beneath the surface genealogy and potential future (see Chapter 5).[8] Tracing is a commitment to rehearsal, to feeling deeply, locating lesson acquisition and digestion, and acknowledging involved interlocutors, revising over time. Black gurl reliable engenders an inventory check and release to begin anew; it is an event that emerged in time over time.⁹

Pedagogies, alongside what they make possible, are about "what we are prepared to teach."¹⁰ Therefore, pedagogies, and in particular their visibility and resonance, have to do with time, attention, practice, doubt, care, discomfort, and surrender on repeat. Layers and new understandings of what constitutes being reliable in Black girlhood continually unfold in accordance with capacity and presence. What follows is a rehearsal of Black gurl reliable with a focus on body-activation. As a multifaceted endeavor, body-activation brings into view what happens when Black girls look and make ourselves available for touch; how somatic artistic expression enlivens bodies and stories of interiority; what it means to witness and facilitate touch as a youthful and seasoned Black girl and student of Black girlhood. Lastly, I discuss what I learned about the granular elements and labor of body-activation and its capacity to sharpen what I describe later as innocent eyes.

Accessing the Archive

I sat trying to catch my breath and grab up all that continued to seep out of my skin. We sat in a circle chatting about their experience of the performance, surprise about my life experiences, and how it felt to see me enact vulnerability. They shared: "I felt it"; "It was like we were going through the exact same thing."¹¹ This performance was not my first sharing of these moments. Each performance, however, opened different subtleties. I memorized original poems and devised a performance skeleton, but their order, like when the dancing occurred or if tears made their way into view, and what feelings arose, was all about the moment.

In a discussion of improvisation in *I Want to Be Ready*, Goldman discusses the undermined regimen and rigor that grounds spontaneous movement. Arguing that improvisation is a skillset that entails "literally giving shape to oneself by deciding how to move in relation to an unsteady landscape," Goldman pivots readers away from spontaneity and intuition to first consider conditions of the body that permit improvisation.¹² Squarely situated in dance studies, the text provides a layered analysis of improvisation and advances it as a freedom practice, one composed of a network of tools. These utensils for dancers include forms or genres of dance and their corresponding rubrics of movement. The tendency of ballet and some modern dancers, for example, is to point the toe and keep light on the feet, while dancers of hip-hop and African forms emphasize flexed extremities and polyrhythm where the hips and feet may move on different beats and at a different pace. The system associated with each respective form educate the body in a particular style of movement. As Omi Osun Joni L. Jones describes about the staying power of form:

> What I and I think others end up relying on is what we've done before. So, the way that we moved our bodies, the way that we've used our voices in previous performances and productions, not even moments of that production itself, but just out in the world other productions—especially if we were rewarded in some way for that. So somebody saying "Ooh, Omi, you have such a rich voice." And so I say, "OK. I'm going to use my rich voice!" And what that does is clamp down the very sense of "Be here. Right now. Be here." . . . Be right here, with your body, and your history, and your truth, and let all of that come forward.[13]

Jones's articulation outlines relations between full presence and technique, and how form embeds memory. Even more, that form plays into our will to pivot from the script, to expand our repertoire. Moreover, Jones references dance and everyday techniques, which in different ways train our bodies and circumscribe our movements. Forms comprise specific vocabulary (grammar) that shows up off and on the stage of dance performance. Repertoire, in and beyond dance then, compels the body to draw from a particular archive of knowledge and use it in a certain way.

Repertoires are all around us. They dwell in bodies, sculpt movement, inform the *why* of movement, its presence and volume. And if, as Tami Spry describes, agency is "the capacity of the agent (in this case an individual) to tell her story of an event," then geographies girls traverse and the messages inscribed onto bodies are arbitrators of our faculty to move.[14] Humans have different emotional and physical capacities.

Variation in these do not limit a cultivation of repertoire. As it pertains to agency and dexterity, however, I am referring to how built environments in the systemic and ideological sense preclude people from full exercise of will and knowing. Repertoires are assembled alongside categories of and meaning assigned to difference. Further, repertoires and their ingredients referee inclination, intuition, and the likelihood of formulating movement that is self-referential.

Mirrors reliable to Black girls forsake respectability and esteem transgression. As a frame, transgression regards social acts commonly regarded as wrong as saturated with opportunity and creativity. Borne of a particular social situatedness taken up at length in the writings and living of individuals committed to Black womn's knowledge creation (see Chapter 1) and autonomy, transgressive politics understand conceptual literacy surrounding the nature of wrong and being marked as such while shifting its root grammar. Antirespectability then becomes a benchmark for self-defined living. Introducing various approaches within this rubric taken up in the service of Black girlhood praxis, Garner et al. insist, "Knowing how to create and hold space for Black girls is important because too often Black girls are not allowed to show up whole and with a self-awareness that magnifies their genius and ingenuity."[15] My responsibility as a youthful seasoned girl and Black Girlhood studies scholar is to identify conditions that make it more possible for girls to be, to be seen, and to know they are believed and labor toward their permanence. When sharing space with other girls, the assignment of reliability morphs to devising an experience where looking intently and sharing become compelling. Following my performance, I surrendered to the moment, used feltsense, and ushered groove[ing] into the driver's seat. This intuitive journey unfolded into a series of exercises, which only recently resurfaced to also be a discussion about repertoire.

FEEL TO ACCESS HOME

Intended to open the body's archive, these exercises consisted of written and physical elements. In *Body, Paper, Stage*, Spry discusses the roles of tools that give and examine texture of the body. She writes, "Here, performance does not 'illuminate' the text, rather [it] assists in the creation of the text; it is in itself performative."[16] In each exercise, the body is summoned to narrate. A set of interdependent exercises that can be taken in sequence or individually, "Feels Like" is a technique used for accessing one's layered archive through embodied and somatic centering. Initially, I crafted these three exercises to distill layers of the body complex—the physical, psychic, and discursive or how the body is made through language, culture, and meaning given to it. Attending to these layers revealed how they collaborated to inform external and internal meaning assigned to girls' lived experience. Taken sequentially, "Feels Like" disentangles experience from meaning and representation from self-valuation. Within each iteration, participants observed the body, history and the body, and the body and presence/essence as webbed networks.

I started with "I am . . . and it feels like." This module of "Feels Like" asks participants to share, through gesture and bodily movement, a sense of their essence and what that feels like. I listened intently and intuited a need to open space for the girls to self-declare, to self-define, and to practice self-expression. Following its spiritual meaning, "I am" is declaration and manifesting language. In writing about Blackness and Zen spiritual practice, Angel Kyodo Williams wrote, "The only way to be truly honest is to stay completely in the moment that we are already in. . . . Every single being's truth and the truth of every given situation are all happening at the same time . . . dynamically creating new truths as they go."[17] On the fly, I shared a version that in the moment rang true for me.

I am . . .	and it feels like . . .
swaying hips making their way around as if making their way around the number eight.	clenched teeth, arms bent not quite at ninety, palms up, legs planted, torso upward shaking

Using statement and gesture combination, we presenced our understandings of self. Varied in tone, emphasis, and shape, we used snaps, hip shifts, props (including each other), and necks to help tell the story of our essences.

Over the course of the workshop, I observed the space girls elected to use. Girls' space-taking and movement grew in size and direction, and calculation before taking action of some kind decreased—important steps toward and signs of body-activation and integration. One poignant example is Christa's use of Deborah and Nicole as props. Her "and it feels like" resembled one of those it's-been-a-long-time hugs. She took her time as if savoring a meal, and fully immersed in that act alone. Christa's reveal of a self that she kept tucked away for safekeeping, in our presence, gave us permission to touch her. Christa felt her way through the movement, and we held space. The echo of this moment filled the room. Although Deborah and Nicole were literally moved by Christa during her sharing, we each learned some of Christa's story and became part of its future narration. Also demonstrated within this moment of self-definition is the possibility that when intentionally vulnerable, a purposeful shove is sometimes warranted, not to be taken personally, and a necessary personification (facet of embodiment) of untethering. As process and product of Christa's repertoire, the activity and specifically that moment marks archival expansion. Too often Black girls' bodies, inclusive of comportment and sartorial choice, get read through a misogynoiristic gaze and are met with judgment, unnecessary mandates, and attempts to fix and train girls. That day, however, Christa's decision, one that communicated who she be and how that feels, received affirmation and assurance.

We began with "I am" to signal our voice, our individual stories, carrying forward and returning some of the weight back to its origins. The second move of this activity was to take that self, how it is presenced in the world, and take a posture/position that echoes being at home with that self. I took to the floor and allowed my body to feel its way into some kind of shape. Girls followed by propping legs on chairs; necks cocking and hanging over the edge of a chair on a slant; standing; sitting atop a table with legs crossed in loose lotus; hands in laps and tucked in armpits. We rehearsed and made subtle adjustments to the degree of a lean, the angle of a released neck, the tightness of fists. We took our time settling into the feel of home and used our senses to hear ourselves and then generate from them. Lying on the ground, hinged at the hips, eyes loosely closed, I listened for changes in breath and posture. Eventually, we all arrived at a position of home with self. Peeking through my arms to take inventory of the room, I noticed and perceived a stillness. Notably, I knew that the pose we each took was our own, symbolic of being ourselves and at home with that.

Feel to Transgress What Happened

Tightening our cypher and stepping further into our archives, I facilitated the practice "I know what it feels like . . ." I created this multistep activity as a (re)memory tool that helps disentangle experience from meaning attached to it. First, we, in no particular style, wrote out a response to the statement "I know what it feels like." There were lists, what looked like free verse poems, and mind maps. We then silently reread our individual makings. From there we identified three words we thought encapsulated the essence of what we remembered about our experiences. Girls chose to underline, circle, place a check mark next to the words and phrases. We sat with what made it to the page, our bodies cross legged, leaning back, arms folded, arms holding ourselves at the knees, arms behind back. I felt into the words. From there, I asked that we create bodily gestures or movement to encapsulate each word or phrase chosen.

    They listened for my guidance. We all sought to bring the story on the page to life and layer it with new significance using sounds, gestures, and audience. We practiced moving each word or phrase chosen through our bodies and tapped into our embodied knowledge by "paying close somatic attention to how and what our body feels when interacting with others in context."[18] We sensed for its meaning in our bodies alongside the message we wanted to bring up and out of us—to share, release, and create anew. With all moves created, we then put them together in an order and pace based on our individual intentions. The words/phrases we identified became what occurred. As I guided and watched for cues from us on what to do next, I took mental jottings of what looked like degrees of touch. Our three combined movements became our testimony, and the total of these experiences and their meaning in motion, simultaneously, became a chorale of feeling, a wind that landed us somewhere new.

As we prepared to share our offerings, girls played with the order, intensity, and duration of their movements. We, in conversation with the moves, decided how long to pound a balled fist, for instance, into an open palm, and how to pace our breathing. While determining the most fitting gestures and movements to use, Nicole asked me how I would communicate being stressed, and I offered a repeated rubbing of my face, accompanied by deep sighs. I also suggested that while thinking through how to bodily narrate their words, they should consider the sound, feel, and outcome of the words or phrases chosen. Only after rehearsing and animating the story with practice and making choices did we pair up to share our stories with each other.

Though the words written could be embodied in erratic movement to reflect all the emotions, Nicole landed on (seemingly) calculated movement. Sitting in the chair, bent over, right arm under chin, hand fisted, eyes forward, feet propped up on the legs of the chair, Nicole kept frozen until she wasn't. When ready, she shifted. Raising her upper body from its folded position to a more obtuse angle, Nicole slid back into the seat. Releasing her arms from their bent position, she lifted them again to meet and cross over her chest. Again, she froze. In her response to the prompt "I know what it feels like," Nicole chose to name emotion-based states and highlighted stress and anger in physical representation. In these exchanges, sound and movement were not accompanied by words. Sentences and explanations were unnecessary. Given the choice to write about their lives and what they know, the decision to include the very things they offered are experiences that have a lingering effect.

The movement portion of the exercise helped in discerning where particular emotions attached to the stories surfaced and where in the body they live. From there, the goal was to translate what is known, reconstruct its meaning, and possibly cultivate release. In arguing for the incorporation of somatics in education and discussing the difference between somatic and cultural knowledge, Brockman asserts, "Somatic knowledge is received from with*in* the human being; cultural knowledge is received from with*out* the human being."[19] Like assumptions, culture is communicated to people to emphasize expectation and stakes. In contrast, "I know what it feels like" is somatic, directly experienced knowledge and moved out from an inner space. Behind their responses lived stories, some spoken aloud and some sensed. Some of these accounts involved loss, racialization, beauty standards, and teacher bias. While attention in "I know what it feels like" is on things that happened upon bodies and within them, a slight modification of the prompt instigates a new emphasis.

With skin the color of a Snickers bar coating, wearing a long-sleeved, blue-jean jacket buttoned almost all the way up, low-top Chucks, and about two inches of an indigo-blue tank hanging over the top of khaki colored cargo pants, Phillipi offered a gesture to fill in the statement, "I am . . . and it feels like . . ."

I am . . .	and it feels like . . .
Mouth widens (smiles)	right hand on hip, lips pursed closed but not puckering, a slight nod followed by intentional eye contact.
Rhythmically bringing her right arm from behind the back and across the chest, she snaps just below her left shoulder.	

When asked to bodily narrate who she is and how it feels to be at home with/in herself, Phillipi's snap snatched our attention. Phillipi broke the neutral stance she had presented throughout the workshop—arms folded in front of chest or arms clasped resting on the lower back—to tell us who she *be*. She literally shifted from a rooted trunk to a swaying tree. No hesitation lived in her movement. Her crisp snap signaled certainty. The volume of her communication echoed in her sharp then subtle changes in movement. Her hand position (on hips) told a story of its own. The stark juxtaposition in bodily positioning confirmed varied responses to the different activities and what emotions materialized.

Her written offering for "I know what it feels like" (Figure 4.1) revealed layers of experience. Her writing didn't highlight nor vocalize religious affiliation of any kind. Yet when asking her to choose her pseudonym, resembling the tone and energy of her snap, she stated Phillipi, "like in the Bible."[20] I'll note that I faltered on the spelling of her designated name because the Bible and I were closer friends in childhood. I decided to lean on her preference and asked whether the spelling of her name had one or two l's; she matter-of-factly retorted, "two."

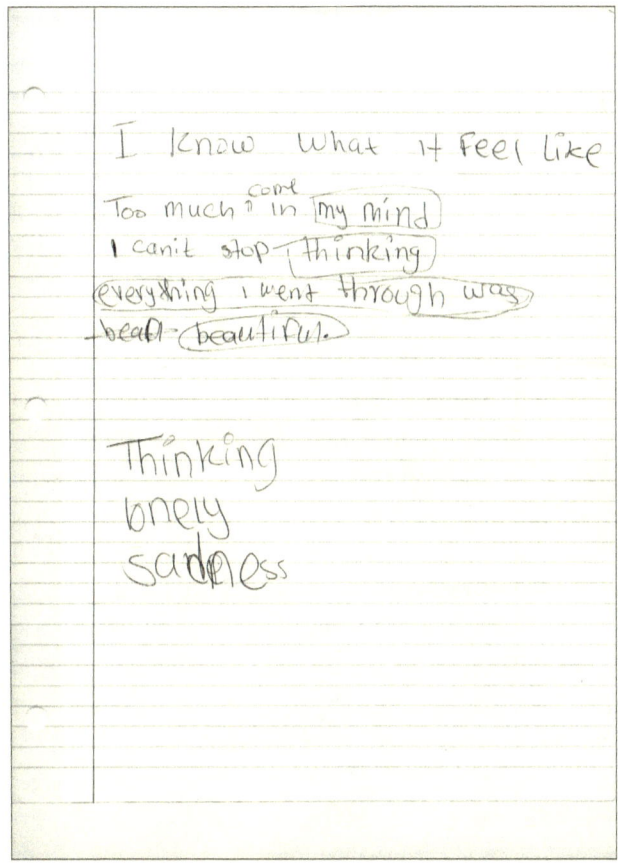

FIGURE 4.1. Phillipi, age fifteen, "I know what it feels like." Author's personal collection

An immigrant from Togo and student who moved to the United States at the start of high school, Phillipi also navigated added academic pressures as an active English language learner. During our workshop debriefing, she connected value in school to her challenges learning English:

ME: Can you tell me about a time you felt unimportant in school?

PHILLIPI: When I first get into school.

ME: What happened?

PHILLIPI: Like I didn't understand English, and it was difficult.

Critical here is the interconnection of language and value for Phillipi. The lack of importance she felt could be tied to others' unwillingness to communicate and/or the limited ways they communicated with her. It could have been about assumptions made about Phillipi because English was not her first language. Despite this adversity, when asked if she liked school, Phillipi said, "I loooove school," and referenced her English Speakers of Other Languages (ESOL) class as a space where she felt valued. Together, her offerings speak to the possibility of receiving judgment in school outside of the ESOL class, perhaps from peers and/or other teachers.

Different from the clarity exhibited in her movements around "I am . . . and it feels like . . .," her choice of the words "thinking," "lonely," and "sadness" offer a synopsis of feeling and affect that transpired from reflection on the prompt. Between her writing, being, and (re)membering, Phillipi oscillated through multiple and layered dimensions of embodiment. For the prompt "I know what it feels like . . . ," her movement was less sharp. Approximating a holding of, up, and together of the self, using her arms, Phillipi engulfed herself and swayed as if to self-soothe or rock to sleep. Led by her shoulders, the sway seemed to almost over tilt until the load required rebalancing. Contrarily, Phillipi's "I am . . . and it feels like . . .," however, potentially triggered a different set of memories in the body. There was no prescriptive way to structure one's response to the prompt.

Christa chose to draft a list of feelings and experiences that up to that moment gave shape to her life. Built into the language of the prompt, these happenings are separate from identity. On paper, Christa's movements embodied the affect caused from being with the words and phrases selected. She stood up and used her right arm to make continuous curved lines, with ease, slowly through the air like writing in cursive. After determining her writing complete, she backed up to sit in a chair. Right leg crossed over the left thigh and arms crossed with hands buried in her pits, she sat still, head slightly tilted downward. During our brainstorm sessions where we played with different movements to capture the essence of the words, Christa asserted, "You can't demonstrate being fatherless." After sharing her story of living through the circled experiences, she announced, "It's like I'm waiting, but I'm not expecting him to show up."

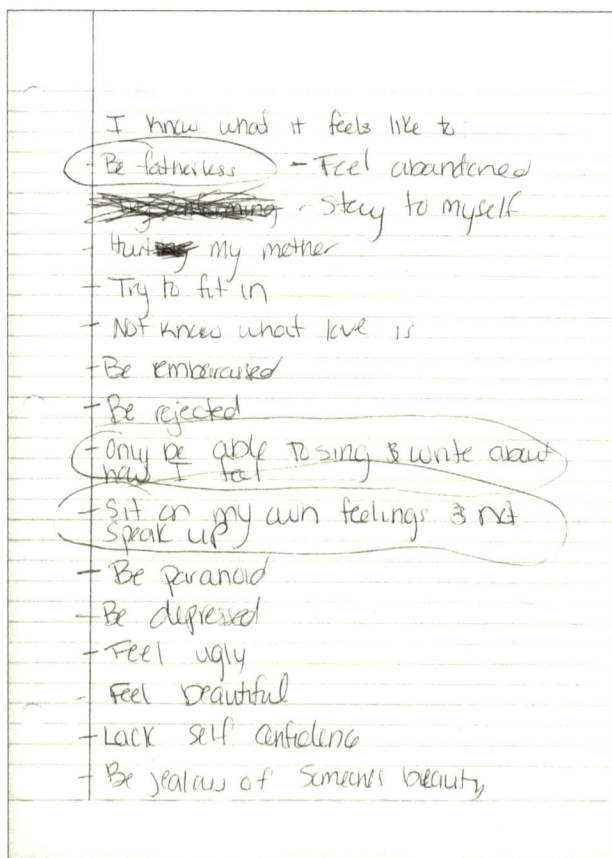

FIGURE 4.2. Christa, age seventeen, "I know what it feels like." Author's personal collection

Instead of trying to embody the word "fatherless," Christa opted to convey what she had been doing since the event of becoming fatherless and how that felt. Conjoining the *what* and the *actions*, something new materialized about the meaning attached to the experience of being fatherless. She also candidly conveys her orientation toward this event and her father—Christa is both waiting *and* not expecting him to show. While being fatherless sat in her experiential archive, shown in Figure 4.2, the sequenced exercise called forth texture around how this experience lived with her. The paradox within her statement gestures back to embodiment. Experience is absorbed in a variety of ways. What stays within our memory and possibly weighs the heaviest is the space-holding that continues independent of desire. Just because Christa is fatherless doesn't mean she feels a lack. Just because she is not expecting him to show up doesn't mean it wouldn't make a difference if he did. When asked to embody the statement, "I am . . . and it feels like . . .," however, she enacted laser-focused movement.

I am . . .	and it feels like . . .
arms fling open, exerting a force that pushes Nicole and Deborah off balance	arms back to the center of her body and across it until her fingertips grasped at her shoulder blades. After making connection—tips to shoulder, she gently sways.

At some point, I held my breath. I know this because when Nicole and Deborah hit the chair from her shove, I felt my eyes widen, and after Christa started swaying, my lips loosened. Christa firmly cleared the space around her in a way that expressed consciousness and buy in to the prompt's request—"imagine being at home with self." The strength exerted to push those near her away also symbolized a commitment to rehearse coming home to self even at the risk of being misunderstood and/or confronted. I wonder now, did Christa sense the energy of the space and intuit that we were all already disarmed, expecting to be tapped into? In our presence, she created a new agreement with herself. She, like all of us, disrobed before the others. This yearning, I speculate, is what lived beneath her actions and the decision to remain fully present and share her choreographed narration without first asking permission to appoint Nicole and Deborah as props. Christa's movement took stock of others' deliberation about who she *be*. About how some ones and some bodies treated her according to what they saw and how she ingested it all. In that moment, however, Christa saw fit to clear the room! Her rhythm, slow, as if taking her time, as if to savor, to rekindle, and tattoo the return on the walls of her archive, to say, "Welcome home."

The archive and the repertoire are not synonyms; rather they are interlocutors. As Taylor insists, "As opposed to the supposedly stable objects in the archive, the actions that are the repertoire do not remain the same."[21] Together, excavating in the public of Black girlhood, our vernacular accentuated, underscored, and conferred our presence and aliveness. Illustrated in these two exercises is the contentiousness of embodiment. Moreover, self-representation is a combination of experience, residual feelings, and self-concept. Girls' articulations of "I am . . . and it feels like . . .," alongside their "I know what it feels like," display the tension Black girls carry between who Black girls are and what makes up that being. Every component of this multipart exercise required we break the repository's shell and in turn expand repertoires. Framed as training, through dance and interacting with the world, Jones describes their distinctions, stating, "your training tells you how to use your voice. You don't abandon that. But you don't let that training eclipse the spontaneity of the instinct in the moment."[22] Since "the present moment counts, not as a transition or a gap between the past and the future but as a rupture that always carries the possibility of breaking free from restrictive discourses and power structures," our bodies enlivening memory transforms how these memories feel in the body as well as the space they take up.[23] "Feels Like" necessarily engendered fracture and as a result, we could rework how memories and experience moved in our bodies and our archive, and the extent to which they inhabited, consumed, guided, and/or informed the degree of touch we allowed.

Feel to Permit Inventory

Happenings, like performance, live with us beyond their humanly measured beginning and ending. They carry on in our skin, muscle, and cellular memory. When reacting to the workshop and activities, Christa described feeling "relieved" and "surprised I still feel this way after so long."[24] Her reaction to the activity confirms the lingering effect of experience. Similarly, Deborah noted, "I forgot about what happened, but it's still there."[25] I surmise the activity unsettled some things that sat tucked away within her archive. Yet, because "the repertoire both keeps and transforms choreographies of meaning," the exercise "Feels Like" afforded the occasion to revisit lived experience and take inventory of the resonance left by these occurrences and their associated meaning.[26] During each aspect of "Feels Like," we wrote about what we know and the feel of what we know. These words, phrases, verbal diagrams, and poems told stories of relationships between our bodies, other people, spaces, and ideas. Within these exercises, our bodies were (re)membering, exhuming, and recasting. Collectively we recalled, lived, and felt who we are and how that feels at that very moment, and also sometimes confronted collision between our self-understanding, the world, and the work of being home with oneself. Spry writes, "the performing body offers a thick description of an individual's engagement with cultural codes and expectations; it is an ancient scroll upon which is written the stories of one's movement through the world."[27] The body in action, therefore, is both a bloom and a composite of areas traversed, experiences that unfolded, and meaning made of such encounters with and in the world. However, interpretations can mutate from activities that stimulate newfangled movements, alternative ways of narrating memory, and knowledge lodged within body's archive.

Threaded into the multiple memories described earlier is the savvy burden of navigating the world in a body assumed Black and female though not inherently cisgender, femme, or feminine. The co-constitutive nature of race and gender enhances girls' likelihood to be pushed out of school, dress coded, and reprimanded for displaying expressive curiosity. Girls' battle with carcerality and confinement occurs bodily despite one's proximity to literal jail or detention. Black girls endure violation without formal recourse or even remorse. The exercise "Feels Like" spurred a naming of inconvenient truths, hardships, and emotional states viscerally and physiologically known. Since knowing is active, learning from these events registered in the form of emotions, felt isolation, skin irritability, ethnic shame, self-policing, and adoption of unreliable mirrors.

Bodily action is not simply reaction to one's environment or internalized assessment of self. For Black girls, these performances are alive, in motion scenes of traversing carceral landscapes as confined geographies in dialogue with self, context, archive (history), and possibility (repertoire expanded). Depending on the degree of perceived wrongness read onto bodies, girls are punished (overtly and covertly), which through repetition, bruises and in other ways punctures girls' embodiment. Our time together revealed that the choice and agreement to feel and be touched facilitates exhumation and creates prospects for noticing and transmuting the connotation attributed to experience.

Conclusion

The process of activating the body opens doors for more internally cultivated measures and intrinsic narration. Being internally directed, as the epigraph at the beginning of this chapter notes, makes way for new relationships with self, memories, and bodies—ours and others. Black girls, irrespective of comportment, face trial. Pinned between narrow configurations of Black girlness, our time together and the practice of touch exceeded the quotidian. The type of Black each girl inhabited in different settings classified girls as too Black, in other spaces not Black enough, and each of these cataloged accounts, wrong. Physical characteristics perceived as too pure, too close to our roots, placed girls at odds with their bodies, other Black people, and the environment. Lorde notes, "to refuse to be conscious of what we are feeling at any time, however comfortable that might seem, is to . . . allow ourselves to be reduced to the pornographic, the abused, and the absurd."[28] When girls look at the world, including all of its smaller units of function, it teaches what is to be known about it and how girls serve that vision. Girls develop an acute sense of how the body is constituted and what wars are waged on its shores due to social institutions and systems of power. As children we quickly learn and continue knowing that having something to say about Black girls ain't the same as having something useful to gift Black girls toward the living they endeavor to do. In contrast, the workshop and its activities cleared room for us to take inventory of what has been absorbed into the body. Additionally, it suspended time in order that we consider what lessons we've acquired from others, what we agree with, and what new lessons we want to gift our ourselves.

When Black girls intimately look at each other, unpacking, reorienting, and connection occurs. This affectionate form of looking engenders touch. Phillipi described a takeaway from the workshop: "Like, it doesn't matter what color you are, all people are the same." Context matters. Within our workshop context, Phillipi's statement connected to our conversation about colorism and the intercultural realities of Black girlhood. Stepping into the circle to affirm herself and be celebrated, she chose her skin to be the body part she wanted to reclaim. When looking at Black girlhood with other girls, Phillipi learned that despite varying ethnic backgrounds, family structure, hue, and even body shape, there are translocal textures to Black gurl living. Asked during post-workshop interviews to offer brief words or phrases to capture how they felt during the workshop, they offered: "rejuvenated," "powerful," "vulnerable," "amazing," and "connected." Each of these words implicitly references a form of weight. Girls find ways to stand firm, perhaps with a slight sway, amid mocking and debasement, but that doesn't mean those messages don't scar the spirit.

When Black girls agree to relate body-to-body, experience-to-experience, disarmed, a crossing occurs.[29] We made room to air out our archives and see ourselves beyond *what happened* to and *what got said* about us. Our covenant compelled that we see each other beyond (and outside) what the world missed while being too busy reducing girls to body/object and behavior. These exercises summoned forth and recalibrated our repertoires. In collective practice, they distended our aptness to read ourselves and Black girlhood with *innocent eyes*. Innocent eyes, I argue, is a complementary perspective to the reorientations presented in Chapter 1 to enrich the quality of embodiment experienced. Innocent eyes undermine actions that appear safe yet jeopardize one's intrarelationship. Embodied retooling using body-activation loosens the reigns of capture. Capture, as defined by Hill and Callier, refers to "the totalizing effects of practices and policies which swiftly and intentionally move students away from schools into prisons, and/or hold them, their families, and communities structurally in place, making ways out of poverty, actualizing autonomy, or moving towards greater senses of freedom—freedom to breathe, stylize as one desires, vote, etc.—near impossibilities."[30] Whereas capture facilitates stuckness, embodied retooling works to thaw the boundary calcified between captive body and flesh with an intention of strengthening embodiment or the (w)holeness of ourselves. To touch through the modes of seeing, being, and being seen, we applied salve to our personal and cultural wounds. Though unaware at the conscious level of creation, in practice, these exercises supported our tapping into the erotic. Lorde details the utility and obstacles of sharing and touch, declaring, "when we look away from ourselves as we satisfy our erotic needs in concert with others, we use each other as objects of satisfaction rather than share our joy in the satisfying, rather than making connection with our similarities and our differences."[31] While our positionalities differed, as did the pressures we brought with us into the workshop, the session afforded an opportunity to adjust and even lighten our loads.

Body-activation involves tagging artifacts to index our archives anew. To stimulate the body is to animate embodied knowledge; it is a technique to awaken flesh in order that the border between captive body and spirit becomes dissolvable. When Black girls will to touch, we—individually and collectively—are beckoned to undress, forefront sentience, and background that which tries to deny our complexity, knowing, and mattering. When time is dedicated to Black girls taking inventory of the mirrors on which we rely, a portal is made for seeing ourselves in each other and new pedagogies materialize. Muhammad and Haddix maintain, "for Black girls and women, literacy enactments not only enable learning how to read print but also how to read the social context and environments."[32] Black girls also benefit from faculties to interpret their bodies as texts and at the end of the day, help them embrace vulnerability as a pathway to embodied living. Extending the important work of critical literacy, touch is a Black gurl pedagogy for mending bodies and a tool that sutures us to each other, beyond time.

I close this chapter with the activity "Body Affirmations." This remixed version of a daily movement and conditioning exercise during the 2011 Urban Bush Women Summer Leadership Institute in New Orleans, "Body Affirmations" does the work of clarification and (re)orientation. It's an agentic practice of clarifying stories we want to embrace about our bodies in general. "Body Affirmations" lovingly gestures us to accept the words of mirrors that love and see us (w)hole. Participation in the exercise is an opportunity to own the ways certain body parts have been engaged undesirably, possibly abused and/or mistreated, while amplifying pleasure toward and beliefs about that body part. Finally, this exercise helps brush off feelings associated with old tracks and invite in new soundscapes for the body parts identified. In SLI, we stood scattered in a room, usually stretching and moving our bodies slowly and intentionally. Spread out around the room, awakening our bodies at the top of the morning, this call and response, led by that morning's conditioning facilitator, kicked off the chant. The base call and response went as follows:

CALL: This gap.

RESPONSE: This gap.

CALL: It's not yours.

RESPONSE: It's not yours.

CALL: It's mine!

RESPONSE: It's mine!

CALL: All mine!

RESPONSE: All mine!

To maintain the sacred and slow deliberate energy created in SLI for warming up and paying homage to our bodies, I invited us to stand eye to eye in a circle. I asked that we each identify a body part that receives unsolicited and/or undesirable attention, a body part that we might quietly disown or dislike. Standing together, I informed them we'd be showing love to that body part through verbal and physical affirmations. Some girls rubbed, laid hands on, accentuated them, or showed them off for us to see so that we might pay respects. In the session, girls served smiles, cheering, and encouraging responses to the call as celebration of each other in body and personhood. And sometimes, as a way to massage the salve more deeply into the skin, a girl offered a remix to add emphasis. We paid our respect to the endurances of feet, bellies, and eyes to withstand gazes with built-in racism, xenophobia, and adultification that undermine our being and becoming. And we held space for all the body parts named and the stories attached but not spoken then, so that we could make room for new narratives and relationships to flourish. We stood before each other and said goodbye to the burdens, pains, and undesirable encounters around this body part.

Black girlhood is sacred; it is work that is done intentionally to allow individual and collective sprouting to happen. In the remix below, I altered the names attached to body affirmations. In doing so, the girls figuratively adorned each other's bodies and attended to them kindly and thoughtfully, through a rub, runway strut, or some other form of taking ownership. At the time, this ephemeral moment felt necessary to the close of the workshop. I felt obliged to make space for us to apply salve to our named and unnamed wounds, as well as the wounds of others. In the now, upholding the sacred and ephemeral nature of the moment remains significant. I endeavor here to preserve that moment just for us, express that something indeed happened, and offer a morsel of the energy pulsing after and while Black girls agreed to touch and be touched.

> [*Standing in a circle, smiles, twirls, and eye contact float around and within. Before someone steps into the center to begin, everyone raises their right fist to signal that this Black girl pledge can begin.*]

PHILLIPI: This stomach.

ALL: This stomach.

CHRISTA: It ain't yours. This smile.

ALL: This smile.

UNIQUE: This skin.

ALL: This skin. And this butt.

NICOLE: This Black girl.

ALL: She ain't yours.

DEBORAH: These legs.

ALL: These legs!

NICOLE: These eyes, not yours!

ALL: They're not yours!

DEBORAH: And this li'l butt. This cute li'l butt.

ALL: This cute li'l butt.

DEBORAH: It's all mine.

UNIQUE: These shoulders.

ALL: These shoulders.

PHILLIPI: These big ole broad shoulders.

DOMINIQUE: And this body.

ALL: This body.

NICOLE: This Black girl.

ALL: This Black girl.

PHILLIPI: She not yours!

ALL: She not yours!

ALL: [*continuous affirming gestures and bodily adornment*] She's mine! All mine!

CHAPTER 5

Teaching Black Girlhood
A Lesson in Cultivating Rigor

> We would have to unlearn an impulse that allows mythologies about each other to replace knowing about one another. . . . We cannot afford to cease yearning for each other's company.
>
> M. Jacqui Alexander, *Pedagogies of Crossing*

Just because I teach Black girlhood doesn't mean it's done teaching me. My name is Dominique C. Hill, and I am still digesting lessons.[1] Teaching Black girlhood is a spiritual process. It requires those present to excavate narratives related to race, gender, sexuality, and other social categories that organize power relations; to imagine; and to see Black girlhood, Black girls, ourselves, in symbiotic relationship. Reliability work is nonnegotiable in the art of teaching Black girlhood because terrible educations are ubiquitous. To teach Black girlhood is to embark on an unbecoming excursion that ensures those present develop a keen sense of tensions, potential, and norms giving shape to the learning process. Embrace of discomfort, process, and stewardship into a cypher, a dream in transit is of great importance. Teaching Black girlhood occurs in all kinds of contexts, for all kinds of reasons, and with all kinds of people. In this chapter, I focus on my time teaching it for the first time in a university setting under the title "Introduction to Black Girlhood Studies" in 2017 at Amherst College while I was a visiting assistant professor of Black studies. Drawing from course artifacts including submitted assignments and journals, I detail connections between the who, how, and where of pedagogy. With specific attention to students' course journals and two assignments that bookend the class—"Assumptions" and "Black Girlhood Statement"—I expound upon the importance of voice and volume in Black Girlhood studies and position them as interlocutors in the processes of being and becoming Black gurl reliable. I close with a found poem, "A Lesson in Black Girlhood Rigor," that draws from the Black Girlhood Statement assignment. A representation of the practice and pedagogy of reliability in action, this chapter illustrates how Black girlhood, if permitted, changes things, people included.

Rub, Rupture, and Relation

Black girlhood—the study and practice of it—is loaded with tension. While making sense of the body in research processes where uneasiness surfaced in physiological and other visceral ways, "the rub" emerged as a concept and phenomenon. Rub is incited by misalignment due to unchecked discomfort, lack of familiarity, value conflict, and/or spiritual rupture. It is a signal that a learning opportunity is nearing or present. Rub is a rawness that, if followed, exposes contradictory configurations held and provokes the body to allow a new repertoire to come forth. I know how to muscle through irritation and soreness of the spirit; it's a rigor taught to me early while navigating the world as a Blackqueer lesbian tomboy girl, from a working-class family of mostly womn, with a rhythm all my own, a mouf that gets me in trouble, and a dream of being a writer and psychologist. It would be in my doctoral program and conceiving my first child (the dissertation), that rub's wounds interrupted my steps and engendered a burning urge around this idea, principle, and pedagogy of Black gurl reliable. The rub, I now know, is an administrator of crossings. So, when the chance came to join in the spiritual work of Black Girl Genius Week 2022 and its inaugural debut at Michigan State University, nerves, rub, and all, I jumped at the opportunity.

On November 10, 2022, I hopped off a plane, attended a conference plenary with Anita Hill, and after roughly three hours of being in Minnesota, signed onto Zoom to participate in "All in Together: A SOLHOT Reunion." This roundtable discussion kicked off the first day of Black Girl Genius Week 2022 at Michigan State University. I arrived at the hotel, praise be for an early check-in, set my background to a purple swirling galaxy and sat ready to give and receive. Part of homegirling is the practice of learning to feel for and hear each other's needs, reflect on the work, see each other, and speak our truths. The decision to homegirl is ongoing work that once embraced unfolds according to the homegirl (not always femme or womn identified) unraveling and saving oneself, all the while participating in practicing Black girlhood. Homegirling is no small undertaking; it is loaded with responsibility, decision-making, and moments of getting something or someone wrong. Just seeing the invitation in my email inbox, my stomach tightened, my palms warmed, my lips quivered at the edges, and my mind started to race. The official invitation for "All in Together" asked me to "participate this year on an ONLINE panel kickoff event on Thursday, November 10th from 6:00–7:30pm and speak for 10–15 about teaching of Black Girlhood Studies."[2] Honored and emotion-filled, I found myself taken by the task and immediately imagined a rolodex of questions and my responses. What have I learned about myself teaching Black girlhood? Where does my teaching live in my body? How do I bring SOLHOT with me in the classroom? What does Black girlhood, being with Black girls, and reconnecting with my body continue to teach that I bring to the practice of teaching Black girlhood? Embedded in the opening epigraph by Alexander is a discussion about becoming and assuming accountability to the world and womn in it. She asserts a need to fend off the impulse to rank oppression and instead prioritize learning from each other.[3] Similar to the work documented in Chapter 4, personal knowing requires a will to touch and be touched.

Now aware and able to allow myself to be seen or touched in Black girlhood spaces, I sensed a need to consult students' words. I used reflections from students in my most recent time teaching Black girlhood—Spring 2022, under the title "Corridors of Black Girlhood"—to ground my talking points and showed up full self. I left the opaque conceptualizations for a different scholarly dialogue and responded to the prompt using the practice of undressing. SOLHOT is where unbecoming and becoming anew occurs. That evening of November 10 in Zoom land, homegirls sat engaged in deep embodied listening and provided receipts to my disclosure about the me who initially showed up to practice

Black girlhood. That Dominique (Dom to beloveds) was not yet—not yet fully back in my body, not yet owning my voice, not yet learned of my call to engage vulnerability work, not yet determinedly communing regularly with spirits through dance, not yet cracked open, not yet (re)membered back together, not yet the Dominique who engraved the ideas on this page.

I left the panel rearranged. My level of vulnerability shook me to satisfaction. In a Lordeian way, I'd shown up fully, revealed myself as in process, and closed a chapter. That day marked another beginning. I reintroduced myself to myself and to SOLHOT homegirls who were familiar with the not yet version of me. To be clear, I remain not yet, but in a different way. This chapter is a token of appreciation and act of gratitude to SOLHOT for its many and varying Black girlhood classes where I and many others learned the skills of full presence and located our distinct gifts (an element of voice).

Who Enters and With Whom Matters

Reliability work is an auspicious concern and aspiration within Black Girlhood studies. This nonprescriptive pedagogy in practice requires effective communication and handling. An organizing idea with many aspects, built into reliability work, is politics of naming, treatment, reading, and storying. Being Black gurl reliable is an ongoing rehearsal of showing up for Black girls, and when teaching Black girlhood, that labor becomes more layered. Media, cultural representations, and a legacy of racial-sexual scripts and values wrongly project a summative estimation about Black girls that is flat and fabricated in the interest of reinforcing existing hierarchies of power and narrative logics that rationalize the mishandling of Black girls. Alexander writes, "We would have to unlearn an impulse that allows mythologies about each other to replace knowing about one another."[4] Within the architecture of Alexander's statement is a call to identify and dispose of abstract metanarratives void of tenderness and direct interaction. To do so, third party referentials must be turned in for firsthand accounts. Related is the history of the term "women of color," which is a political one that sidesteps identity to foreground responsibility to one another amid assumptions that haunt present and future encounters while allowing for reintroduction and meaningful relation.

With an expanded repertoire from mistakes made and practicing Black girlhood in SOLHOT and other Black girl serving spaces, being misunderstood and/or judged by other Black womn, and learning to pick up the pieces of myself and others, I entered the fall semester of 2017 prepared to teach "Introduction to Black Girlhood Studies." In a class of thirteen students, two-thirds personally owned the identity Black girl and/or having experienced girlhood; roughly a third at some point disclosed being within the queer spectrum; two adopted the location girl and gender nonconforming; all referenced high stress, anxiety, and/or depression; and many were first-generation college students and/or first-generation United States citizens. Voice immediately appeared in the classroom as a key ingredient to the process of studying Black girlhood. While identity is not the basis for taking a Black girlhood course, the recent trend around compulsory identity, where youth utilize identity categories as the basis for belonging, academic courses taken, and even "appropriate" activism, it affects what students are willing to share, admit, and explore. When Black girls with personal histories that included parents and grandparents who had immigrated from Ghana, Nigeria, and Ethiopia; experiences in boarding schools and all-girl schools; and Christian, gender nonconforming, African American, and queer backgrounds are alongside other non-Black, queer, racially mixed girls, and they all come together to engage Black girlhood, capaciousness is a requisite.

To enlarge the archive and repertoire of Black girlhood when teaching Black girlhood, reliability work must be enacted. From my time teaching Black girlhood in 2017, I spotted the beautiful tensions held between Black girl the figure, the idea, and living breathing Black girls. In the classroom, there are girls in the pages, in the songs, on the screen, in the spoken word poems, in the room. There are individuals who are read as Black and female but do not assume the pronoun she. Also present are individuals who have been young womn so long, they spend the semester unworking the ideas that girl and womn are synonymous, that girlhood and childhood are interchangeable, and that girlhood is Black womn pain.

As a facilitator of students' study of Black girlhood and Black girls as an academic field, I see my responsibility as manifold. My primary charges include introducing students to Black Girlhood studies; facilitating processes that help to unearth and interrogate preconceived notions about Black girls; expanding students' understandings of theory and education; and cultivating a curiosity about identity, power, and creativity that applies to themselves as well as to how they study Black girlhood. I accept these duties also knowing that who shows up, the curiosities they bring, and what they are willing to give to the learning endeavor will guide which of these responsibilities become course focal points and which get relegated as learning bonuses or "if we get there, awesome." During the field's expansion, students fill classrooms with experience, questions, and theory. These classrooms are also determinative sites of Black Girlhood studies' formation. Some of the subgroups within the classroom include individuals who know girlhood directly and/or who relate to having a girlhood cut short, denied on the playground or stoop; individuals interested in issues of social justice; and those inquisitive about Blackness, Black femininity, and Black womnhood. These beings all come to class looking for answers to their specific points of interest. Though the class supplies some insights, their acumen is negotiated by our class ethos and the investment to embrace "struggling over your identification with it. Struggling over your feelings about Black girls and Black girlhood. I'm talking 'bout finding pleasure with/among Black girls and Black girlhood, that alone is a revolution."[5] Labor within Black girlhood, according to this track from the Humility Mixtape by DJ Sarah Grace is working through chafing that occurs between ideas projected about Black girls and actually being with Black girls, as well as between those notions personally believed about Black girls and what becomes possible in the practice of girlhood. Black girlhood is labor that can go invisible, and when noticed, can be met with suspicion and unbelievability. Therefore, locating pleasure in Black girlhood is a necessary labor that can get pushed aside or is undermined.

The *who* and *what* we, those teaching Black girlhood, bring with us matters and contributes to the vibe of the party, the educational venture, and the shape it takes. According to the 1997 song "Party Ain't a Party," performed by Queen Pen, a party is contingent upon energy

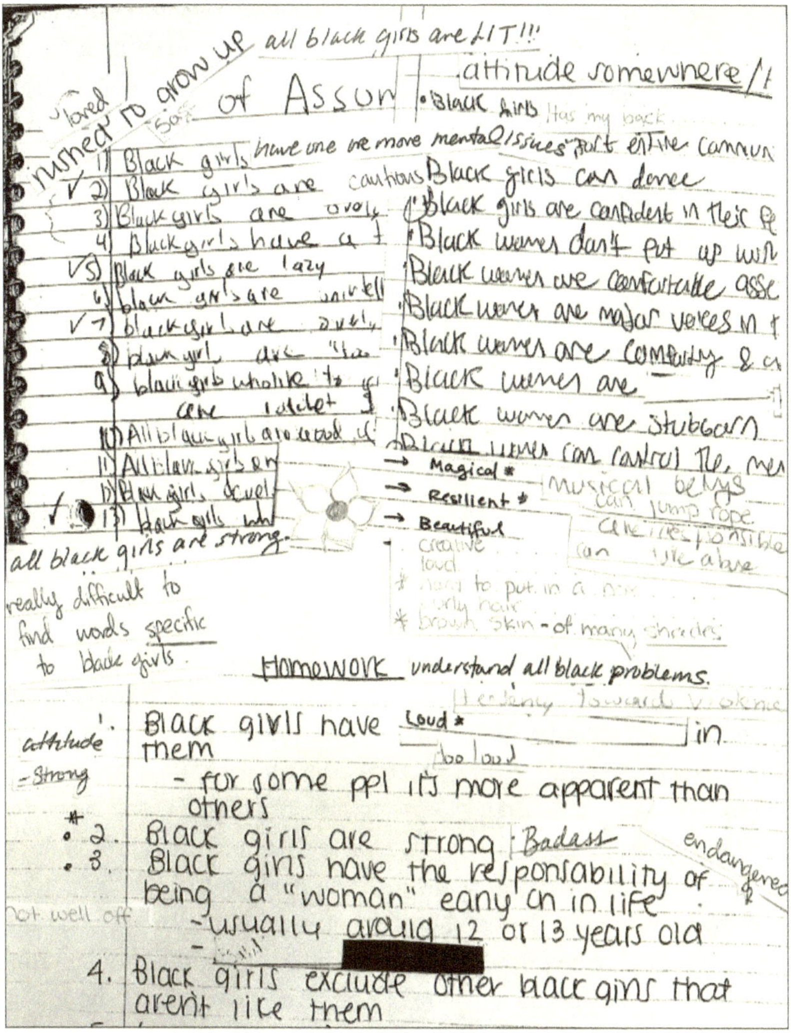

FIGURE 5.1. Original collage of collective assumptions about Black girls from handwritten journal entries of students in "Introduction to Black Girlhood Studies" (Fall 2017). Author's personal collection

activated by who's in attendance, the collective vibe built, and actions taken within the space.[6] Likewise, a party is a good time filled with options such as romantic and/or sexual connections, wanted attention, and a good time. A party is created from an amalgamation of sounds, actions, and spirits in space.

Similarly, a lesson ain't a lesson till students arrive. Before that, there are ideas, curricular sketches, and aspirations. When the students enter the space, the geography of education changes. The becoming (or not) of an academic party, a deep engagement with content, is only partially about the educator's preparation (see Chapter 4). Though I cannot name all of who and what walks with me, I am clear that I am not alone. I know I also bring with me to classroom spaces a commitment to lifelong learning, a love for Black girls, a knowingness that schooling and education are not synonymous, and an embodied feminist pedagogy, along with a will to touch and be touched by students, ancestors, and my educational background. Devising ways to find out who and what we bring with us is vital.

Being Black gurl reliable is layered and, within the process of teaching Black girlhood, necessitates contemplation about and active recognition of what is requested by girls present while keeping in mind the politics and stakes of the bigger picture. Undressing is useful for establishing a baseline of experiential and collaborative learning. Through what is described here as touch and what Alexander in the opening epigraph describes as a covenant to be with, distortions become surmountable as they usher in ways of being that jettison "practices of domination."[7] Such agreements require internal measures, divergent tools, and reading the relevance of difference. Application of awareness took me to my toolkit to access the practice of undressing that in the classroom is best accompanied by (re)orientations to academic learning.

At the crux of Black Girlhood studies is a responsibility to (re)acquaint girls and womn, with the body generally and our individual bodies. This reintroduction is meant to widen the range of what is seen about and as part of Black girlhood, inclusive of stories drummed up about what is seen, and how the body shows up to practice it. Out of my dissertation research emerged five initial (re)orientations that condensed into three along the way. They are "You, all of you, are welcome here and expected to show up"; "Lean into the process"; and "Challenge yourself to go beyond." My autodidact study of the "finding voice method" in theatrical jazz aesthetics advised my approach to the workshops (see Chapter 4) and the above (re)orientations emanate from my application of this method to the work of undressing. Upon starting a postdoctoral fellowship in 2014, I began incorporating these (re)orientations into my syllabi and classroom pedagogy as a means of making transparent my particular pedagogy and aspirational learning culture to students.[8] At first glance, students tended to overlook them and dismiss them as rhetorical. However, these tenets extend from the advice from Cynthia Oliver I shared in the book's introduction—"If you are going to do it. You gotta DO IT"—and arrange learning norms along lines of transgression, full presence, and progression over perfection. Equally, these ingredients are foundational to adopting the rigor of undressing, especially within an academic setting.

Undressing as Temperature Check

Introduced in Chapter 2, undressing in public is a practice located within the spectrum of embodied vulnerability and pedagogies of transgression. Despite variation in procedure and method, undressing consists of purposeful vulnerability with aims of identifying, challenging longstanding stories about the self, as well as others, that limit connection, embracing the paradox of self and stories, and promoting genuine bond. Initiated to address false narratives mapped onto me as a postdoctoral fellow and as a means to build rapport with Black and Brown girls in an enrichment teaching context, embodied vulnerability flowered as a pedagogy intended to better steer how (white) students interfaced with my body. The combination of revisiting my life as a young and youthful girl, learning about the womn in my family as girls, and being entrusted to guide girls—poets, not born in the United States, angry, the color of dark roast coffee, queer, PKs (preacher's kids), native Spanish speakers, some shy, all committed to going to college—put me in a deep state of reflection and envisioning. Concurrently, life had me on a journey of creating a repertoire around embodiment and vulnerability more broadly.

Black Girlhood Hieroglyphics

Beneath the skin of Black girlhood live etchings, sketches, tattoos, linguistic, signs, visual semiotics registering popularized and socially circulated Black girl iconography. Soaked in basins of racial capitalism, racialized gender, white supremacy residue, anti-Blackness, fear, and difference misarranged as deviant, these assumptions inhabit the body, take root at the hypodermic level of Black girlhood, and assist in the propagation of racial-sexual scripts. I instructed students—some Black, representing varying ethnicities, mostly non-white, some white passing, many queer—to "create a list of visceral/immediate assumptions that come to mind about Black girls. Choose five to examine and provide a written reflection exploring where those assumptions come from, what they connect to, and how, if at all, they influence your engagement with Black girls."[9] These assumptions, though not the total story of Black girlhood, create multifarious landscapes for girls to navigate, and contour to Black girl geographies.

Black Girlhood studies and teaching Black girlhood, attuned to these contours, is about "the radical and creative potential of Black girlhood, the knowledge we/they build, and where—if we are courageous enough—we can go."[10] A word referring to folk in and beyond SOLHOT committed to the work of studying Black girlhood and expanding the field of Black Girlhood studies, "audacity" is about being aware of the work of the world around us while investing in the building of a world with a different set of criteria. Work in our class was about coming to terms with how the educational settings traversed created an investment in the social institution of education, high regard for college as a marker of intellect and achievement, a learned sense of how best to do student, or some combination of these. Despite students being mostly Black, mostly self-identifying along the girl–womn spectrum, it was also the case that many spent time—deliberately or inadvertently—avoiding certain Black girl scripts. Those who didn't self-identify as Black, girl, or Black girl hesitated to share their responses to the prompt. Living in the seams of the above assumptions are questions that inform the field and the labor of teaching Black girlhood in a way that foregrounds celebration and unlearning. Some of these questions include: What foreclosures are manufactured through bodily policing? In what ways does the quality of being outspoken order Black girls faring in educational settings? What social change becomes possible if defiance was a nurtured skill? Where can girls be themselves and try on different expressions and embodiments without punishment for supposedly being grown, an oreo, fas', or some other Black girl trope?

The incorporation of introspection regarding beliefs about Black girls afforded an opportunity to interrogate the specifics of the Black girl/s we saw in our minds when listing our assumptions, to revisit the girl we initially saw as the reference point for the course, and to see them tethered. Who is in the room matters in all educational instances because who is present helps to invigorate the material and the digestion of course content. Similarly, when it comes to teaching Black girlhood, temperature checks become a way of laying bare who is present, what experiences they bring to their learning, and possibly what strain and rub may be on the horizon.

Writing to Save Room to Hear and Sound Self

Teaching Black girlhood warrants an openness to conflict and contradiction.[11] As principle and practice, embracing paradox shows more than tells the variety of Black girlness, features difference as a gem, and scales Black girlhood across and beyond childhood to have students consider it in its fullness. To hold space for students' beliefs, thoughts, memories, theorization, and unlearning, I required them to keep a class journal. Students had to devise at least one weekly entry while addressing "a question posed on the syllabus, in class, and/or a self-initiated question or prompt."[12] Some of them decorated their journals; some used classic Five Star and composition notebooks; some wrote in letter format; others wrote in poetic prose. My hope was that they engaged the material at the levels of the personally educative and academic. A bonus of this assignment would be deepened awareness of themselves—most, not all, went there by the end. I wanted them to explore and come to own parts of themselves previously hushed and tucked away. Accordingly, I didn't evaluate spelling, grammar, or other things related to technical writing. Since learning is about the what and how, I needed them to come face-to-face with stories they circulated and internalized about Black girls, about themselves, about girls they alleged as different from them, about academic rigor and the space made within it for Blackness, for girl talk, for Black girlhood.

The journal was sacrosanct; it served as a freestyle cypher between the self/page/professor, a rehearsal, and to some, the main event as it pertained to engagement. At different times, I also brought in an idea from someone's journal, or a common theme expressed, and used it as a class building block. Initially, I read the journals individually, taking note of prompts they elected to explore, identity references, and recurring topics in students' writing. Some of these included freedom, body politics, sexuality, becoming and unbecoming, being Black in predominantly white school environments, self-love and care, and unlearning. From there, I looked at the prompts chosen by self-identified Black and non-Black students, noting the language chosen and the distance and proximity to Black girlhood it symbolized. I also noticed that irrespective of students' social identities, the course's pedagogical approaches summoned students to confront beliefs beyond those about Black girls, exhume messages they carry with them that shape their presence in the world, and encourage self-definition. For example, a student from Fiji who identified ethnically as Indian and Chinese, wrote, "journaling forces me to get personal. It lets me say the things I feel might sound 'dumb' to my peers," while a self-identified Black queer girl expressed, "It has made me aware of my existence and body in this space, this white world of privilege and how to be. I feel I am realizing a power I've always had but forgot."[13] The journal made space for them to locate themselves amid social realities and modes of domination.

Black Gurl Vernacular

Through Black girlhood praxis, I've honed the skill of listening to silence. Mindful of the many formations of silence and my awareness that it is wise to listen for and to "raised eyebrows, side and rolled eyes, change in pitch, a lip smack, and shared hugs," I presume it's not *if* there is something being said, rather *what* tools are being deployed to speak.[14] In their final journal reflection, a student shares a revelation: "This journaling experience has taught me that I really do have things to say. I've been using the excuse 'I just have nothing to say' in response to my quietness, but I truly think it's more like 'I don't want to say what I'm thinking.'"[15]

Voice takes the form of literal leg splits, doing hair, volume turned up on necks, bussin' out in song, gut laughter, and lots of questions. Taught how to survive predominantly white schools in a nonwhite body, I also sensed hesitation and willingness, anxiety and eagerness, interest and fear, and sought to mobilize an expansive notion of silence, one different from the silence Lorde warns against. Different from being quiet, silence here refers to a quality or aesthetic as well as abnegation. In "The Transformation of Silence to Language and Action," Lorde discusses silence's connection to fear and in anticipation that one will dodge a bullet—judgment, isolation, denied access—of some kind. Silence here is a form of self-foreclosure where "we can sit in our corners mute forever . . . while our children are distorted and destroyed, while our earth is poisoned; we can sit in our safe corner mute as bottles, and we will still be no less afraid."[16] Stitched into an earlier student reflection is the imperative of deliberate space and time to decipher the reason beneath one's actions and silence to recognize the sound and texture of one's voice to also know when it's muted and energized.

Sound refers to an aesthetic that rises out of "a wider repertoire of how Black girls sound as a potentially creative source of knowledge."[17] Brown et al. discuss sounds' particular relevance to voice and Black girlhood celebration, stating, "we used sound, a sense so often leveraged against Black girls and women as a means of punishment and separation, as an embodied source of listening to our hearts in the beats and the breaks of doing collective work."[18] Sound and voice are interlinked. When girls are tone policed, punished for the volume of their laughter and hair, voice is muffled.

Black gurl vernacular is about the literal and figurative speech spoken and created by Black girls and practiced in Black girlhood. It consists of unstudied speech or mother tongue, modes of voice and what they make realizable. School and specifically the cumulative effects of learning to do school well silhouettes girlhood and voice in ways that must be attended to, scrutinized, and accounted for in the field. When discussing the complexities of voice, Black girls, womn, and those read as Black and female though not inherently cisgender, femme, or feminine in the class talked about voice as something moderated by sociocultural spaces like school and familial spaces. In other ways, they described it as something integral to the body—one's hair, style of dress, and proximity to popularly circulated scripts. Other times, voice emerged as something they were in search of locating, a confidence and self-accessing technology. As one student writes, "in a way, journaling served as a much-needed conversation between me, myself, and I."[19] Likewise, voice functioned as a portal to qualities they believed to be unattainable at that moment. Lastly, when discussing voice, it was often in relation to other Black girls.

To edify students' theorization of voice in Black girlhood, what follows is a performative dialogue, "Someday Is Today." I draw inspiration for this dialogue from students' final journal entries and the title from one written as a poem titled "Someday I'll Love [GGO]." GGO are the students' initials. Riffing off a self-referential line in the poem (see below), I refer to this author using the pseudonym Messiah Borne. I add the last name Borne in support of her prophecy. The draft, which appears in her journal, was revised and included in her final portfolio. "Someday I'll Love [GGO]" was dream and declaration. Messiah writes:

> Someday. Ill love GGO
> And when that day comes, I will not wait for anyone
>   To celebrate me
> Because by then
> I will know
> That I am worthy of celebration . . .
> Even when they don't praise me like they should . . .
> Like I won't resurrect on the third day
> Like I ain't the messiah herself[20]

I maintain the structure of her poem and handwriting as a form of voice. Confession and forecast, Messiah identifies where she was then and where she plans to be in the future:

> Someday, I'll love GGO
> And when that day comes
> they cannot touch me
> cannot reach me . . .
> I will be me in my own right
> I will be read
> and magical
> all at once[21]

The word "someday" conjures forth a Messiah who salutes the fullness of herself and no longer needs pedestalled outside validation. Taking seriously Messiah's incantation, I crafted "Someday Is Today." Alongside the methods of embodied listening and sensing and born of final reflection entries from students in Introduction to Black Girlhood Studies that semester who self-identified as Black girls, womn, individuals having experienced a Black girlhood, some combination, or all of these, this recipe moves Messiah's not yetness into present tense. Imagined as a cypher of girls speaking, the text below names the challenges, interceptions, and labor around Black gurl embodiment with a focus on voice. In this context, voice encompasses self-definition through sartorial decisions, comportment, and internal dialogue; it is about the weight those bodily associated with Black girlhood experienced around taking up space and claiming the fullness of themselves. As a note on layout, words in italics are direct statements that appeared in students' journals. "Someday is today" is a set of ingredients, a bridge between a Black girl yesterday named by the girls in that Fall 2017 iteration of the course and the many tomorrows of Black girlhood.

Someday Is Today

Ask yourself,
What do I need, right now?

I guess I came to save myself

They say my hips too big
I say my hips too big
And the cycle continues

My lack of movement and expression—
self-imposed.

I know that if I stepped out of this
identity (if I stopped playing good
girl) *I would instantly be criticized and*
stereotyped by my classmates, teachers,
and parents.

Ask yourself,

How will I find joy today?

How will I celebrate us, today,
this instant?

Miss Mary Mack or double Dutch,

These were just fun games and I liked to play them.

                                                Keep up the joy.

I could take up space with my hands, voice, and legs—
my body remembers.

And I didn't have to feel sorry about it—I recall.

                                                When the joy is not there

                                                Worry won't make it appear.

                                                Be.

Most of the stress that I mention revolves around academia and me studying things that I don't particularly enjoy or am not passionate about. So I've been asking myself how I can learn to live in the moment and not for a particular outcome.

                                                Make more space for you.

I guess I came to save myself, both from the poisonous parts of myself and from any outside forces that can encourage me to turn against my inherent girlhood.

                                                Make more space for,
                                                More space for y/our story,
                                                Space for celebration.

There are some things that I wouldn't have written about a year ago that I'm writing about today.

                                                Let go of the people you decide to leave behind.

I write to get it out.

                                                Hold on tight to the people you decide to keep close.

I really don't like expressing negative feelings and "burdening others" (a mindset I am trying to unlearn).

	Keep talking to you.
	Keep digging inside.
	Imagine,
I need to embrace my awkward Black personality and make more space for myself to not be silenced by my white peers.	
	How it feel to not wait?
I can still feel how I silence myself. Unlearning that takes practice.	
	It's okay, homegirl.[22]
As an extremely awkward Black girl who stutters when she talks in front of too many people, who cannot dance, and has no idea how to handle her hair out of braids, realizing these qualities didn't make me any less Black was something I really needed to hear when I was younger	
	It's okay, homegirl.
Next to go is the self-hatred.	
	No specific, no special way to be a Black girl,
	No particular steps to show up Black girl.
	Be Black girl you.
... That comment instigated a conversation in which I defended my hair without compromising for anyone.	Remember, practice makes progress.
	What do you want to feel?
I realized, she doesn't need me to do anything for her. . . . As I'm writing this I'm texting her and it feels so nice to just reconnect, not to worry about her future or "fixing" her, but just letting her do her and letting her know that I have her back when she needs an ace.	How do you want to feel?

And hopefully the courage comes to me soon to tell my family because I love my girlfriend and I wanna shout it from the rooftops.

. . . It's a shame a hairstyle might not get me a job. I'm aware of that.

My story can only be told by me and the stories of other Black girls can only be told by them,

Someday, I'll love us.

And when that day comes, I will not wait for anyone.

Practice creating that feeling.

We have to be what the world refuses to be for us.

It's okay, homegirl.

Build you a business girl, a world even,

hire who you please.

Get a *squad*.

Get loose.

Whenever you decide, we here.

Wherever you decide, we have your back.

Whatever you decide, be sure it's your decision.

Like ninety-one-year-old *Mrs. Nickerson* or beloved BJ, the young girl trying to skateboard in the sand or the seasoned and youthful one trying to dig a cloud out the dirt, do as you please.

It's okay to be.

We've decided, someday is today.

Teaching Black Girlhood Requires Love

Hooks said, "when we understand love as the will to nurture our own and another's spiritual growth, it becomes clear that we cannot claim to love if we are hurtful and abusive."[23] Such a willingness also stipulates a determination to imagine and cultivate a future where we are alive and operating in full presence. Black Girlhood studies, Kwakye, Hill and Callier note, was "birthed out of love . . . birthed out of a desire to know what we used to know and uncover it and give it back to us so we may know again"; Black Girlhood studies vies for a future where Black girls, womn, and loved ones inhabit the world in full presence.[24] To teach Black girlhood then is about the contents and contexts of Black girlhood as well as time and space to study and rehearse reliable touch.

When teaching Black girlhood, I aspire to bring to life contours and conversations relevant to those in and beyond the room. I make room for Black girls not yet born, those busy mothering parents, in elementary school, those summoning the overworked lawyer to the dancefloor for a contest, stylizing themselves on the outside to mirror their essence, those at the playground, in a garden or field, behind metal doors with tiny windows, and asleep inside the womn burdened by social scripts and expectations. I've taught girls whose first language is not English, who while moving about the world are held responsible and read as adolescents, adults, tweens, womn, ambiguous, and more. Teaching Black girlhood in rooms not exclusively Black, girl, or Black girl is an exercise of active listening and consistent improvisation. To make the most of our time together, transgression is normalized and permits a falling away of distinctions made for the sake of disciplinary agreements and academic discourses that in real time take on different qualities.

To teach Black girlhood is to send out and accept the invitation to hold in the same palm theory informed by practice and unsettling logics that bar pleasure and embodied living in the lives of Black girls. To be in the practice of building learning processes where students are asked to be with self, course content, music, and bodies entails acceptance of potential confusion and disparaging reactions. For example, through anonymous quick course assessment activities and within their closing journal entries, students in this class described the course as "disorganized," "overwhelming," and also a place where they were permitted to "reflect on childhood a lot more deeply and often than in the past ... [that] has opened up a dialogue between us [student and parents]." Despite the initial sting I often experience with students' feedback, taking a step back, I recognize the cumulative class experience and reflections signaled something generative happened in our class. It is true that getting to the useful bits was a journey that was often messy and uncomfortable.

As a last expression of theory derived from students' study of Black girlhood, I close with a found poem because it is an appropriate architecture for Black girlhood. As Ewing states, "inherent in a poem is a comfort with paradox and subtlety, with nuance and even the moments of apparent self-contradiction or uncertainty that characterize all human life."[25] Devised while listening to Black feminist artists and self-proclaimed Black girl MCs like We Levitate on SoundCloud, and other artists like Mother Nature, Sammus, and Jamila Woods, I take guidance from June Jordan and aspire to practice truth telling and amplify impact with minimal words.[26] Language for this poem comes from two related assignments. The first, an anonymous end-of-class free write in response to the prompt "Black Girls/Black Girlhood studies are teaching me ..." collected weekly at the end of the first four weeks of the course. The second, "Black Girlhood Statement," is submitted at the end of the course as a succinct understanding of the field, based on course materials and personal reflections, that articulates its purpose, perspective on Black girls, pedagogies within in the field, and intellectual and/or personal import. "A Lesson in Black Girlhood Rigor" encapsulates action items, reminders, and ingredients for cultivating a regimen of Black girlhood that has staying power, an ability to sustain in cold temperatures, thoroughness rooted in persistent movement and being, in the name of internal satisfaction and vibrant spirit.

A Lesson in Black Girlhood Rigor

I.
trust
you hafta play and open yourself up
rigor be what Black girlhood requires
sound and body speak
speech need no words
play. show. be.
how you know
Black girlhood is
feelings song dance thoughts
cacophony and chorale
no one thing to say
no one thing to be
Before Black, we was
us
Fat fly awkward queer loud shy bitches smart sassy mothers
alladat none of it and more re/member
Black gurl opulent
girl no more
Every gurl all accounted for

II.
(re)orient
everything a lesson
hafta unlearn and add seasonin
reason
not with lies to and bout Black girls
manufactured worlds nor scripts
curricula nor pulpits
devoted to womn forgetting and girls lamenting
Build a gospel
Black Girlhood Studies teaches

center blackgurlwomn
slow down
give gratitude
Breathe upon entry
Emotion and academia ain't nemesis
sip on this in plain view

III.
conjure
set fiya to dat simmer
throw it all in da pot
Add spice sass and introspection
watch lies slide off dey bone
Ladle em up and out de way
watch emotional and creative intelligence rise to a boil
feel a sting in the right eye
stir in respect and (re)memory
graze the raging boil with fingertips
recognition is key
bring body to meet steam
bring questions to meet onion
see butter loosen walls
see water soggy burdens
breathe order out of place

IV.
allow
you hafta
reinterpret revisit reinvent
new pathways to activate
soil for self-saving
seeds of relation and revelation
prayers enliven and quicken Black girls
equal parts magic and real bodies

V.
know
hafta be y/our origin know Black girlhood and manifestation of
epistemology
Black girlhood be sanctuary
for us, by us
praise. play. repeat
for us, by us
repetition creates rigor
re/membering is worship
Black gurl existence
one step toward celebration
praise for twerk with
tone sets not tone policing
today we know
tomorrow we remember
now we presence
Black girlhood demands

CONCLUSION
Gifts of Being with Black Girlhood

Black girlhood is an ember and conductor—of freedom and worldmaking trails. This book is a testimony and artifact of such work. *Black Gurl Reliable* inaugurates embodiment as a vital facet of justice and examines de jure and de facto policies within carceral landscapes that sculpt Black girlhood and contribute to Black gurl embodiment. As I write this book, my fingers attempt to locate words to make sentences that neatly gather my ideas and tie them up in a bow. But how do I "neatly" wrap up a book while wars wage across the world? While I cite and write with June Jordan, a spirit guide, who had and still has so much to say about love and the interdependence of being loving and being accountable, and while the outcome of the 2024 United States presidential election was a vote for hate, corporatism, heteropatriarchy, and hijacking of human rights? How do I write the layers of something just unfolding, something I cannot name with precision, something that sometimes jerks me out of words and toward the rhythm of my breath? What rehearsals and practices need we indulge with urgency and persistence? What attitudes and sensibilities do we adopt to orient us (humans) to move, vote, and act, next time, in the interest of our lives, from collective knowing that we are all connected? How do I coherently acknowledge in writing something that sometimes sits in my tear ducts, sometimes numbs my feet, other times thrusts me off the couch and toward a poem, to call a loved one, or to vigorously dance and shake until calm emerges? This asking and sitting with are part of reliability work. These questions must live in tow of the words turned sentences and carried with me to listen to, embody, and address once able. Even as this performance nears a curtain close, it is unfinished, honest, and absolutely untidy. And yet, I am crystal quartz clear, nurturance of embodiment is vital to our personal, social, cultural, global living and aspiring vibrance.

Demonstrated throughout *Black Gurl Reliable* is embodiment's indispensability to the charge of Black mattering and the feminist project—a multidimensional commitment to reducing, disrupting, and dissolving domination. As I write, I am reminded that to embody a practice of interconnection is foundational to Black gurl reliable and social transformation. Black girlhood expands the feminist project and discussions of embodiment and pedagogy, as well as Black and feminist geographies, in three vital ways. First, this book makes visible distinct modes of body-based policing and technologies that facilitate foreclosure of self-definition at the expense of baseline survival. Second, through interrogation of carceral geographies, stakes and repeat offenses of disembodying experiences reveal "stuckness" as a quotidian form of death experienced by Black girls and throughout Black girlhood. Third is a naming and exposition of pedagogies of embodiment and tools (e.g., body-activation, mirror theory, reframing of innocence, undressing in public) raised from or textured by practicing Black girlhood that make accessible routes toward living whole, self-determined, and in right relationship with one's spirit. In the face of confinement, it is plausible to get jammed and concede to the adoption of unreliable readings as the truth of one's potential. As shapeshifters, Black girls "must always stay on the side of change, possibility, movement, and the future, or they would not be so adept at shifting the normative shapes and spaces that threaten their (and our) lives."[1] The tools introduced and practiced within these pages support shapeshifting, as well as retooling of the body from unrelenting geographies and contexts that erode Black gurl embodiment. Likewise, these practices are useful for fostering intimacy or enthusiastic embodied vulnerability, in and beyond Black girlhood.

Black Gurl Reliable, though not explicitly a spatial project, advances Black girlhood as an important transgressive Black geography. Specifically,

Black girlhood's capaciousness makes room for speculation and retooling through intergenerationality and defiance of borders beside their corresponding social arrangements related to age and rubrics around which lives "deserve" to be celebrated, for instance. Additionally, Black girlhood as a geography is a terrain wherein dimensions of embodiment are respected and positioned as immutable to Black spatiality. In practice, pedagogies of transgression are proof of Black life and worldmaking. Insights particular to embodiment highlight the fundamental need for bodily resets to interrupt pathways of stuckness. Confinement is a web of curricular and cultural processes performed in macro and micro ways.

Beyond the institutional and structural, confinement takes place interpersonally, culturally, and intrapersonally through conditioning strategies. In the face of confinement, pedagogies of foreclosure are systematized schemes that ignite internal disquiet and build walls within and without. Required to traverse the line of being too much (usually in terms of physical features or comportment) and not enough (with respect to markers of Black authentication and in school treatment from authority), girls must find a rhythm all their own to live healthily, (w) holy, and in relationship to themselves. Retooling of the body is valuable to shifting meaning and value attributed to our bodies and each other, and thereby reorient, as needed, to maintain Black gurl embodiment.

There is no one way to establish and/or locate a misplaced rhythm. Black girls practice and imagine freedom through movement, alignment, and adornment. Despite anti-Black school policies, power-wielding systems that delimit self-articulation, and authority figures who emphasize obedience and cultural erasure, Black girls exercise bodily agency. Black gurl aesthetics inclusive of sartorial choices and behavior, against the above backdrop, are instances of Black resistance legacies. These modes of dissent and their strategies teach us, if we catch the lesson, how to hold onto ourselves.

Starting with an inkling about the body's root significance to Black girlhood and interest in the ways contexts, especially educational ones, manipulate girls' embodiment, I ventured down a path that landed me at an impasse. This crossroad, loaded with questions, memories, and intimation, roused a reckoning: be with the journey and all it brings, stick to the research, only its so-called logical parts, or abandon it all.

In Bernice Johnson Reagon's keynote "Black Women's Issues," given at Barnard College on November 11, 1980, she stewards those present through history, activism, and stances taken in Black women's legacy.[2] In my most recent listening of it, I was struck by the intergenerational conversation about mothering, footprints, and activism. Gripped by her words, I wandered in and through my dreams. Quickly I returned to my dream of wanting to be a writer, and in elementary school confessing to beloved Lucille Clifton my passion for poetry, where at the end of our half day together, she declared me right then and there a poet. In "Site of Memory," Morrison uses water and specifically flooding as a metaphor for memory to uncover its connection to imagination and the physical body. She writes, "All water has perfect memory and is forever trying to get back to where it was. . . . It is emotional memory—what the nerves and skin remember as well as how it appeared. And a rush of imagination is our [writers] 'flooding.'"[3] I used the ingredient of memory and the process of (re)memory to engender an intentional organic venture that relied upon intuition and feltsense. Agreeing to study Black girlhood was one thing. Understanding education as a mode of practicing freedom and a commitment to self-determination was another thing, with the latter insisting that I follow my intellectual oddities and unravelings. I foregrounded intuition because to tell a story of Black girlhood is to tell many braided stories and because "stories stand as the corporeality of memory."[4]

Groove[ing] is an attitude, practice, and aesthetic. It is kin (specifically a daughter) to the fundamental element of improvisation and the "finding voice method" in theatrical jazz aesthetics. It escorted me toward queries related to the body and Black girlhood. With each turn, undulation, foot stomp, thigh pat of the process, the volume in my body cranked and cracked open new sightings for Black gurl embodiment and potential obstructions. Experiences of confinement and their corresponding technologies like Jane Crow oppressions, spirit-murdering, and the mass manufacturing of anti-Black mirrors tattoo Black girls' spirits. Their cumulative effects modulate embodiment. Since stuckness only needs the feeling of captivity, groove[ing], a process and stance taken, induces transgression and maintains one's inner rhythms (innocence). More, to be in body, in right relationship with one's self—embodied. As auto/ethnography—a deliberate examination of one or many cultures at the level of a body—a prerequisite of this experience was saying yes to undressing in public where sites of potential confinement morph into corridors of creation. Or as Alexander notes, "at these crossroads of subjectivity and collectivity, Sacred knowing and power, memory, and body that we sojourn so as to examine their pedagogic content to see how they might instruct us in the complicated undertaking of Divine self-invention."[5]

While I often sat alone pressing keys to make words appear on a Google Doc or pressed pencil to paper in order that my knowing materialize in the world in a specific way, I was not (am never) alone. My spiritual and writing practices, homegirls, ancestors, and Black feminist auto/ethnography ensure I'm in good company. I also kept in touch with homegirls who, like me, know Black girlhood's power, need, and genius. One of those homegirls is DJ B.E. (Blair E. Smith) who I reached out to because I know she too writes into and works with reliability.[6] First sharing space through a virtual workshop series with Alexis Pauline Gumbs, our interactions branched out beyond those spaces orchestrated by others to include biweekly creativity sessions where we shared our dreams and original poetry. Our watering of each other birthed a practice we called BodiesNBeats. DJ B.E. and I been moving with and because of our parallel and indivisible yearnings—to love, to save ourselves, to practice celebration.

Unsuspectingly, we were practicing what she theorizes about as "being in a with." A methodology, form of Black girlhood praxis, and Black feminist practice of collectivity, "being in a with" stands firm on the idea that "practice cannot be done without being with and doing it with Black girls and people who love them."[7] Drawing from Smith who was inspired by Reagon's speech "Black Women's Issues," to "be in a with" entails envisioning and building together in the name of changing the course of our realities. Withness takes many forms. In April 2022, Blair E. Smith participated in the Black Feminist Poetics and Performance series at Colgate University. This inter- and cross-disciplinary initiative highlighted Black feminist contributions to the arts, artivism, and feminist praxis through sonics, poetry, and performance. During this five-day residency, my class, "Corridors of Black Girlhood," and the broader Colgate campus got to be in conversation with Smith's scholarship and sonic productions. To close out our course symposium, later in the semester Smith delivered the virtual keynote, "Being in a With: Dreaming Black Girlhood Anew," where she practiced reliability through the facet of tracing. Specifically, Smith narrated how and why she arrived at embodying the position of DJ: "I like to work and DJ from the heart. I DJ because of my family . . . I DJ because of them. Black girls, people who love me, who have called on me to make them occasional mixtapes, listen to their songs, DJ, organize music shows for local artists and parties. I do it because it keeps me alive and loving fiercely."[8] Echoed in Smith's tracing of taking up the gift of DJing is the idea that to "be in a with" is a form and an agreement to care and to carry forward what gets created, named, and/or felt there. Though we have not collaborated on an academic paper about reliability, we have been tracing and thinking together. I have been listening to her sound Black girlhood, sound herself to life and love. I have been taking her sounds and ingesting them, letting them roam my hallways, and animate my limbs into gyration, melodic undulation, and vigorous twerk. I know first-hand that to move with nourishes and unsettles. To "be in a with" involves feeding a space while maintaining one's idiosyncrasy as a necessary feature to the life of the space. I am only recently coming to lucidly comprehend this particular both/and demand. Moving with stretched my repertoire and I am changed in ways that cannot be put to words. It wasn't until I got to this very chapter, that I (re)membered all the layers of us being with each other. Maybe it was hearing Reagon's clear caution about lifework and legacy asserting that "the only thing we can extract is the commitment for movement and change and motion."[9]

Perhaps it was my almost monthly return to Lorde's "Uses of the Erotic" and the surge of energy I felt while reading the lines, "And that deep and irreplaceable knowledge of my capacity for joy comes to demand from all of my life that it be lived within the knowledge that such satisfaction is possible."[10] Or maybe it was my rereading of Jordan critiquing the conceptualization of independence in the US, and the oversimplified movements of the 1970s espousing liberation and perpetuating rules of engagement enacted by US racial capitalism. Maybe it was Jordan's frankness, her refusal to exalt an either/or that took me back into the translocality of Black girlhood and the commitment to visualizing something generous enough to account for but not hold captive the people who chose to be with it. Maybe it was my sitting with Alexander's discussion of Divine self-invention where "the work of rewiring the self is neither a single nor individual event. Practitioners must be present and participating in a community" that brought my trace cycle to a pause as I fixated on the process and pathway of tracing.[11] Since both/and is foundational to my theorization, practice, and embodiment, I know all these moments helped me to get here.

Absolutely, the gifts of reliability work and moving with others give distinct shape and texture to my scholarship, language, and research agenda. My navigation of corridors is one steeped in vulnerability, (re)memory, and transgression. It was through the rub experienced all the while clumsily practicing Black girlhood that certain utensils applied throughout this text showed up as gifts and part of my toolkit. While groove[ing] is an internal and intuitive compass used to traverse space and determine the most reliable move to make in a given moment, this aesthetic supports one's *how* of movement. During her keynote, Reagon talks about the importance of being able to look the legacy of Black womn in the eyes, the indispensable action, and the tools to stay the course. Describing the cultural and personal significance of the work of Fannie Lou Hamer, she asks, "At what point do you give up what you are doing every day to put in a stake for another day that is different from that day you are giving up and jeopardizing?"[12] She continues narrating the relationship between history, Black living, and purposive action, insisting that folk know their distinct contribution. It is with more grasp of my peculiar touch, growing toolkit, and open heart that I offer provisional closure to this rendering of politics and possibilities of transgression in Black girlhood. Following Reagon's advisement to aspire that our work allows us to look in the eyes of those who lit a light and left tools for our journeys, the four letters below are also receipts of me making ground on being able to look Mama Crystal, BJ, June Jordan, Audre Lorde, Pat Parker, Toni Cade Bambara, and others in the eye while telling them about what I been up to since they took a seat on the other side of the rainbow, wrapped in gratitude to people and spaces I have been more accountable to because of my engagement with the study and practice of Black girlhood. These letters trace my travel through sites of confinement, confrontations with foreclosure, transgressions taken in the name of retooling myself, and cautionary lessons for anyone able to wield power upon Black girls, Black girlhood, and Black Girlhood studies.

Dear Students,

Those former and to come, welcome to some of the roots that live beneath my classroom, advising, and guiding pedagogy. If you took a class with me, read the syllabus, and still found yourself befuddled by my style and approach to education, some of the answers rest in the pages preceding this one. I am most grateful Black girlhood opened in me and (re)membered us back together. And because of this homecoming and all that came and became no more, I do not apologize for taking its lessons everywhere I go. Whether you took, or will take, "Introduction to Qualitative Research," "Corridors of Black Girlhood," "Feminist Methodologies," "Introduction to Women's, Gender, and Sexuality Studies," or some other class, you are presented in written and/or verbal form with three asks, what I call "Professor Hill's (Re)Orienting Tools." In shorthand these read: You, all of you, are welcome and expected to show up; Lean into the process; and Challenge yourself to go beyond. Through my work in Black girlhood, these principles materialized as building blocks for a classroom that attends to complexities of identity, the learning process (not just the content), and their interconnection.

After a decade+ of working with Black girls in various capacities and studying Black girlhood as a practice and academic field, I am a different being, lover, and professor. To be honest, I didn't always know how to show up fully to myself and definitely not in the presence of other girls, womn, gurl-womn—a necessary truth to name and not leave implied.[13] The ways of being in the world given back to me by Black girlhood and spaces that co-create worlds with Black girlhood are too grand to be kept in Black-girl specific spaces. And despite or perhaps because of their specificity, they show those working with its principles, politics, and investments how to apply them in all kinds of settings and circumstances. From saying "Yes" to studying Black girlhood and being in relationship, I emphatically said and continue to say

"Yes" to saving myself and moving in purpose, some of which has to do with educating, and specifically classroom instruction. To be "in a with," as Smith theorizes, is to be with someone somewhere dreaming and sounding off into futures. For Smith, this withness is with SOLHOT, Black girls, Black feminists and womanists, and love.

Black Girlhood studies demands engagement. More than participation, engagement joins initiative and full presence. As disclosed earlier, I was not always in engagement mode with Black girlhood or even myself. The expectation is not that you are in engagement mode 100 percent of the time. Rather, that you are aware of and accountable for your level of engagement and that discomfort does not dissuade your rehearsal of being with others—other students, organizers, loved ones, Black girls, et cetera.

Student, if you have not yet crossed paths with me in the classroom, take the above information as a frame of reference; no tellin' how you'll experience me or who I'll be in the classroom by the time we actually meet. It's also quite possible our first meeting won't be under the auspices of a class nor that the classroom will be our final exchange. If you are coming in this direction, consider the following recommendations: Accept the idea (even if you don't know what it means fully) that childhood and girlhood are not synonymous; that volume is connected to body is connected to power is connected to embodiment; that Black girls be pedagogues; and that your presence in a room matters. Though I don't advise it, you can pretend not to know these things, but you cannot say you weren't told.

Hey Body,

We been at this thang called friendship for a while and it's only recently, I'd say eight years or so, that I've asked for your trust again to establish a partnership. I know, I know, I needed to first take accountability for my mishandling of us. Funny thing is, I am you and you be me, but this was not always known and showed up in my actions. I've since come to terms with my negligence and acquiescence to the misuse of us from others. I've also revisited misinformation passed around about what a body is, its utility in life, and the incessant nagging to always be cautious of it. I guess the elders, teachers, and ministers didn't know what I now know—we are one. What they planted in me, again osmosis, made it easy, damn near common sense that I declare us separate entities. When people wanted a piece of us and took without asking, I decided to protect some part of us I constructed as not you, not us. Each extraction solidified the division taught at church, at school, and by community members I still deeply respect.

Even after coming back into the fullness of me and acknowledging our integrative nature, before the digestion of this lesson, I overworked you/us, tuned you/us out, and rented you/us out for insufficient remuneration. In all honesty, I elected you my employee and told myself that you were here for my benefit. That is, until you set the record straight and refused to move, breathe, feel in the same ways. Right around this same time, I navigated a tumultuous romantic break up, met SOLHOT, and was left to sit with us. Parallel to this sitting, I dug into Black girlhood. There, I came face-to-face with some inconvenient truths. Since the physical dimension of us got us into lots of unforeseen trouble, I suppressed our material curiosities unless initiated by others, usually for sexual purposes. Though my mother lectured me about the dangers of body art (piercings especially), the labels "at-risk," "inner-city youth," and "working class" tagged my skin like graffiti. Whether at home, in school, in the streets, or in some other context, our body served as measurement for access or denial to certain terrain. Plus, when I got in there, wherever there was, our comportment determined degree of pleasure and possibility. Unfortunately, this, for us, resulted in me resisting certain schemes but not always well enough to keep us in good standing.

So, when we got to SOLHOT, unbeknownst to us, especially our heady version, the wild girl, the tongue out dancer, the one who snuck to watch the latest music videos and grew inquisitive about nude bodies in the presence of other bodies, was ready to pop out. Meanwhile, another dimension of us, Corset—the one learning how to do school well and gain access to "respectable" exit routes—had our volume dialed down to a whisper and quickly yoked the wild one up.[14] When Wild woke, we woke, and rupture started. I'm sure you felt the civil war happening, the start and stop like learning to drive a stick shift car.[15] I tried to reconcile what was happening. As Jordan reminds, "and that is indeed the plan: To defuse and to deform the motivating truth of critical human response to pain," so I had to sit with all we braved. I apologize for the polished abuse that unfolded.[16] I apologize for what I could not say nor own. I apologize that I didn't know how to feel my way into nor ride the wave of what was happening in the moment. I could not embrace the gift of surprise that comes with groove[ing] and being directed by sensing into the moment. I apologize for the cruelty that came with us being in the care of Corset. Awaking to tyrannies swallowed, silences hoarded, and what followed in tow, poetry and dance returned to us.[17] In the mirror, at the club, tongue out, feet flexed, being. Initially, it felt awkward, especially in the presence of strangers. Unraveling in open spaces started out as a triple-dog dare until it became ritual and reverence. The more we practiced, the more I could hear you. The more I could hear you, I could hear us, as if we were polyphonic, an instrument with multiple simultaneous voices, messages, but one.

What a ride. I know the truth, we are one, and I know better now. We are better. I appreciate your patience, accountability, and grace. I'm also particularly grateful for SOLHOT and practicing Black girlhood; they managed to get the attention of Corset. Even when a part of us wasn't listening, Body, you kept your signals on to feel for and reach me/us. Thank you.

Dear Christa,

It's been a minute. Since we last saw each other—you rocking that side swooped bang and your to-the-side and high on the head ponytail, me with a red fade, lots happened. I'd love to know the details of your lots but for now, I'll summarize mine as best as possible. First, remember our conversation about Blackness, being a Black girl, and school? Let's just say that workshop and in particular, your bodily retelling and releasing, well, it's been nagging me in the most persistent, beautiful, and challenging way. Your willingness to allow a story to bubble up from your body's archive and tell it with full intensity moved me.

I knew enough to listen to you and assume I was missing something. Upon being thrust back into that moment and asked to locate meaning, I immediately returned to your body language. Almost instantly, it appeared in my mind's eye. Like an invisible ink image on a wall, I turned off the light that hid you in plain sight and there you were. I get it now. You were trying my word on for size, testing my capacity to be reliable. When you said (though not with words at all), "I betchu won't," you were right. That moment with you continues to birth so many ideas inside me. From it came conversations, writing, and a scavenger hunt within myself along with deep consistent introspection. While I tripped and fumbled miserably, I carried you carefully and close. I spent time with you and surrendered to the digestion of the lesson you offered me that Saturday morning. In the physical, I have not seen you since 2012. But Christa, you walk with me. You live in my heart and in the tentacles of a field named in our honor—Black Girlhood studies.

Gurllll you been irkin' me something fierce (I can hearsee you smirking, "You welcome"). In all sincerity, Thank You Christa. What I know from you and practice accordingly is that you were insisting on being recognized and handled with care (elements of Black gurl reliable). You embodied a courage and playfulness while sharing stories that illuminated varying textures of injustice. Without explicit instruction, your style of sitting and moving a reality through your body pronounced you knew something to be off about your encounters and the world needing to take note and do better. I also recall a "set of documents." I am unsure of the name under which they were filed but what stayed with me was the frustration described around certain types of comportment. I recollect a shame, an almost turning away from forms of Black gurling seemingly a bit more aggressive, more sexual, more street, if you will. Do you recall that file? Has it been thrown away?

During our workshop conversation, a few of you named Black girl scripts and distinguished between those girls wanting to go to college and others. I sensed a pressure, perhaps, that seemed to make you (and others with the same vision) a different kind of girl. I remember time traveling to the corner of my east side street, waiting on the bus before daybreak, and backing up until the fence stopped my movement out of fear the white man circling the block might attempt to snatch me. The immensity. That weight and squeeze you felt are real and real heavy. I surmise though, that the divergent paths taken by Black girls didn't make us varying types but Black girls navigating tailor-made densities that stipulated undivided attention and sometimes created blind spots in our reading of each other.

In case you needed the reminder then or could use it now, you are not a problem, and we are not wrong. There isn't enough time and space here to tell all I've endured to uncover and then choose to water the seed you left here with me. The full expression of some things can only be done and felt, not written. What I can say for certain is that seed is now a plant. I can also say I listen with my body for when it needs water, sunlight, music, etc. In our session of processing the workshop, you said, "I guess you could say in that moment, I was Christa. Whoever she is. In that space writing and moving I felt connected." Wherever you are and whatever you're doing, I affirm you are being Christa, whoever that is, now.

Dear Future Black Girlhood Scholars,

Welcome to a study that is also a practice with a political commitment at its core. Welcome to a developing set of dreamscapes that as we speak are being scaled across bodies, classrooms, dancefloors, after-school initiatives, conferences, and hemispheres. How you enter and dwell in this area of study matters. No doubt the discipline you're in, your advisor and dissertation chair matter; they create a container for your research and framing of it. And this message is for you. Emphasis on the *you*. Whether you commune with young and youthful, youthful and seasoned Black girls; whether you give yourself permission to loosen the reigns of adulthood, Black womnhood, identity, age; whether you do this work while in and present to your body all informs the work itself. This is what I mean.

Lots of my life journey is sprinkled within these pages in print for you to think with, trouble, expand upon, and utilize as you see fit. It may feel "natural," whatever that means, to say I am a Black girlhood scholar. It may also feel commonplace, possibly archaic, to use the phrase Black Girlhood studies as other phrases and pluralities take hold. Keep in mind that Black Girlhood studies is already plural, already diasporic in foundation, already accounting for and pushing the boundaries of terms like *girl*, *age*, and more. You've entered this work when the phrase **Black girlhood** has taken root and started germinating; when there are now symposiums and academic initiatives focusing on the subject; where there's a field named and referenced across many disciplines. There was a time when Black girlhood did not sit on the tongues of scholars, when journals nor special issues focused on Black girls explicitly. Yet there have always been Black girls, Black womn attuned to and living from what the girls inside them been knowing, games invented and played to teach lessons, adults, usually Black womn, busy worldmaking with the tools at their disposal for girls to come, and the world trying to make folk marked Black and female (which is not the sum total of who resonates with

Black girlhood nor the term Black girl) a reason, a possession, an indicator, a cause, a spectacle. And because "we lack a language that accurately describes what it means to work with Black girls in a way that is not about controlling their bodies and/or producing [w]hite, middle-class girl subjectivities," we [Black Girlhood scholars] are summoning a grammar, crafting its lexicon, bringing it into view, so that Black girlhood is made known and kept sacred.[18]

With all things come politics, stakes, and possibilities. Consider what those are for the moves you make and be sure to move with others. As you do this work, the body you have will matter but it does not predetermine your actions nor framing of the work. Whether you identify and/or are attributed as Afro, Black and queer, Brown but white passing, white, in some way impeded emotionally, physically, or in some other way, gender nonconforming, most crucial are the politics that undergird y/our work. It's about the questions we seek to explore, the assumptions, ideas, and people we bring with us along the way. Our work is about the way we see, what tools we use to see, who we see with and alongside. The academy will have folk out here complaining about its ways and simultaneously adopting these very conventions as the only way forward. Grandma Dorothy asked li'l Toni, "what are you pretending not to know today, Colored Gal?" and I invite you to move on what you know and once knew but back pocketed in the name of perhaps this degree.[19]

Allow the field and your wonders to move through and open you in ways that surprise you. I look forward to all that you bring to the pot, the album—spice, herbs, meats, and other flavors. Surrender and groove. Art and love are essential ingredients to the celebration of Black girlhood. They live here, in these pages, and in the field. No matter the disciplinary point through which you enter this world, consider the many corridors here, named and not yet. Focus on the questions to be asked and how they illuminate the messages inscribed on/in/to the skin of girls, womn, and Black girlhood. Notice how your body responds to the voices of girls. And if your scholarship demands that most of your intimate time be in poorly lit spaces and/or ones where girls need be located, conjured, imagined even, make time to share space with some young and youthful girls and allow yourself to just be with them, their laughter and theory, your laughter and yearning, and appreciate the feelings incited.

Should you elect to teach or find yourself teaching Black girlhood in a college classroom, after-school program, with family, accept that you will be stretched in new ways. Know that it matters who is in the room and why they came, because, like working with girls in real time, your ideas will crash and burn. If you find yourself discouraged, return to this book, hell you can just flip to the first page of the introduction. Surely, seeing some of my misfires, confusion, and beginning again will minimally offer comfort and hopefully some kind of guiding light. If you happen to adopt groove[ing] as your pedagogical approach, be prepared to receive some pushback, to feel in over your head, and to appear (and even be) disorganized. Allow it all.

While sometimes students are put off by such an experience, others "grow to challenge narratives outside this class that solely [focus] on Black girl lamentation."[20] Be in the moment and live for the times when you are peeled back and away from yourself. Welcome in and even facilitate the hard and heavy. When students have sensed my full presence at some point, they, even if not all, decide to give others access to their inner workings and unraveling about Black girlhood, girls, themselves. In these instances, even when I'm working through my fear—about what students are picking up, if they feel supported, and course evaluations to come (because they influence contract renewal and promotion to tenure, just being honest)—but choose to step anyway, a gift and a lesson surfaces. Sometimes as a youthful and seasoned Black girl and Blackqueer lesbian womn professor teaching Black girlhood and committed to wandering and feeling through life, sometimes being Black gurl reliable opens a new corridor inside a girl. Names are portals and political. Recognition is multifaceted, and as you've seen throughout this book, it comes with no prescription. Instead, registered recognition must be sensed. For instance, when in the spring 2022 semester I taught the course "Corridors of Black Girlhood," students referred to each other using a name that resembled the one on the roster but shortened in length. I intuited a need to ask how to properly address them in name. I knew all too well the ways formal documentation becomes sites of erasure and misreads. Said differently, formal documents, legal names, for instance the ones that appear on forms, are not always *the* story nor the one a person wants told first or at all. I also know that everyone can't call me what my grandma calls me and expect that I answer. And sometimes names have nothing to do with gender identity. This class moment could've gone any range of places and I was fine with that. What became necessary to me was that this Black girl told me the proper address and when given, I moved accordingly. I'd later learn that such a moment, and the moments that followed where I addressed her using her full name, shifted the terrain under both our feet. Purpose, a pseudonym, says, "It only really started in your class, but I have started saying my full name. It's weird, but a good weird. It's almost like there's more of me? I really like it and want to extend that thank you." In my response I say, "Your name be fierce, the whole thing, and the same is true for you," while the meaning carried in those words was "thank you for telling me the name your spirit knows to listen for." Almost a year after our course together, in an email with the subject "random note," Purpose resurfaces the moment stating, "Sidenote: I can't understate how much you encouraging me to use my whole name has changed my life. It's been almost a year now and it's starting to feel strange to hear one part without the other."[21]

No doubt, Black girlhood is generous enough to hold girls, womn, play, critique, pleasure, obstructions made and those given to a body to live with, a/sexuality, diaspora, and the dissonance that emerges from prioritizing open geography rather than poised containment. Black Girlhood studies deserves our creativity, love, and courage to launch a politic that ensures its vibrance (read: usefulness), audacity, and rarity. To do our best Black girlhood work, like the action taken to create Black women's studies, "requires not only intellectual intensity, but the deepest courage."[22] The nurturance of Black Girlhood studies demands our commitment to forging a futurenow that is more expansive, reliable, and inviting to Black girls young and youthful, youthful and seasoned, and not yet.

Notes

Preface

1. The phrase "Black and female though not inherently cisgender, femme, or feminine" is used here to mark the distinction between attributive identity and self identity. Individuals who are read as female and/or assigned as female at birth (AAFAB) are not necessarily feminine presenting and may not personally identify along the manufactured linear path of gender. Embodiment is connected to the reading of bodies and one's intimacy with self. The term *female* is used here to denote the reading of a body and its physical characteristics within a society operating in a binary orientation. The "though not inherently . . ." affirms the capaciousness of the body and personhood; acknowledges the social tendency to conflate external readings of people as synonymous with their personal identity; and indexes gender, sex, and gender performativity as interrelated not interchangeable.
2. As discussed in Andrew Jefferson, Simon Turner, and Steffen Jensen, "Introduction: On Stuckness and Sites of Confinement," *Ethnos: Journal of Anthropology* 84, no. 1 (February 2019): 1–13.
3. Ruth Nicole Brown, *Black Girlhood Celebration: Toward a Hip-Hop Feminist Pedagogy* (Peter Lang, 2009).
4. Evelyn C. White, foreword to *Black Like Us: A Century of Lesbian, Gay, and Bisexual African American Fiction*, 2nd ed., ed. Devon W. Carbado, Dwight A. McBride, and Donald Weise (Cleis Press, 2012), xiv.
5. Lyndon K. Gill, "Situating Black, Situating Queer: Black Queer Diaspora Studies and the Art of Embodied Listening," *Transforming Anthropology* 20, no. 1 (2012): 32–44.
6. Gayatri Gopinath, "Diaspora," in Keywords Editorial Collective, *Keywords for Gender*, 67.
7. Karishma Desai, "Girl," in Keywords Editorial Collective, *Keywords for Gender*, 101.
8. Black womn, feminists, womanists, and queer people have long used the word *girl* to signify many things. In the last decade, the everyday usage of this term

has entered scholarly discussion and Black girlhood conversations. While it is nothing new for *girl* to stand in as more than a figure and not necessarily someone a certain age or gender identity, those involved in Black girlhood work over the last decade have been deliberate about its expansive utilization and theorizing its meaning. See crunktastic, "Black Girl Is a Verb: A New American Grammar Book," Crunk Feminist Collective, March 28, 2016, https://www.crunkfeministcollective.com/2016/03/28/black-girl-is-a-verb-a-new-american-grammar-book, and Julia S. Jordan-Zachery and Duchess Harris, eds., *Black Girl Magic beyond the Hashtag: Twenty-First-Century Acts of Self-Definition* (University of Arizona Press, 2019), 15.

Introduction

1. During an interview, Theatrical Jazz practitioner and emeritus Black performance studies scholar Omi Osun Joni L. Jones recounts Laurie Carlos's insistence to "put on a good bra." In Black vernacular, a good bra is one that is perhaps supportive and/or aesthetically pleasing. Importantly, a "good bra" is signification of a moment, experience, performance of great import. Here, I use it in a similar way—to signal that Christa was calling for me to stretch in a new way, to develop a new set of skills for interfacing with her specifically and Black girls broadly. Dominique C. Hill and Omi Osun Joni Jones, "'Put on Your Good Bra!'" HowlRound Theatre Commons, April 13, 2017, https://howlround.com/put-your-good-bra.
2. crunktastic, "Black Girl Is a Verb: A New American Grammar Book," Crunk Feminist Collective, March 28, 2016, https://www.crunkfeministcollective.com/2016/03/28/black-girl-is-a-verb-a-new-american-grammar-book. An extension of Hortense Spillers' theorization and outlining of the grammar crafted about Blackness and bodies determined Black and female, The Crunk Feminist Collective declare "Black girl" a verb. Embodying Ruth Nicole Brown's 2009 articulation of Black girlhood as not contingent on age or identity, they locate Black girl within actions and something that is both accessible to Black womn and something we can choose to do. Hortense J. Spillers, "Mama's Baby, Papa's Maybe: An American Grammar Book," *Diacritics* 17, no. 2 (1987): 65–81. https://doi.org/10.2307/464747; Ruth Nicole Brown, *Black Girlhood Celebration: Toward a Hip-Hop Feminist Pedagogy* (Peter Lang, 2009).
3. Charlotte Sieling, dir., "I Am," *Lovecraft Country*, season 1, episode 3, written by Misha Green, aired September 27, 2020, https://www.imdb.com/title/tt9548458.
4. Sieling, dir., "I Am."
5. "Soul II Soul – Keep on Moving," posted to YouTube by SoulIISoulVEVO, June 2, 2009, https://www.youtube.com/watch?v=1iQl46-zIcM.
6. See Ruth Nicole Brown, *Black Girlhood Celebration: Toward a Hip-Hop Feminist Pedagogy* (Peter Lang, 2009).

7. See Abbey Lincoln, "Who Will Revere The Black Woman? [1966]." *Ebony*, February 12, 2013, http://www.ebony.com/who-will-revere-the-black-woman-405; and Aishah Shahidah Simmons, "Who Will Revere US? (Black LGTBQ People, Straight Women, and Girls) (Part 3)" *The Feminist Wire* (blog), April 25, 2012. https://thefeministwire.com/2012/04/who-will-revere-us-black-lgtbq-people-straight-women-and-girls-part-3.
8. Rebecca Epstein, Jamilia Blake, and Thalia González, *Girlhood Interrupted: The Erasure of Black Girls' Childhood* (Georgetown Law Center on Poverty and Inequality, 2017), https://genderjusticeandopportunity.georgetown.edu/wp-content/uploads/2020/06/girlhood-interrupted.pdf.
9. Taylor Ardrey, "Kaia Rolle Was Arrested at School When She Was 6. Nearly Two Years Later, She Still 'Has to Bring Herself out of Despair,'" *Insider*, March 17, 2021, https://www.insider.com/6-year-old-black-girl-arrested-school-disturbing-trend-criminalization-2021-3.
10. For examples see Marcia Davis, "Black Lives Matter – Including Black Women's, Activists Remind Nation," *Washington Post* (Washington, DC), May 20, 2015, https://www.washingtonpost.com/lifestyle/magazine/black-lives-matter--including-black-womens-activists-remind-nation/2015/05/19/e155a514-fe43-11e4-833c-a2de05b6b2a4_story.html; Kurt Chirbas, Erik Ortiz and Corky Siemszko, "Baltimore County Police Fatally Shot Korryn Gaines, 23, Wound 5-Year-Old, Son," *NBC News*, August 3, 2016. https://www.nbcnews.com/news/us-news/baltimore-county-police-fatally-shoot-korryn-gaines-boy-5-hurt-n621461.
11. Jennifer C. Nash. "Unwidowing: Rachel Jeantel, Black Death, and the 'Problem' of Black Intimacy," *Journal of Women in Culture and Society* 41, no. 4 (2016): 751–74.
12. For examples see Madeline Ross, "Mother Accuses Catholic School of Having a Racist Hair Policy after Claimed Her Daughter Was Banned from the Playground and Canteen Because She Braided a Heart into Her Cornrow Hairstyle," *MailOnline*, January 19, 2023, https://www.dailymail.co.uk/news/article-11653975/Mother-accuses-Catholic-school-having-racist-hair-policy-daughter-banned-playground.html; Daniel Reynold, "Gay HS Senior Barred from Walking at Graduation for Wearing Pants," *Advocate*, June 2, 2020, https://www.advocate.com/youth/2020/6/03/gay-hs-senior-barred-walking-graduation-wearing-pants; Katie Mettler, "Mass. School Punishes Twins for Hair Braid Extensions. Their Parents Say It's Racial Discrimination." *Washington Post*, May 15, 2017. https://www.washingtonpost.com/news/morning-mix/wp/2017/05/15/mass-school-punishes-twins-for-hair-braid-extensions-their-parents-say-its-racial-discrimination.
13. See Legal Defense Fund, "Natural Hair Discrimination: Frequently Asked Questions," NAACPLDF, accessed February 26, 2024, https://www.naacpldf.org/natural-hair-discrimination; "States with Hair Discrimination (CROWN) Laws

in 2024: Interactive Map." GovDocs, September 23, 2024, https://www.govdocs.com/states-with-hair-discrimination-laws/.

14. Dove and JOY Collective, "Dove CROWN Research Study for Girls" (Dove and JOY Collective, 2021), https://static1.squarespace.com/static/5edc69fd622c36173f56651f/t/623369f7477914438ee18c9b/1647536634602/2021_DOVE_CROWN_girls_study.pdf.

15. Kayla Patrick, Adaku Onyeka-Crawford, and Nancy Duchesneau, "'And They Cared': How to Create Better, Safer Learning Environments for Girls of Color," Education Trust, August 20, 2020, 2, https://edtrust.org/rti/and-they-cared-how-to-create-better-safer-learning-environments-for-girls-of-color.

16. See Christianne Corbett, Catherine Hill, and Andresse St. Rose, *Where the Girls Are: The Facts about Gender Equity in Education* (American Association of University Women [AAUW] Educational Foundation, 2008); Susan K. Dyer, "Beyond the 'Gender Wars': A Conversation about Girls, Boys, and Education" (Washington, DC, September 14–15, 2000). AAUW Educational Foundation, Washington, DC, https://files.eric.ed.gov/fulltext/ED453100.pdf.

17. Bettina L. Love, *We Want to Do More than Survive: Abolitionist Teaching and the Pursuit of Educational Freedom* (Beacon Press, 2019), 7.

18. Cordelia Freeman and Sydney Calkin, "Feminism/Feminist Geography," in *International Encyclopedia of Human Geography*, 2nd ed., ed. Audrey Lynn Kobayashi, 35–41 (Elsevier, 2020).

19. Chris Bobel and Samantha Kwan, *Body Battlegrounds: Transgressions, Tensions, and Transformations* (Vanderbilt University Press, 2019), 2.

20. Beth E. Richie, "Carcerality," in Keywords Editorial Collective, *Keywords for Gender*, 41.

21. Ruthie Gilmore, qtd. in Michelle Daigle and Margaret Marietta Ramirez, "Space," in Keywords Editorial Collective, *Keywords in Gender*, 217.

22. Patricia Williams, "Spirit-Murdering the Messenger: The Discourse of Fingerpointing as the Law's Response to Racism," *University of Miami Law Review* 42, no. 127 (1987): 156.

23. "Body Politics," Encyclopedia.com, accessed Dec. 18, 2024, https://www.encyclopedia.com/social-sciences/encyclopedias-almanacs-transcripts-and-maps/body-politics.

24. Jefferson, Turner, and Jensen, "Introduction," 2.

25. Jefferson, Turner, and Jensen, 3.

26. Beth E. Richie and Kayla M. Martensen, "Resisting Carcerality, Embracing Abolition: Implications for Feminist Social Work Practice," *Affilia* 35, no. 1 (February 2020): 13.

27. Richie, "Carcerality," 41.

28. As expressed in the preface, womn, including womnhood without an *a* or *e* acknowledges its expansiveness and contestation of gender and sexuality; the absence of these vowels is symbolic of an absence of a singular origin story of

identifying with the category, including womnhood. Womn disrupts perceived linearity between the categories of girl and woman. Equally, this particular spelling enmeshes individual and group while expanding who gets indexed as a participant of Black girlhood.

29. For reference, see Nishaun T. Battle, "From Slavery to Jane Crow to Say Her Name: An Intersectional Examination of Black Women and Punishment," *Meridians* 15, no. 1 (December 1, 2016): 109–36; and Chenelle A. Jones and Renita L. Seabrook, "The New Jane Crow: Mass Incarceration and the Denied Maternity of Black Women," *Race, Ethnicity and Law*, vol. 22 (2017): 135–54.
30. Pauli Murray and Mary O. Eastwood, "Jane Crow and the Law: Sex Discrimination and Title VII," *George Washington Law Review*, no. 34 (1965): 235.
31. Murray and Eastwood, 235.
32. See for instance, Black Girls Rock, Black Girls Run, Girl Trek, Justice 4 Black Girls.
33. Camilla Hawthorne, "Black Matters Are Spatial Matters: Black Geographies for the Twenty First Century," *Geography Compass* 13, no. 11 (2019): 7.
34. Hawthorne, 3.
35. Chamara Jewel Kwakye, Dominique C. Hill, and Durell M. Callier, "10 Years of Black Girlhood Celebration: A Pedagogy of Doing," *Departures in Critical Research* 6, no. 3 (2017): 1.
36. Brown, *Black Girlhood Celebration*, 35.
37. Brown, *Black Girlhood Celebration*, 1.
38. Aishah Shahidah Simmons, "Who Will Revere US? (Black LGTBQ People, Straight Women and Girls) (Part 3)" *The Feminist Wire* (blog), April 25, 2012, https://thefeministwire.com/2012/04/who-will-revere-us-black-lgtbq-people-straight-women-and-girls-part-3.
39. Barbara Omolade, "A Black Feminist Pedagogy," *Women's Studies Quarterly* 15, no. 3/4 (1987): 31.
40. Shawn Wilson, *Research Is Ceremony: Indigenous Research Methods* (Fernwood, 2008), 33.
41. In her discussion of politics and feminist theory, Sarah Ahmed expresses the importance of putting the "who" back into work and action, or "trying to locate the person who is doing the knowledge." Sarah Ahmed, "What Is Feminist Research Series with Sara Ahmed," YouTube, posted by Feminist Research Institute UC Davis, June 6, 2018, https://www.youtube.com/watch?v=djc8TEUhPiA.
42. M. Jacqui Alexander, *Pedagogies of Crossing: Meditations on Feminism, Sexual Politics, Memory and the Sacred* (Duke University Press, 2005), 7.
43. DaMaris Hill, *A Bound Woman Is a Dangerous Thing: The Incarceration of African American Women from Harriet Tubman to Sandra Bland* (Bloomsbury Publishing, 2019), xiii.
44. Jefferson, Turner, and Jensen, "Introduction," 7.

45. bell hooks, *Teaching to Transgress* (Routledge, 1994), 12.
46. Toni Cade Bambara, "The Education of a Storyteller," in *Deep Sightings and Rescue Missions: Fiction, Essays, and Conversations*, ed. Toni Morrison (Pantheon Books, 1996), 248.
47. Bambara, 248.
48. Bambara, 248.
49. Bambara, 249.
50. Bambara, 248.
51. Durell M. Callier and Dominique C. Hill, *Who Look at Me?! Shifting the Gaze of Education Through Blackness, Queerness, and the Body* (Brill Sense, 2019).
52. Bambara, "The Education of a Storyteller," 255.
53. Omi Osun Joni L. Jones, Lisa L. Moore, and Sharon Bridgforth, eds., *Experiments in a Jazz Aesthetic: Art, Activism, Academia, and the Austin Project* (University of Texas Press, 2010), 7.
54. Documentation is important to process. Outside of curating my own course of study, I participated in many opportunities curated by practitioners of the form. Prior to graduating, my understanding came through conversations, viewing performances created using the form, and studying written texts about it. After graduating, I attended a masterclass in 2015 with Sharon Bridgforth that invited attendees to tend to our bodies. We addressed spiritual challenges, elements of our creative processes, and the people who teach us as well as members of our art family or "who yo people is?" as she framed it. This masterclass required me to ask myself harder questions to clarify what I wanted my art to do, how I see myself as an artist, and who is holding me in the process. And June 13–15, 2024, I attended the first ever Theatrical Jazz Aesthetics (TJA) conference at the University of Minnesota. I note this here because as I grew as a student of the form, it grew in academia to the point of making possible an undisciplined conference centered around doing, being, and witnessing the form in action. The experience of oscillating between movement classes, workshops, and performances created a sensory-filled experience of understanding the expansiveness of TJA while seeing vividly principles I describe below and practice in the working of this text. While I don't go in detail about that experience here, I find it important to confess that since this experience, I am not the same, that the change currently lives in how I do life and has not yet made it beyond language for the body. "Theatrical Jazz Conference," Pillsbury House and Theater, accessed Dec. 19, 2024, https://pillsburyhouseandtheatre.org/homepage/theatrical-jazz-conference.
55. Cynthia Oliver, email message to author, February 27, 2012.
56. Debbie Rosas and Carlos Rosas, *The Nia Technique: The High-Powered Energizing Workout That Gives You a New Body and a New Life* (Broadway Books, 2004), 27.
57. Omi Osun Joni L. Jones, *Theatrical Jazz: Performance, Às̩e̩, and the Power of the Present Moment. Black Performance and Cultural Criticism* (Ohio State University Press, 2015), 4.

58. Founded in 2002, tAP or The Austin Project is a collaborative project started by TJA practitioner and professor Dr. Omi Osun Joni Jones, dedicated to using art, mostly writing, for social change. Comprising womn of various ages, backgrounds, sexualities, and race—though most are womn of color—tAP brings these womn together to create, unpack themselves, and build themselves again. Jones, Moore, and Bridgforth, eds., *Experiments in a Jazz Aesthetic*, 9.
59. Sara Ahmed, *Queer Phenomenology: Orientations, Objects, Others* (Duke University Press, 2006), 1.
60. Joni L. Jones, "Making Space," in Jones, Moore, and Bridgforth, *Experiments in a Jazz Aesthetic*, 6.
61. Jones, "Making Space," 6.
62. As an example, see Dominique C. Hill, "Assata's (Groove[ing]) Daughter: An Embodied Lyrical Autoethnography of Resistance," *International Review of Qualitative Research* 14, no. 2 (2021): 337–43.
63. Sharon Bridgforth, phone conversation with author, January 31, 2012.
64. Jones, *Theatrical Jazz*, 10.
65. Jones, *Theatrical Jazz*, 255.
66. Cynthia Dillard, *Learning to (Re)member the Things We've Learned to Forget: Endarkened Feminisms, Spirituality and the Sacred Nature of Research and Teaching* (Peter Lang, 2012), 8–10.
67. Toni Morrison, "The Site of Memory," in *The Source of Self-Regard: Selected Essays, Speeches, and Meditations* (Knopf Publishing, 2019), 237.
68. Christina Elizabeth Sharpe, *In the Wake: On Blackness and Being* (Duke University Press, 2016), 17.
69. Toni Cade Bambara, *The Salt Eaters* (Random House, 1980), 3, 10.
70. Barbara Christian, "The Race for Theory," *Feminist Studies* 14, no. 1 (1988): 67–79.
71. Eve Tuck, "Citation Is Political," workshop at Curriculum Inquiry Fellowship and Writing Retreat, June 13, 2027, Ontario Institute for Studies in Education, University of Toronto, Toronto, Ontario.
72. Eric Gottlieb, "The Role of the Page in Jazz: *dyke/warrior-prayers*' Theatrical Jazz Aesthetic; an Interview with Sharon Bridgforth." *Liminalities* 18, no. 2 (2022): 6.
73. Eve L. Ewing, "The Quality of the Light: Evidence, Truths, and the Odd Practice of the Poet-Sociologist," in *Black Women's Liberatory Pedagogies: Resistance, Transformation, and Healing Within and Beyond the Academy*, ed. Olivia N. Perlow et al. (Springer International Publishing, 2018), 199.
74. Donna Haraway, "Situated Knowledges: The Science Question in Feminism and the Privilege of Partial Perspective," *Feminist Studies* 14, no. 3 (1988): 581.
75. Irma McClaurin, ed. *Black Feminist Anthropology: Theory, Politics, Praxis, and Poetics* (Rutgers University Press, 2001), 54–56.
76. Aisha Durham, "On Collards," *International Review of Qualitative Research* 10, no. 1 (2017): 23.

77. Angel Kyodo Williams, *Being Black: Zen and the Art of Living with Fearlessness and Grace* (Penguin Compass, 2000), 8.
78. Nathan Stucky and Cynthia Wimmer, "Introduction: The Power of Transformation in Performance Studies Pedagogy," in *Teaching Performance Studies*, ed. Nathan Stucky and Cynthia Wimmer (Southern Illinois University Press, 2002), 1–2.
79. Callier and Hill, *Who Look at Me?!*, 53.
80. Jones, Joni L. "Performance Ethnography: The Role of Embodiment in Cultural Authenticity," *Theatre Topics* 12, no. 1 (2002): 7.
81. Irma McClaurin, "Black Feminist Auto/Ethnography That Makes You Want to Cry," *Insight News*, June 27, 2012, https://www.insightnews.com/news/local/black-feminist-auto-ethnography-that-makes-you-want-to-cry/article_50b309a6-8bb0-5ad1-9c8f-3a424ac3a020.html.
82. Callier and Hill, *Who Look at Me?!*, 12.
83. Tami Spry, *Body, Paper, Stage: Writing and Performing Autoethnography* (Routledge, 2011), 64.
84. Alexander, *Pedagogies of Crossing*, 8.

Chapter 1

A portion of this chapter was originally published in Dominique C. Hill, "And Who Will Revere the Black Girl," *Gender & Society* 35, no. 4 (2021): 546–56. This title is informed by Ntozake Shange's, "Dark Phrases," in *For Colored Girls Who Have Considered Suicide / When the Rainbow Is Enuf: A Choreopoem* (Scribner Poetry, 1997), 4.

1. Collins Dictionary, "Policy," https://www.collinsdictionary.com/us/dictionary/english/policy.
2. Dominique C. Hill and Durell M. Callier, "Troubling Innocence: Staging Scenes of Black Youth Pleasures and Possibilities," in *Beyond Innocence: Refusing the Limits of Contemporary Childhood*, ed. Julie C. Garlen and Neil T. Ramjewan (Lexington Books, 2024), 229.
3. "Nikki Giovanni and James Baldwin in conversation on 'SOUL!' (PART 2) | ALL ARTS Vault." *Soul!*, produced by Ellis B. Haizlip, WNET, 1971. Posted to YouTube by ALL ARTS TV, Dec. 17, 2022, https://www.youtube.com/watch?v=P-g2t5bom2d4. This 1971 conversation between Nikki Giovanni and James Baldwin about Black life, art, and the possibilities for social change illustrates one site of struggle, Black family, around the power of ideological assumptions in cementing intercultural relations. Counterintuitive to heteropatriarchy, and despite the rationale Baldwin provided, Giovanni maintains that an alternative reality emerges or at least is more likely only alongside a different set of premises.

4. June Jordan, *Who Look at Me* (Thomas Y. Crowell Company, 1969), 31.
5. I draw particularly on Black feminist artists' articulations of wrong. Likewise, whether or not the term is used, subversion of this status and resistance to social practices, rules, and structures that reinforce it is of great importance to the history and contemporary approaches to Black feminism and other theories of knowledge invested in eradicating oppression and domination.
6. Sojourner Truth, "Two Speeches (United States, 1851, 1867)," in *The Essential Feminist Reader*, ed. Estelle B. Freedman (Modern Library, 2007), 11.
7. W. E. B. Du Bois, *The Souls of Black Folk: Essays and Sketches* (A. G. McClurg, 1903; reprinted by Johnson Reprint Corp., 1968).
8. Pat Parker, "Group," in *Movement in Black: The Collected Poetry of Pat Parker, 1961–1978* (Crossing Press, 1983).
9. June Jordan, "Poem about My Rights," in *Directed by Desire: The Collected Poems of June Jordan*, ed. Jan Heller Levi (Copper Canyon Press, 1980), 309.
10. June Jordan, "Wrong or White," in *Life as Activism: June Jordan's Writings from the Progressive* (Litwin Books, 2014), 28.
11. Ruth Wilson Gilmore, *Golden Gulag: Prisons, Surplus, Crisis, and Opposition in Globalizing California* (University of California Press, 2007), 28.
12. Hortense J. Spillers, "Mama's Baby, Papa's Maybe: An American Grammar Book" (1987), in *The Transgender Studies Reader Remix*, edited by Susan Stryker and Dylan McCarthy Blackston (Routledge, 2022), 64.
13. Jordan, "Poem about My Rights," 309.
14. Kayla M. Martensen, "Review of Carceral State Studies and Application," *Sociology Compass* 14, no. 7 (2020): e12801.
15. Audre Lorde, "Good Mirrors Are Not Cheap" in *Undersong: Chosen Poems Old and New*, rev. ed. (Norton, 1992), 67.
16. Lorde, 67.
17. "Combahee River Collective: A Black Feminist Statement," *Off Our Backs* 9, no. 6 (June 1979): 7.
18. Katherine McKittrick, *Demonic Grounds: Black Women and the Cartographies of Struggle* (University of Minnesota Press, 2006), 61.
19. Abbey Lincoln, "Who Will Revere The Black Woman? [1966]." *Ebony*, February 12, 2013, http://www.ebony.com/who-will-revere-the-black-woman-405.
20. See Moya Bailey, "They Aren't Talking about Me . . ." *The Crunk Feminist Collective* (blog), March 14, 2010, https://www.crunkfeministcollective.com/2010/03/14/they-arent-talking-about-me; and Moya Bailey, "More on the Origin of Misogynoir," Tumblr, April 27, 2014, https://moyazb.tumblr.com/post/84048113369/more-on-the-origin-of-misogynoir.
21. Cathy J. Cohen, "Punks, Bulldaggers, and Welfare Queens: The Radical Potential of Queer Politics?" *GLQ: A Journal of Lesbian and Gay Studies* 3, no. 4 (1997): 438.

22. Durell M. Callier, "Gendered Violences and Queer of Color Critiques in Educational Spaces: Remembering Sakia, Carl, and Jaheem," in *Encyclopedia of Educational Philosophy and Theory*, ed. Michael A. Peters (Springer Singapore, 2017), 914–19.
23. Durham, "On Collards," 22–23.
24. Stephanie Troutman and Ileana Jiménez, "Lessons in Transgression: #BlackGirlsMatter and the Feminist Classroom," *Meridians* 15, no. 1 (December 1, 2016): 7–39.
25. Omi Osun Joni L. Jones, introduction to *love conjure/blues*, ed. Sharon Bridgforth (RedBone Press, 2004), xv.
26. Jones, xv.
27. Jones, xiii.
28. Jones, xiv.
29. Joyce A. Ladner, *Tomorrow's Tomorrow: The Black Woman* (Anchor Books, 1972).
30. Sara Lawrence Lightfoot, "Socialization and Education of Young Black Girls in School," *Teachers College Record* 78, no. 2 (1976): 1–18.
31. See Corbett, Hill, and St. Rose, *Where the Girls Are*.
32. See Venus E. Evans-Winters and Jennifer Esposito, "Other People's Daughters: Critical Race Feminism and Black Girls' Education," *Educational Foundations*, no. 24 (2010): 11–24; Shawn Arango Ricks, "Falling through the Cracks: Black Girls and Education," *Interdisciplinary Journal of Teaching and Learning* 4, no. 1 (2014): 10–21.
33. Alongside the cultural boom of initiatives like #BlackGirlsRock, Black Girls Run, Black Girl Trek, and #BlackGirlMagic, scholars, often working in traditions including but not limited to hip-hop feminism, womanism, and Africana and Black feminism, pushed the academic agenda of Black girlhood through special issues like "Black Girls and Girlhood" (2020) in *Black Scholar*, "Black Girlhood and Kinship" (2019) in *Women, Gender, and Families of Color*, and "Saving Our Lives, Hear Our Truths: Exploring the Theory, Praxis, and Creativity of Black Girlhood Studies" (2017) in *Departures in Critical Qualitative Research*, as well as conferences and convenings like the Black Girl Movement Conference (2016), Locating the Geographies of Black Girlhoods in Education (2021), the Formation Conference (2023), Black Girl Genius Week (BGGW) and the now annual #JusticeForBlackGirls National Conference. Moreover, there are networks, labs, and other initiatives dedicated to varying facets of Black girlhood, Black girl lived experiences, and intergenerational relationships between young and youthful, youthful and seasoned Black girls and womn. Some of these include the Black/Girlhood Imaginary Working Group, the History of Black Girlhood Network (HBGN), and Black Girlhood Studies Lab. The point here is not to be exhaustive but to showcase the ways and directions Black girlhood as a subject of analysis and scholarship takes flight post 2010.

34. Aria S. Halliday, ed., *The Black Girlhood Studies Collection* (Women's Press, 2019).
35. Corinne T. Field and LaKisha Michelle Simmons, "Introduction: Looking for Black Girls in History," in *The Global History of Black Girlhood*, edited by Corinne T. Field and LaKisha Michelle Simmons, 1–28 (University of Illinois Press, 2022); Nazera Sadiq Wright, *Black Girlhood in the Nineteenth Century* (University of Illinois Press, 2016).
36. Kyra D. Gaunt, *The Games Black Girls Play: Learning the Ropes from Double-Dutch to Hip-Hop* (New York University Press, 2006), 58.
37. Tamara T. Butler, "Black Girl Cartography: Black Girlhood and Place-Making in Education Research," *Review of Research in Education* 42, no. 1 (March 1, 2018): 31.
38. Butler, 31.
39. Tammy C. Owens et al., "Towards an Interdisciplinary Field of Black Girlhood Studies," *Departures in Critical Qualitative Research* 6, no. 3 (2017): 119.
40. Kimberlé Crenshaw, Priscilla Ocen, and Jyoti Nanda, "Black Girls Matter: Pushed Out, Overpoliced and Underprotected," Columbia Law School Faculty Scholarship Archive, January 1, 2015, https://scholarship.law.columbia.edu/faculty_scholarship/3227.
41. Kimberlé Crenshaw, Priscilla Ocen, and Jyoti Nanda, "Black Girls Matter: Pushed Out, Overpoliced and Underprotected," Columbia Law School Faculty Scholarship Archive, January 1, 2015, https://scholarship.law.columbia.edu/faculty_scholarship/3227.
42. Monique W. Morris, Stephanie R. Bush-Baskette, and Kimberlé Crenshaw, *Confined in California: Women and Girls of Color in Custody* (African American Policy Forum, 2013).
43. Subini Ancy Annamma et al., "Black Girls and School Discipline: The Complexities of Being Overrepresented and Understudied," *Urban Education* 54, no. 2 (February 2019): 211–42; Edward W. Morris and Brea L. Perry, "Girls Behaving Badly? Race, Gender, and Subjective Evaluation in the Discipline of African American Girls," *Sociology of Education* 90, no. 2 (April 2017): 127–48; Connie Wun, "Angered: Black and Non-Black Girls of Color at the Intersections of Violence and School Discipline in the United States," *Race Ethnicity and Education* 21, no. 4 (July 4, 2018): 423–37.
44. T. L. Cook, "Violated and Victimized: The Juvenile Justice System and Black Girls," in *Black Girls and Adolescents: Facing the Challenges*, ed. Catherine Fisher Collins (Praeger, 2015).
45. Kayla J. Smith, "Reforming Black Girlhood and Sexuality at the Missouri State Industrial Home for Negro Girls, 1930–1948," *Crimson Historical* (2021): 77–90; Mary Zaborskis, "Queering Black Girlhood at the Virginia Industrial School," *Signs: Journal of Women in Culture and Society* 45, no. 2 (2020): 373–94.
46. Kali Nicole Gross, "African American Women, Mass Incarceration, and the Politics of Protection," *Journal of American History* 102, no. 1 (2015): 25–33.

47. See Stacey C. Ault, "Critical Post-Traumatic Growth among Black Femme High School Students within the School to Prison Pipeline: A Focus on Healing," *International Journal of Human Rights Education* 5, no. 1 (2021), https://repository.usfca.edu/ijhre/vol5/iss1/7; Saidiya V. Hartman, *Wayward Lives, Beautiful Experiments: Intimate Histories of Social Upheaval* (W.W. Norton, 2019); Maisha T. Winn, *Girl Time: Literacy, Justice, and the School-to-Prison Pipeline* (Teachers College Press, 2019).
48. Treva B. Lindsey, *America, Goddam: Violence, Black Women, and the Struggle for Justice* (University of California Press, 2022), 225.
49. Laura Boutwell, "'I Don't Want to Claim America': African Refugee Girls and Discourses of Othering," *Girlhood Studies* 8, no. 2 (2015): 103–18.
50. Reighan Gilliam, "Representing Black Girlhood in Brazil: Culture and Strategies of Empowerment," *Communication, Culture and Critique* 10, no. 4 (2017): 609–25.
51. Janelle Griffith, "Alleged Strip Search of 4 Black Middle School Girls Prompts Third-Party Investigation," *NBC News*, January 30, 2019, https://www.nbcnews.com/news/us-news/alleged-strip-search-4-black-middle-school-girls-prompts-third-n964856.
52. Audre Lorde, *Sister Outsider* (Oxford University Press, 1983), 74.
53. Jillian Hernandez, *Aesthetics of Excess: The Art and Politics of Black and Latina Embodiment* (Duke University Press, 2020), 11.
54. Kwakye, Hill and Callier, "10 Years of Black Girlhood Celebration," 10.
55. The BlackLight Project, "Mission," BlackLight Newark, March 10, 2011, https://blacklightnewark.wordpress.com/about-2/mission.
56. Sheri K. Lewis, "Pushing the Limits in Black Girl–Centered Research: Exploring the Methodological Possibilities of *Melt* Magazine," in *The Black Girlhood Studies Collection*, edited by Aria S. Halliday (Women's Press, 2019).
57. A Long Walk Home, "A Long Walk Home | Our Mission," accessed October 29, 2023. https://www.alongwalkhome.org/about-us.
58. Barbara Smith, introduction to *Home Girls: A Black Feminist Anthology*, ed. Barbara Smith (Rutgers University Press, 2000), xxii.
59. Ruth Nicole Brown, *Hear Our Truths: The Creative Potential of Black Girlhood*, Dissident Feminisms (University of Illinois Press, 2013), 47.
60. Savannah Shange, "Black Girl Ordinary: Flesh, Carcerality, and the Refusal of Ethnography," *Transforming Anthropology* 27, no. 1 (April 2019): 6.
61. Laila Nashid, "Understanding Digital Narratives of Black Girlhood Through Social Media Aesthetics," *Girlhood Studies* 17, no. 2 (2024), 87.
62. Nashid, 91.
63. Porshé R. Garner, "The Sounded-Word Aesthetics: Black Girl Covenant and the Fire Commandments," *International Journal of Qualitative Studies in Education* 34, no. 6 (July 3, 2021): 549–61.

64. DaMaris Hill, *Breath Better Spent: Living Black Girlhood* (Bloomsbury, 2022), 39.
65. Jasmine Elizabeth Johnson, "A Politics of Tenderness: Camille A. Brown and Dancers' BLACK GIRL: Linguistic Play," *Black Scholar* 49, no. 4 (October 2, 2019): 23.
66. Lashon Daley, "Coming of (R)age: A New Genre for Contemporary Narratives about Black Girlhood," *Signs: Journal of Women in Culture and Society* 46, no. 4 (2021): 1053.
67. As examples see Aisha S. Durham, "Between Us: A Bio-Poem," *Meridians* 8, no. 2 (2008): 177–82; and Robin M. Boylorn, "On Being at Home with Myself: Blackgirl Autoethnography as Research Praxis," *International Review of Qualitative Research* 9, no. 1 (2016): 44–58.
68. Kenly Brown, Lashon Daley, and Derrika Hunt, "Disruptive Ruptures: The Necessity of Black/Girlhood Imaginary," *Meridians* 21 no. 1 (2022): 75–76.
69. Julia S. Jordan-Zachary and Duchess Harris, *Black Girl Magic Beyond the Hashtag: Twenty-First Century Acts of Self-Definition* (University of Arizona Press, 2019), 33.
70. For more some examples see Durham, *Home with Hip Hop Feminism* (Peter Lang, 2014); Robin M. Boylorn, "'Sit with Your Legs Closed!' and Other Sayin's from My Childhood." in *Handbook of Autoethnography*, ed. Tony E. Adams, Stacy Holman Jones, and Carolyn Ellis, 375–82 (Routledge, 2021); Ashley L. Smith-Purviance et al., "Toward Black Girl Futures: Rememorying in Black Girlhood Studies," *Girlhood Studies* 15, no. 3 (2022): 67–83; Breonna Riddick, "Searching for Home: Autoethnographic Reflections of a Black Girl," *Qualitative Inquiry* 28, no. 10 (2022): 1087–91.
71. Smith-Purviance et al., "Toward Black Girl Futures."
72. Gaunt, *The Games Black Girls Play*, 2.
73. E. Patrick Johnson, "Black," in *Keywords for American Cultural Studies*, eds, Bruce Burgett and Glenn Hendler (New York: New York University Press, 2014), 34.
74. Maima Chea Simmons. "'There's More Than One Way to Be Black': The Literacy Experiences of Black African Immigrant Girls in the United States." In *Black Girls' Literacies: Transforming Lives and Literacy Practices*, edited by Detra Price-Dennis and Gholnecsar E. Muhammad, 98–112. Routledge, 2021.
75. Wright, *Black Girlhood*.
76. See Corinne T. Field et al., "The History of Black Girlhood: Recent Innovations and Future Directions," *Journal of the History of Childhood and Youth* 9, no. 3 (2016): 383–401.
77. Tammy C. Owens, "Black Sites of Speculation: A Case for Theorizing Black Childhood as a Subject in Black Adult Narratives," in *Children and Youth as Subjects, Objects, Agents: Innovative Approaches to Research Across Space and Time*, eds. Deborah Levison et al. (Cham: Springer International Publishing, 2021), 144.

78. Harriet Jacobs, *Incidents in the Life of a Slave Girl* (Dover Publications, 2001), 27.
79. Nazera Sadiq Wright, "Black Girl Interiority in Toni Cade Bambara's *Gorilla, My Love*," *Black Scholar* 50, no. 4 (2020): 5.
80. bell hooks, "Visionary Feminism," in *Feminism Is for Everybody: Passionate Politics* (Pluto Press, 2000), 112.
81. June Jordan, "A New Politics of Sexuality," in *Some of Us Did Not Die: New and Selected Essays of June Jordan* (Basic/Civitas Books, 2002), 135.
82. Fannie Barrier Williams, "The Colored Girl," *The Voice of the Negro* 2, no. 6 (1905): 401.
83. Williams, "The Colored Girl," 402.
84. Alice Walker, *In Search of Our Mother's Gardens—Womanist Prose* (Harvest/Harcourt, 1983). In *In Search of Our Mothers' Gardens*, Alice Walker offers multiple examples that reveal the interrelated nature of feminism and womanism, especially as it pertains to Black womn. This is but one example of a key debate within feminist theorizing.
85. Dominique Hill and Durell M. Callier, "Troubling Innocence: Staging Scenes of Black Youth Pleasures and Possibilities," in *Refusing the Limits of Contemporary Childhood*, ed. Julie C. Garlen and Neil T. Ramjewan, 219–40 (Lexington Books, 2024).
86. Desai, "Girl," 103.
87. *Merriam-Webster Dictionary*, "Innocent," accessed February 13, 2023, https://www.merriam-webster.com/dictionary/innocent.
88. Wilma King, *Stolen Childhood: Slave Youth in Nineteenth-Century America* (Indiana University Press, 1995).
89. "'Embodying the Black Inner Child Through Innocent Eyes' – Embodied Social Justice Certificate 2021," Posted to YouTube by Shamell Bell, Aug. 31, 2021, https://www.youtube.com/watch?v=gef4n49MYvs.
90. Janaka Bowman Lewis, *Light and Legacies: Stories of Black Girlhood and Liberation* (University of South Carolina Press, 2023), 149.
91. Devon W. Carbado et al., eds. *Black Like Us: A Century of Lesbian, Gay, and Bisexual African American Fiction*, 2nd ed. (Cleis Press Start, 2011), xiv–xv.
92. Jones, *Theatrical Jazz*, 11.
93. McKittrick, *Demonic Grounds*, 61.
94. Jordan, "Poem about My Rights," 309. This phrasing acknowledges the specificity and dignity of being a human with a specific history and life experience that resonates beyond the self, is part of a Black diaspora, but also not assumed to be generalizable in all cases in this case of Blackgirlness.
95. Callier and Hill, *Who Look at Me?!*, 78.

Chapter 2

Epigraph. Pat Parker, "Group," in *Movement in Black: The Collected Poetry of Pat Parker, 1961–1978* (Crossing Press, 1983), 136.

1. Elaine B. Richardson. *P.H.D. to Ph.D.: Po Ho on Dope: How Education Saved My Life* (Parlor Press, 2013). An earlier version of this chapter was titled "P.I.N.S to PhD."

Inspired by Dr. Richardson's story and narration of it, I thought to riff on her book title to mark a transformation, though different from hers, to continue a conversation about (re)memory in practice, and because her raw rendering is an embodiment of the transgressive practice I write about in this chapter—undressing in public. While the evolution of the chapter birthed a new title, *P.H.D. to Ph.D.* remains a grounding text for this chapter.

2. This monologue first appears in my dissertation as a "site of memory" and my first attempt at writing a synopsis of this experience. Two years later, it would be the opening monologue of my one woman show "Rupturing Silence"; when it debuted, that was the first time my family heard this level of detail about my time in juvie. Then and now, I offer it to give detail to what was seen by other's eyes and the corresponding lessons I internalized through this experience.
3. Dillard, *Learning to (Re)member*, 19.
4. Sara Ahmed, *Living a Feminist Life* (Duke University Press, 2017), 23.
5. Dillard, *Learning to (Re)member*, 15.
6. Laura L. Ellingson, *Embodiment in Qualitative Research* (Routledge, 2017), 13.
7. Sharpe, *In the Wake*, 20.
8. Harvey Young, *Embodying Black Experience: Stillness, Critical Memory, and the Black Body*, Theater: Theory/Text/Performance (University of Michigan Press, 2010), 7.
9. Ahmed, *Living a Feminist Life*, 23.
10. McKittrick, *Demonic Grounds*, 33.
11. David Naimon, "Interview with Nikky Finney," *Between the Covers Podcast*, June 1, 2020, https://tinhouse.com/podcast/nikky-finney-love-childs-hotbed-of-occasional-poetry.
12. Nikky Finney, *Love Child's Hotbed of Occasional Poetry: Poems & Artifacts* (TriQuarterly Books/Northwestern University Press, 2020), 211.
13. Finney, *Love Child's Hotbed*, 214.
14. Kristi Holsinger, "Confinement, Girls," in *The Encyclopedia of Juvenile Delinquency and Justice*, ed. Christopher J. Schreck et al. (John Wiley & Sons, 2017): 2.
15. Jill Scott. "Watching Me," track 15 on *Who Is Jill Scott? Words and Sounds, Vol. 1* (Hidden Beach Recordings, 2000).
16. In *The Body Keeps the Score*, van der Kolk writes, "When our senses become muffled, we no longer feel fully alive." Bessel A. van der Kolk, *The Body Keeps the Score: Brain, Mind and Body in the Healing of Trauma* (Penguin Press, 2015), 91.
17. Alexander, *Pedagogies of Crossing*, 310.
18. Ahmed, *Living a Feminist Life*, 24.
19. Ahmed, 23.
20. Spillers, "Mama's Baby, Papa's Maybe," 65; Jarvis R. Givens et al., "Modeling Manhood: Reimagining Black Male Identities in School," *Anthropology and Education Quarterly* 47, no. 2 (2016): 167.
21. Hartman, *Wayward Lives*, 469.

22. See Lisa Marie Cacho, "'You Just Don't Know How Much He Meant': Deviancy, Death, and Devaluation," *Latino Studies* 5, no. 2 (2007): 182–208.
23. Elizabeth Alexander, *The Black Interior: Essays* (Graywolf Press, 2004), 5.
24. Pat Parker, "Revolution: It's Not Neat or Pretty or Quick," in *This Bridge Called My Back: Writings by Radical Women of Color*, 2nd ed., ed. Cherríe Moraga and Gloria Anzaldúa (Kitchen Table, Women of Color Press, 1983), 11.
25. Kakali Bhattacharya, foreword to *Decolonial Feminist Research: Haunting, Rememory, and Mothers*, ed. Jeong-eun Rhee (Routledge, 2021), xii.
26. Sharpe, *In the Wake*, 17.
27. Alexander, *Pedagogies of Crossing*, 276.
28. Sara Ahmed, *Queer Phenomenology*, 1.
29. Sharpe, *In the Wake*, 11.

Chapter 3

Portions of this chapter were originally published in Dominique C. Hill, "And Who Will Revere the Black Girl," *Gender and Society* 35, no. 4 (2021): 546–56; and Dominique C. Hill, "Rethinking Spaces of Confinement Through Black Girl Embodiment," *Oxford Research Encyclopedia of Education*, March 25, 2021, https://doi.org/10.1093/acrefore/9780190264093.013.1321.

Epigraph. Vanessa Van Dyke, personal communication, December 13, 2021. In alignment with the consent received to conduct two oral history interviews with Vanessa Van Dyke, I use all proper names.

1. Despite once being on the internet in original policy form (Faith Christian Academy, https://www.fcalions.org/wp-content/uploads/2013/02/FCA-Large-Student-Handbook-12-13.pdf), the wording from 2013 can only be traced back through news coverage and Vanessa's recounting. In addition, school affiliation is now required to access certain documents located on the portal, including dress-code policies and the student handbook. These articles use the same language from the policy: Dominique Hobdy, "Florida School Threatens to Expel African-American Girl for Wearing Natural Hair," *Essence*, October 27, 2020, https://www.essence.com/news/florida-school-threatens-expel-african-american-girl-wearing-natural-hair; "Update: African-American Girl Won't Face Expulsion over 'Natural Hair,'" ClickOrlando, November 27, 2013, https://www.clickorlando.com/news/2013/11/27/update-african-american-girl-wont-face-expulsion-over-natural-hair; Clare Kim, "Student Faces Expulsion for 'Natural Hair,'" NBC News, Nov. 26, 2013, https://www.nbcnews.com/id/wbna53673866.
2. Vanessa Van Dyke, interview with author, December 13, 2021.
3. Jordan, "Poem about My Rights," 311.
4. Callier and Hill, *Who Look At Me?!*, 4.

5. For some studies conceptualizing education inequality and experiences through Black feminist, womanist, intersectional and critical feminism see Kristina Henry Collins, Nicole M. Joseph, and Donna Y. Ford, "Missing in Action: Gifted Black Girls in Science, Technology, Engineering, and Mathematics," *Gifted Child Today* 43, no. 1 (2020): 55–63; Venus E. Evans-Winters and Jennifer Esposito, "Other People's Daughters: Critical Race Feminism and Black Girls' Education," *Educational Foundations* 24, no. 1/2 (2010): 11–24; Donna Y. Ford et al., "Blacked Out and Whited Out: The Double Bind of Gifted Black Females Who Are Often a Footnote in Educational Discourse," *International Journal of Educational Reform* 27, no. 3 (2018): 253–68.
6. Shannon Malone Gonzalez, "Black Girls and the Talk?: Policing, Parenting, and the Politics of Protection," *Social Problems* 69, no. 1 (2022): 22–38.
7. Deborah K. King, "Multiple Jeopardy, Multiple Consciousness: The Context of a Black Feminist Ideology," *Signs: Journal of Women in Culture and Society* 14, no. 1 (1988): 47.
8. Bianca A. White, "The Invisible Victims of the School-to-Prison Pipeline: Understanding Black Girls, School Push-Out, and the Impact of the Every Student Succeeds Act," *William & Mary Journal of Race, Gender, and Social Justice* 24, no. 3 (2017): 641.
9. Nancy Heitzeg, "Education or Incarceration: Zero Tolerance Policies and the School to Prison Pipeline," *Forum on Public Policy Online* 2009, no. 2 (2009): 1–21.
10. Wanda Pillow, "'Bodies Are Dangerous': Using Feminist Genealogy as Policy Studies Methodology," *Journal of Education Policy* 18, no. 2 (2010): 146.
11. Jefferson, Turner, and Jensen, "Introduction: On Stuckness," 7.
12. Annamma et al., "Black Girls and School Discipline," 227.
13. Annamma et al., "Black Girls and School Discipline," 232
14. Alaina Neal-Jackson, "Muting Black Girls: How Office Referral Forms Mask Dehumanizing Disciplinary Interactions," *Journal of Educational Administration and History* 52, no. 3 (July 2, 2020).
15. Morris, *Pushout*.
16. Patrick, Onyeka-Crawford, and Duchesneau, "'And They Cared,'" 9.
17. Wun, "Angered," 428.
18. John R. Slate, Pamela L. Gray, and Brandolyn Jones, "A Clear Lack of Equity in Disciplinary Consequences for Black Girls in Texas: A Statewide Examination," *Journal of Negro Education* 85, no. 3 (2016): 250–60.
19. Ricks, "Falling Through the Cracks," 14.
20. Black News, "8-Year Old Black Girl Was Not Allowed to Take School Pictures Because of Her Hair," BlackNews.com, October 11, 2019, https://blacknews.com/news/marian-scott-8-year-old-black-girl-not-allowed-school-pictures-red-braids-hair.

21. National Women's Law Center, "DRESS CODED: Black Girls, Bodies, and Bias in D.C. Schools" (NWLC, 2018), https://nwlc.org/wp-content/uploads/2018/04/5.1web_Final_nwlc_DressCodeReport.pdf; Jasmine Aline Persch, "Girl, 7, Switches Schools after Her Dreadlocks Are Banned," Today.com, September 6, 2013, http://www.today.com/parents/girl-7-switches-schools-after-her-dreadlocks-are-banned-8C11095779. Furthering the configuration of natural Black hair as a "distraction" to educational achievement, then-7-year-old Tiana Parker of Tulsa, Oklahoma, is punished for her dreadlocks. The style, which she'd worn for an entire year, took pride in, and was kept up by her father, was claimed "could distract from the respectful and serious atmosphere it strives for"; the school told her father, Terrence Parker, that his child's hair was not "presentable."

22. Leah Asmelash, "'I Felt Dehumanized': A Black NC Softball Player Says She Was Forced to Cut off Her Hair Beads," WVTM, May 17, 2021, https://www.wvtm13.com/article/black-sports-cut-hair-softball/36441779. On April 19, 2021, high school sophomore and softball player Nicole Pyles became the target of anti-Black and gendered microaggressions. After playing a full inning and hitting a double, her beads were suddenly an issue. Nicole's teammates collaborated to use some bands to secure the beads, and she tucked them into her sports bra. Allowed to return to the field, she helped her team strike out their opponent until it was her turn at bat.

23. Jamilia J. Blake et al., "Unmasking the Inequitable Discipline Experiences of Urban Black Girls: Implications for Urban Educational Stakeholders," *Urban Review* 43, no. 1 (2011): 97.

24. Lauren Shure, Cirecie West-Olatunji, and Blaire Cholewa "Investigating the Relationship between School Counselor Recommendations and Student Cultural Behavioral Styles," *Journal of Negro Education* 88, no. 4 (2019): 454–66.

25. West-Olatunji, Shure, and Cholewa, 460.

26. Linda Grant, "Black Females 'Place' in Desegregated Classrooms," *Sociology of Education* 57, no. 2 (1984): 98–111.

27. Signithia Fordham, "'Those Loud Black Girls': (Black) Women, Silence, and Gender 'Passing' in the Academy," *Anthropology and Education Quarterly* 24, no. 1 (1993): 3–32.

28. Edward W. Morris, "'Ladies' or 'Loudies'?: Perceptions and Experiences of Black Girls in Classrooms," *Youth and Society* 38, no. 4 (2007): 490–515.

29. Morris and Perry, "Girls Behaving Badly?," 128.

30. Alaina Neal-Jackson, "A Meta-Ethnographic Review of the Experiences of African American Girls and Young Women in K-12 Education," *Review of Educational Research* 88, no. 4 (2018): 508–46.

31. Dorothy Hines-Datiri and Dorinda J. Carter Andrews, "The Effects of Zero Tolerance Policies on Black Girls: Using Critical Race Feminism and Figured Worlds to Examine School Discipline," *Urban Education* 55, no. 10 (2020): 1.

32. Asilia Franklin-Phipps, "Entangled Bodies: Black Girls Becoming-Molecular," *Cultural Studies Critical Methodologies* 17, no. 5 (October 2017): 384–91. https://doi.org/10.1177/1532708616674993.
33. Danielle Apugo, Andrene J. Castro, and Sharyn A. Dougherty, "Taught in the Matrix: A Review of Black Girls' Experiences in US Schools," *Review of Educational Research* 93, no. 4 (2023): 559–93; Patricia Hill Collins, *Black Feminist Thought: Knowledge, Consciousness, and the Politics of Empowerment* (Routledge, 1990).
34. Heitzeg, "Education or Incarceration," 2.
35. Hines and Wilmot, "From Spirit-Murdering," 66.
36. Johanna Wald and Daniel J. Losen, "Defining and Redirecting a School-to-Prison Pipeline," *New Directions for Youth Development* 2003, no. 99 (2003): 13.
37. Layli Maparyan, *The Womanist Idea*, Contemporary Sociological Perspectives (Routledge, 2012), 6.
38. Maparyan, 13–14.
39. Maparyan, 10.
40. Audre Lorde, "Good Mirrors Are Not Cheap," 67.
41. Lorde, 67.
42. Lorde, 67.
43. Lorde, 67.
44. Lucille Clifton, "What the Mirror Said," in *The Collected Poems of Lucille Clifton 1965–2010*, ed. Kevin Young and Michael S. Glaser, 199 (BOA Editions, 2012).
45. Clifton, 199.
46. Clifton, 199.
47. Clifton, 199.
48. Frances E. White, *Dark Continent of Our Bodies: Black Feminism and the Politics of Respectability* (Temple University Press, 2001), 9.
49. Fred Moten, "Blackness," in *Keywords in African American Studies*, ed. Erica R. Edwards, Roderick E. Ferguson, and Jeffrey OG Ogbar, 27–29 (New York University Press, 2018), 28.
50. Ysaye M. Barnwell, *No Mirrors in My Nana's House* (Houghton Mifflin Harcourt, 1988), 25.
51. Barnwell, 5.
52. Barnwell, 11.
53. Bambara, "The Education of a Storyteller," 250.
54. Jordan, *Who Look at Me*, 4.
55. Jordan, *Who Look at Me*, 5.
56. Jordan, "Poem about My Rights," 309.
57. Jordan, "Poem about My Rights," 310–11.
58. Jordan, "Poem about My Rights," 312.
59. Vanessa Van Dyke, interview with author, December 13, 2020.

60. HuffPost, "Vanessa VanDyke [sic] Could Be Expelled After Having Her Hair Mocked," November 26, 2013, https://www.huffpost.com/entry/vanessa-vandyke-expelled_n_4345326.
61. The handbook has since been taken down, making official citation of original policy unavailable. However, similar wording about the policy can be found at Hobdy, "Florida School."
62. Vanessa Van Dyke, interview with author, December 13, 2021.
63. HuffPost, "Vanessa VanDyke."
64. Vanessa Van Dyke, interview with author, December 13, 2020.
65. Hines and Wilmot, "From Spirit-Murdering," 62–69.
66. Hines and Wilmot, 65.
67. Crenshaw et al., "Black Girls Matter," 24.
68. Samuel C. McQuade, James P. Colt, and Nancy B. B. Meyer, *Cyber Bullying: Protecting Kids and Adults from Online Bullies* (Praeger Publishers, 2009), 3.
69. Vanessa Van Dyke, interview with author, December 31, 2020.
70. McQuade et al., *Cyber Bullying*, 3.
71. Richie and Martensen, "Resisting Carcerality," 14.
72. Vanessa Van Dyke, interview with author, December 31, 2020.
73. Vanessa Van Dyke, interview with author, December 31, 2020
74. Vanessa Van Dyke, interview with author, December 31, 2020
75. Audre Lorde, "The Transformation of Silence into Language and Action," in *Identity Politics in the Women's Movement*, ed. Barbara Ryan (New York University Press, 2001), 42.
76. Vanessa Van Dyke, interview with the author, December 13, 2021.
77. Vanessa Van Dyke, interview with the author, December 13, 2021.
78. Connie Wun, "Unaccounted Foundations: Black Girls, Anti-Black Racism, and Punishment in Schools," *Critical Sociology* 42, no. 4-5 (2016): 742.
79. Idara Essien and Luke Wood, "I Love My Hair: The Weaponizing of Black Girls Hair by Educators in Early Childhood Education," *Early Childhood Education Journal* 49, no. 3 (May 2021): 401–12.
80. Janice Williams, "Black Girls' Hair Extensions Are a Distraction," *Newsweek*, May 22, 2017. https://www.newsweek.com/malden-ma-dress-code-charter-school-policy-613691.
81. Persch, "Girl, 7, Switches Schools."
82. Callier and Hill, *Who Look at Me?!*, 52.
83. "Nina Simone – Here Comes the Sun (Francois K. Remix)," posted to YouTube by jonathan Moor, May 19, 2009, https://www.youtube.com/watch?v=jSVscnLdUxk.
84. "Solange - Don't Touch My Hair (Video) ft. Sampha," posted to YouTube by solangeknowlesmusic, October 2, 2016, https://www.youtube.com/watch?v=YTtrnDbOQAU.

85. HuffPost, "Vanessa VanDyke."
86. SOLHOT We Levitate, "Black Girl Jewelry Series Featuring BGGW 2016 Homegirls," posted to SoundCloud by We Levitate, November 16, 2016, https://soundcloud.com/solhot-next-level/sets/solhot-we-levitate-presents. During Black Girl Genius Week's studio session, the topic collectively brainstormed was Black girl jewelry. Those in the session, including me, took to writing verses theorizing Black girl jewelry. From literal hair accessories like barrettes and beads to discussing ancestors and family wisdom passed down as adornment, those present spoke the significance of Black girl jewelry. I use it here to refer to actual accessories and implicitly the wisdom Vanessa already inhabited about the interconnection between her hair and spirit.
87. Vanessa Van Dyke, interview with author, December 13, 2021.
88. Jefferson, Turner, and Jensen, "Introduction: On Stuckness," 3
89. Vanessa Van Dyke, interview with author, December 13, 2020.
90. Since the attention received and Vanessa's ongoing activism around hair and bullying, the school's handbook is no longer available to the public. With the increasing number of hair cases nationwide, schools have moved to placing dress-code-related info behind firewalls, requiring community login, and/or removing the policies from websites altogether.
91. Thabile Vilakazi, "Students Protest School's Alleged Racist Hair Policy," CNN World, September 1, 2016. https://www.cnn.com/2016/08/31/africa/south-africa-school-racism/index.html.
92. "'Racist School Hair Rules' Suspended at SA's Pretoria Girls High," *BBC News*, August 30, 2016, https://www.bbc.com/news/world-africa-37219471.
93. Vilakazi, "Students Protest."
94. See my previous publications, specifically "Rethinking Spaces of Confinement through Black Girl Embodiment," "A Black Girl's Crown Changes the Game," and "And Who Will Revere the Black Girl," where I examine various cases between 2008 and 2018 not discussed here related to Black girls and punishment for particularities around hair adornment.
95. Vilakazi, "Students Protest."
96. Ingrid Banks, *Hair Matters: Beauty, Power and Black Women's Consciousness* (New York University Press, 2000).
97. Shange, "Black Girl Ordinary," 6.
98. CROWN Act of 2020, H.R.5309, 116th Cong. (2020).
99. The Official CROWN Act, "About," accessed November 26, 2024, https://www.thecrownact.com/about.
100. See Chandelis Duster and Rosa Flores, "Darryl George: Texas Judge Rules School District Can Restrict the Length of Male Students' Natural Hair," CNN, February 22, 2024, https://www.cnn.com/2024/02/22/us/darryl-george-crown-act-trial-texas-reaj/index.html.

101. Jordan, "Poem about My Rights," 311.
102. "Our Story," Vanessa's Essence, accessed February 4, 2023, https://vanessasessence.com/pages/our-story.
103. Vanessa Van Dyke, interview with author, December 13, 2021.
104. Vanessa Van Dyke, interview with author, December 13, 2021
105. Sabrina Kent, interview with author, December 13, 2021.
106. Persch, "Girl, 7, Switches Schools."
107. Jenisha Watts, "7-Year-Old's Mother Speaks on Cut Braid," *Essence*, October 29, 2020. https://www.essence.com/news/seven-year-olds-mother-speaks-out-about.
108. Rachel Paula Abrahamson, "See What Happened After a Girl Was Denied a Class Picture Because of Her Hair," Today.com, November 18, 2019, https://www.today.com/parents/michigan-girl-denied-yearbook-photo-because-her-hair-t164152.
109. Leah Asmelash, "A Black Softball Player Says She Was Forced to Cut Off Her Hair Beads at a Game. Her Family Wants to Change the Rule They Say Is Discriminatory," CNN, May 14, 2021, https://www.cnn.com/2021/05/14/us/hair-discrimination-softball-durham-trnd/index.html.
110. "AAPF. "#SAYHERNAME." African American Policy Forum, accessed July 4, 2022, https://www.aapf.org/sayhername.
111. Christine Hauser and Patrick McGee, "Black Student's Suspension over Hairstyle Didn't Violate Law, Texas Judge Rules," New York Times, Feb. 22, 2024, https://www.nytimes.com/2024/02/22/us/darryl-george-locs-hair-trial-texas.html.
112. Dominique C. Hill, "A Black Girl's Crown Changes the Game," *Gender and Society* (blog), July 15, 2021, https://gendersociety.wordpress.com/2021/07/15/a-black-girls-crown-changes-the-game.
113. Sabina Ghebremedhin and Christina Carrega, "Timeline: Inside the Investigation of Breonna Taylor's Killing and Its Aftermath," ABC News, November 17, 2020, https://abcnews.go.com/US/timeline-inside-investigation-breonna-taylors-killing-aftermath/story?id=71217247.

Chapter 4

Epigraph. Toni Cade Bambara, ed., *The Black Woman: An Anthology* (Washington Square Press, 2005), 1.

1. Audre Lorde, *Sister Outsider*, 40.
2. Urban Bush Women, "Summer Leadership Institute," accessed November 17, 2023. https://www.urbanbushwomen.org/summer-leadership.
3. Francesca T. Royster, "Queering the Jazz Aesthetic: An Interview with Sharon Bridgforth and Omi Osun Joni Jones," *Journal of Popular Music Studies* 25, no. 4 (2013): 547.
4. Royster, "'Queering the Jazz Aesthetic," 53–54.
5. Lorde, *Sister Outsider*, 54.
6. Lorde, 58.

7. Callier and Hill, *Who Look at Me?!*, 4.
8. As example, see Dominique C. Hill, "Black Girl Pedagogies: Layered Lessons on Reliability," *Curriculum Inquiry* 48, no. 3 (2018).
9. Alexander, *Pedagogies of Crossing*, 8.
10. Alexander, 8.
11. Workshop recording, September 29, 2012, author's personal collection.
12. Danielle Goldman, *I Want to Be Ready: Improvised Dance as a Practice of Freedom* (University of Michigan Press, 2010), 5.
13. Royster, "'Queering the Jazz Aesthetic," 547.
14. Spry, *Body, Paper, Stage*, 58.
15. Porshé R. Garner et al., "Uncovering Black Girlhood(s): Black Girl Pleasures as Anti-Respectability Methodology," *American Quarterly* 71, no. 1 (2019): 191.
16. Spry, *Body, Paper, Stage*, 28–29.
17. Williams, *Being Black*, 8.
18. Spry, *Body, Paper, Stage*, 64.
19. Jeff Brockman, "A Somatic Epistemology for Education," *Educational Forum* 65, no. 4 (Summer 2001): 331.
20. Workshop recording, September 29, 2012, author's personal collection.
21. Diana Taylor, *The Archive and the Repertoire: Performing Cultural Memory in the Americas* (Duke University Press, 2003), 20.
22. Royster, "Queering the Jazz Aesthetic," 547.
23. Bhattacharya, foreword to *Decolonial Feminist Research*, xiv.
24. Workshop recording, September 29, 2012, author's personal collection.
25. Workshop recording, September 29, 2012, author's personal collection.
26. Taylor, *The Archive and the Repertoire*, 20.
27. Tami Spry, "Illustrated Woman: Autoperformance in 'Skins: A Daughter's (Re)Construction of Cancer' and 'Tattoo Stories: A Postscript to "Skins,"'" in *Voices Made Flesh: Performing Women's Autobiography*, ed. Lynn C. Miller, Jacqueline Taylor, and Heather Carver (University of Wisconsin Press, 2003), 120.
28. Tami Spry, "Illustrated Woman," 120.
29. Alexander, *Pedagogies of Crossing*, 299.
30. Hill and Callier, "Troubling Innocence," 223.
31. Lorde, *Sister Outsider*, 59.
32. Gholnecsar E. Muhammad and Marcelle Haddix, "Centering Black Girls' Literacies: A Review of Literature on the Multiple Ways of Knowing of Black Girls," *English Education* 48, no. 4 (2016): 299–336.

Chapter 5

Epigraph. Alexander, *Pedagogies of Crossing*, 269.

1. "Just Because" is an exercise in SOLHOT. Created by a fellow homegirl and often utilized when teaching Black girlhood as well as when desiring to bring students into a lesson on perception, "Just because" is a way of distinguishing

between perception and being, exterior and interiority. In this case, I wanted to make clear that learning is also in the labor of teaching Black Girlhood studies and that I, as a practitioner of Black girlhood and student of Black girls, am forever reflecting on lessons offered.
2. Personal communication, email conference invitation, September 27, 2022.
3. Alexander, *Pedagogies of Crossing*, 19.
4. Alexander, *Pedagogies of Crossing*, 269.
5. We Levitate: Saving Our Lives Hear Our Truths, "Black Girl Insistence, or, When You Wanna Be in Conversation with Fred Moten about SOLHOT," posted to SoundCloud by We Levitate, 2017, accessed August 10, 2022, https://soundcloud.com/solhot-next-level/black-girl-insistence-or-when-you-wanna-be-in-conversation-with-fred-moten-about-solhot-fr.
6. "Party Ain't a Party (Official Music Video)," posted to YouTube by QueenPenVEVO, Nov 22, 2009, https://www.youtube.com/watch?v=CF95dXw_1_c.
7. Alexander, *Pedagogies of Crossing*, 4.
8. Until 2022, irrespective of course content, these (re)orientations appeared on my syllabi with a clause about what each means and could look like. Beginning in August 2022, I moved them off the syllabus to the opening lecture presentation and reinforce them throughout the semester in relation to engagement.
9. Dominique C. Hill, "BLST/SWAG 246—Introduction to Black Girlhood Studies," unpublished syllabus, Amherst College, Amherst, 2017.
10. Kwakye, Hill, and Callier, "10 Years of Black Girlhood Celebration," 1.
11. Produced in 2006, "Save Room" by John Legend was a plea about the permission needed for love to flourish. I use the term "save room" here to reference the work of creating spaciousness for processing, interrogating self and content, and even changing one's mind. This reference of saving room harkens back to Legend with a focus on the journal as a space for saving room by listening for and making the self-known. John Legend, "Save Room," track 1 on *Once Again* (GOOD Music, Sony Music, and Columbia Records, 2006).
12. Hill, "BLST/SWAG 246."
13. Student course journals, December 10 and 11, 2017, author's personal collection.
14. Brown, *Hear Our Truths*, 184.
15. Student journal entry, December 2017, author's personal collection.
16. Lorde, *Sister Outsider*, 42.
17. Brown, *Hear Our Truths*, 188.
18. Ruth Nicole Brown et al., "Doing Digital Wrongly," *American Quarterly* 70, no. 3 (2018): 397.
19. Student course journal, December 11, 2017, author's personal collection.
20. Student course journal, December 11, 2017, author's personal collection.
21. Student course journal, December 11, 2017, author's personal collection.
22. In the introduction to *Home Girls*, Smith discusses "homegirl" as a political reference to maintain a known connection between Black women and Black

culture amid insistence that to declare oneself a Black feminist, to own one's lesbianism, and to do both is to be without home, without community (xxii). I use it here and within this dialogue to hold fast to Smith's idea with the same insistence for Black girls. No matter aesthetic, sartorial choices, phenotype, sexuality, etc., Black girls are an essential ingredient to Black culture.
23. bell hooks, *All about Love: New Visions* (William Morrow, 2000), 6.
24. Kwakye, Hill, and Callier, "10 Years of Black Girlhood Celebration," 2.
25. Ewing, "The Quality of the Light," 200.
26. "We Levitate: Saving Our Lives Hear Our Truths aka SOLHOT #Next Level," SoundCloud artist's page, accessed August 31, 2023. https://soundcloud.com/solhot-next-level.

Conclusion

1. Aimee Cox, *Shapeshifters: Black Girls and the Choreography of Citizenship* (Duke University Press, 2015), 234.
2. Bernice Johnson Reagon, "Black Women's Issues," Barnard College, Reid Lectureship Women's Issues Luncheon, November 11, 1980, http://archive.org/details/pacifica_radio_archives-IZ0711.
3. Morrison, "The Site of Memory," 243.
4. Durham, *Home with Hip Hop Feminism*, 105.
5. Alexander, *Pedagogies of Crossing*, 299–300.
6. Hill, "Black Girl Pedagogies," 390.
7. Blair E. Smith, "Being in a With: Dreaming Black Girlhood Anew" (webinar, Colgate University, Hamilton, NY, April 28, 2022).
8. Smith, "Being," 2022.
9. Reagon, "Black Women's Issues."
10. Lorde, *Sister Outsider*, 57.
11. Alexander, *Pedagogies of Crossing*, 310.
12. Reagon, "Black Women's Issues."
13. In the song "To Be Honest" by the girl band We Levitate, they present the phrase "To be honest," as Black gurl vernacular and a pathway toward ascension (or levitation). "To be honest," when uttered, is followed by truth telling that in some forges new possibilities. Written here, "to be honest" precedes testimony that together offers a textual undressing of me that embodies Black gurl reliable. We Levitate: Saving Our Lives Hear Our Truths, "To Be Honest," posted to SoundCloud by We Levitate, 2016, accessed on August 10, 2023, https://soundcloud.com/solhot-next-level/to-be-honest.
14. The Corset is a split (dimensional quality of self) animated and presented in my one-woman show "Rupturing Silence." The Corset is the iteration who is buttoned up, capable of moving through intellectual spaces exhibiting minimal unwanted emotion, Black gurl sass, or other qualities marked inappropriate in professional spaces. The particular aesthetic of the Corset is the amalgam of

calculations made amid policing Black girls in preparation of Black womnhood, Black womn tropes, dichotomous projections between race and gender, Blackness and sexuality, and the politics of intellectual spaces. In many ways, the Corset is a possibility of the outcome of suppressing Black girls' self-expression and denial of self-definition.

15. In June Jordan's 1980 essay "Civil Wars," she unpacks civil wars as ones where those under attack respond politely, almost apologetically, and where a country, a community, is at odds from the inside. As an extension of this metaphor, the civil war I reference here combines both conceptualizations—it is a war inside of me where abuse was enacted cordially. June Jordan, "Civil Wars (1980)," in *Civil Wars: Observations from the Frontline of America*, 178–88 (Simon and Schuster, 1995).
16. Jordan, "Civil Wars (1980)," 179.
17. Lorde, *Sister Outsider*, 40.
18. Brown, *Black Girlhood Celebration*, 2.
19. Bambara, "Education of a Storyteller," 246–47.
20. Course evaluation, Spring 2022, author's personal collection. A direct quote taken from my Spring 2022 course evaluations, it reveals the field's centering of celebration, which moves students' conceptualization of Black girlhood beyond what happens to Black girls.
21. Personal communication, student emails to author, October 19, 2022, and April 27, 2023.
22. Gloria Hull and Barbara Smith, introduction to *All the Women Are White, All the Blacks Are Men, but Some of Us Are Brave: Black Women's Studies*, 2nd ed., edited by Gloria T. Hull and Barbara Smith, xvii–xxxii. The Feminist Press at the City University of New York, 2015, xxv.

Bibliography

AAPF. "#SAYHERNAME." African American Policy Forum, accessed July 4, 2022. https://www.aapf.org/sayhername.

Abrahamson, Rachel Paula. "See What Happened after a Girl Was Denied a Class Picture Because of Her Hair." Today.com, Nov. 18, 2019. https://www.today.com/parents/michigan-girl-denied-yearbook-photo-because-her-hair-t164152.

Ahmed, Sara. *Living a Feminist Life*. Duke University Press, 2017.

Ahmed, Sara. *Queer Phenomenology: Orientations, Objects, Others*. Duke University Press, 2006.

Ahmed, Sara. "What Is Feminist Research Series with Sara Ahmed." YouTube, posted by Feminist Research Institute UC Davis, June 6, 2018. https://www.youtube.com/watch?v=djc8TEUhPiA.

Alexander, Elizabeth. *The Black Interior: Essays*. Graywolf Press, 2004.

Alexander, M. Jacqui. *Pedagogies of Crossing: Meditations on Feminism, Sexual Politics, Memory, and the Sacred*. Perverse Modernities. Duke University Press, 2005.

Annamma, Subini Ancy, Yolanda Anyon, Nicole M. Joseph, Jordan Farrar, Eldridge Greer, Barbara Downing, and John Simmons. "Black Girls and School Discipline: The Complexities of Being Overrepresented and Understudied." *Urban Education* 54, no. 2 (February 2019): 211–42. https://doi.org/10.1177/0042085916646610.

Apugo, Danielle, Andrene J. Castro, and Sharyn A. Dougherty. "Taught in the Matrix: A Review of Black Girls' Experiences in US Schools." *Review of Educational Research* 93, no. 4 (2023): 559–93.

Ardrey, Taylor. "Kaia Rolle Was Arrested at School when She Was 6. Nearly Two Years Later, She Still 'Has to Bring Herself out of Despair.'" *Business Insider*, March 17, 2021. https://www.businessinsider.com/6-year-old-black-girl-arrested-school-disturbing-trend-criminalization-2021-3.

Asmelash, Leah. "A Black Softball Player Says She Was Forced to Cut Off Her Hair Beads at a Game. Her Family Wants to Change the Rule They Say Is Discriminatory." CNN, May 14, 2021. https://www.cnn.com/2021/05/14/us/hair-discrimination-softball-durham-trnd/index.html.

Asmelash, Leah. "'I Felt Dehumanized': A Black NC Softball Player Says She Was Forced to Cut Off Her Hair Beads." WVTM, May 16, 2021. https://www.wvtm13.com/article/black-sports-cut-hair-softball/36441779.

Ault, Stacey C. "Critical Post-Traumatic Growth among Black Femme High School Students within the School to Prison Pipeline: A Focus on Healing." *International Journal of Human Rights Education* 5, no. 1 (2021). https://repository.usfca.edu/ijhre/vol5/iss1/7.

Bailey, Moya. "More on the Origin of Misogynoir." Tumblr, April 27, 2014. https://moyazb.tumblr.com/post/84048113369/more-on-the-origin-of-misogynoir.

Bailey, Moya. "They Aren't Talking about Me . . . ." *The Crunk Feminist Collective* (blog), March 14, 2010. https://www.crunkfeministcollective.com/2010/03/14/they-arent-talking-about-me.

Bambara, Toni Cade, ed. *The Black Woman: An Anthology*. Washington Square Press, 2005.

Bambara, Toni Cade. "The Education of a Storyteller." In *Deep Sightings and Rescue Missions: Fiction, Essays, and Conversations*, edited by Toni Morrison. Pantheon Books, 1996.

Bambara, Toni Cade. *The Salt Eaters*. Vintage Contemporaries. Vintage Books, 1992.

Banks, Ingrid. *Hair Matters: Beauty, Power and Black Women's Consciousness*. New York University Press, 2000.

Barnwell, Ysaye M. *No Mirrors in My Nana's House*. Houghton Mifflin Harcourt, 1988.

Battle, Nishaun T. "From Slavery to Jane Crow to Say Her Name: An Intersectional Examination of Black Women and Punishment." *Meridians* 15, no. 1 (December 1, 2016): 109–36.

Bhattacharya, Kakali. Foreword to *Decolonial Feminist Research: Haunting, Rememory, and Mothers*, edited by Jeong-eun Rhee. Routledge, 2021.

BlackLight Project. "Mission." BlackLight Newark, March 10, 2011. https://blacklightnewark.wordpress.com/about-2/mission.

Black News. "8-Year Old Black Girl Was Not Allowed to Take School Pictures Because of Her Hair," Blacknews.com, October 11, 2019. https://blacknews.com/news/marian-scott-8-year-old-black-girl-not-allowed-school-pictures-red-braids-hair.

Blake, Jamilia J., Bettie Ray Butler, Chance W. Lewis, and Alicia Darensbourg. "Unmasking the Inequitable Discipline Experiences of Urban Black Girls: Implications for Urban Educational Stakeholders." *Urban Review* 43, no. 1 (March 2011): 90–106. https://doi.org/10.1007/s11256-009-0148-8.

Bobel, Chris, and Samantha Kwan. *Body Battlegrounds: Transgressions, Tensions, and Transformations*. Vanderbilt University Press, 2019.

"Body Politics." Encyclopedia.com, accessed Dec. 18, 2024. https://www.encyclopedia.com/social-sciences/encyclopedias-almanacs-transcripts-and-maps/body-politics.

Boutwell, Laura. "'I Don't Want to Claim America': African Refugee Girls and Discourses of Othering." *Girlhood Studies* 8, no. 2 (2015): 103–18.

Boylorn, Robin M. "On Being at Home with Myself: Blackgirl Autoethnography as Research Praxis." *International Review of Qualitative Research* 9, no. 1 (2016): 44–58.

Boylorn, Robin M. "'Sit with Your Legs Closed!' and Other Sayin's from My Childhood." In *Handbook of Autoethnography*, edited by Tony E. Adams, Stacy Holman Jones, and Carolyn Ellis, 375–82. Routledge, 2021.

Bridgforth, Sharon. *love conjure/blues*. RedBone Press, 2004.

Brockman, Jeff. "A Somatic Epistemology for Education." *Educational Forum* 65, no. 4 (Summer 2001): 328.

Brown, Kenly, Lashon Daley, and Derrika Hunt. "Disruptive Ruptures: The Necessity of Black/Girlhood Imaginary." *Meridians* 21, no. 1 (2022): 75–100.

Brown, Ruth Nicole. *Black Girlhood Celebration: Toward a Hip-Hop Feminist Pedagogy*. Peter Lang, 2009.

Brown, Ruth Nicole. *Hear Our Truths: The Creative Potential of Black Girlhood*. Dissident Feminisms. University of Illinois Press, 2013.

Brown, Ruth Nicole, Blair Ebony Smith, Jessica L. Robinson, and Porshé R. Garner. "Doing Digital Wrongly." *American Quarterly* 70, no. 3 (2018): 395–416. https://doi.org/10.1353/aq.2018.0028.

Butler, Tamara T. "Black Girl Cartography: Black Girlhood and Place-Making in Education Research." *Review of Research in Education* 42, no. 1 (March 1, 2018): 28–45. https://doi.org/10.3102/0091732X18762114.

Cacho, Lisa Marie. "'You Just Don't Know How Much He Meant': Deviancy, Death, and Devaluation." *Latino Studies* 5, no. 2 (2007): 182–208.

Callier, Durell M. "Gendered Violences and Queer of Color Critiques in Educational Spaces: Remembering Sakia, Carl, and Jaheem." In *Encyclopedia of Educational Philosophy and Theory*, edited by Michael A. Peters, 914–19. Springer Singapore, 2017. https://doi.org/10.1007/978-981-287-588-4_429.

Callier, Durell M., and Dominique C. Hill. *Who Look at Me?! Shifting the Gaze of Education through Blackness, Queerness, and the Body*. Personal/Public Scholarship, vol. 3. Brill Sense, 2019.

Carbado, Devon W., Dwight A. McBride, Donald Weise, and Evelyn C. White, eds. *Black Like Us: A Century of Lesbian, Gay, and Bisexual African American Fiction*, 2nd ed. Cleis Press, 2012.

Chirbas, Kurt, Erik Ortiz, and Corky Siemszko. "Baltimore County Police Fatally Shot Korryn Gaines, 23, Wound 5-Year-Old, Son." NBC News, August 3, 2016. https://www.nbcnews.com/news/us-news/baltimore-county-police-fatally-shoot-korryn-gaines-boy-5-hurt-n621461.

Christian, Barbara. "The Race for Theory." *Cultural Critique* 6 (1987): 51–63.

Clifton, Lucille, "What the Mirror Said." In *The Collected Poems of Lucille Clifton 1965–2010*, edited by Kevin Young, and Michael S. Glaser, 199. BOA Editions, 2012.

Cohen, Cathy J. "Punks, Bulldaggers, and Welfare Queens: The Radical Potential of Queer Politics?" *GLQ: A Journal of Lesbian and Gay Studies* 3, no. 4 (May 1, 1997): 437–65. https://doi.org/10.1215/10642684-3-4-437.

Collins, Kristina Henry, Nicole M. Joseph, and Donna Y. Ford. "Missing in Action: Gifted Black Girls in Science, Technology, Engineering, and Mathematics." *Gifted Child Today* 43, no. 1 (2020): 55–63.

Collins, Patricia Hill. *Black Feminist Thought: Knowledge, Consciousness, and the Politics of Empowerment*. Routledge, 1990.

"Combahee River Collective: A Black Feminist Statement." *Off Our Backs* 9, no. 6 (1979): 6–8.

Cook, Tomasina L. "Violated and Victimized: The Juvenile Justice System and Black Girls." In *Black Girls and Adolescents: Facing the Challenges*, edited by Catherine Fisher Collins. Praeger, 2015.

Corbett, Christianne, Catherine Hill, and Andresse St. Rose. *Where the Girls Are: The Facts about Gender Equity in Education*. American Association of University Women (AAUW) Educational Foundation, 2008.

Cox, Aimee Meredith. *Shapeshifters: Black Girls and the Choreography of Citizenship*. Duke University Press, 2015.

Crenshaw, Kimberlé, Priscilla Ocen, and Jyoti Nanda. "Black Girls Matter: Pushed Out, Overpoliced and Underprotected." Columbia Law School Scholarship Archive, January 1, 2015. https://scholarship.law.columbia.edu/faculty_scholarship/3227. Published by the African American Policy Forum and the Center for Intersectionality and Social Policy Studies.

crunktastic. "Black Girl Is a Verb: A New American Grammar Book." Crunk Feminist Collective, March 28, 2016. https://www.crunkfeministcollective.com/2016/03/28/black-girl-is-a-verb-a-new-american-grammar-book.

Daigle, Michelle, and Marietta Margaret Ramirez. "Space." In Keywords Feminist Editorial Collective, ed., *Keywords for Gender and Sexuality Studies*, 216–19.

Daley, Lashon. "Coming of (R)age: A New Genre for Contemporary Narratives about Black Girlhood." *Signs: Journal of Women in Culture and Society* 46, no. 4 (2021): 1035–56.

Davis, Angela Y. *Women, Race & Class*. Vintage Books, 1983.

Davis, Marcia. "Black Lives Matter – Including Black Women's, Activists Remind Nation." *Washington Post* (Washington, DC), May 20, 2015. https://www.washingtonpost.com/lifestyle/magazine/black-lives-matter--including-black-womens-activists-remind-nation/2015/05/19/e155a514-fe43-11e4-833c-a2de05b6b2a4_story.html.

Desai, Karishma. "Girl." In Keywords Feminist Editorial Collective, *Keywords for Gender and Sexuality Studies*, 13: 101–5.

Dillard, Cynthia B. *Learning to (Re)Member the Things We've Learned to Forget: Endarkened Feminisms, Spirituality, & the Sacred Nature of Research & Teaching.* New York: Peter Lang, 2012.

Dove and The JOY Collective. "The CROWN Research Study." Dove and The JOY Collective, 2019. https://static1.squarespace.com/static/5ed-c69fd622c36173f56651f/t/5edeaa2fe5ddef345e087361/1591650865168/Dove_research_brochure2020_FINAL3.pdf.

Dove and The JOY Collective. "Dove CROWN Research Study for Girls." Dove and The JOY Collective, 2021. https://static1.squarespace.com/static/5ed-c69fd622c36173f56651f/t/623369f7477914438ee18c9b/1647536634602/2021_DOVE_CROWN_girls_study.pdf.

Du Bois, W. E. B. *The Souls of Black Folk; Essays and Sketches.* A. G. McClurg, 1903. Reprinted by Johnson Reprint Corp., 1968.

Durham, Aisha. "Between Us: A Bio-Poem." *Meridians* 8, no. 2 (2008): 177–82.

Durham, Aisha. *Home with Hip Hop Feminism.* Peter Lang, 2014.

Durham, Aisha. "On Collards." *International Review of Qualitative Research* 10, no. 1 (May 1, 2017): 22–23. https://doi.org/10.1525/irqr.2017.10.1.22.

Duster, Chandelis, and Rosa Flores. "Darryl George: Texas Judge Rules School District Can Restrict the Length of Male Students' Natural Hair." CNN, February 22, 2024. https://www.cnn.com/2024/02/22/us/darryl-george-crown-act-trial-texas-reaj/index.html.

Dyer, Susan K. *Beyond the "Gender Wars": A Conversation about Girls, Boys, and Education.* American Association of University Women (AAUW) Educational Foundation, September 14–15, 2000.

Ellingson, Laura L. *Embodiment in Qualitative Research.* Routledge, 2017.

"Embodying the Black Inner Child Through Innocent Eyes – Embodied Social Justice Certificate 2021." Posted to YouTube by Shamell Bell, Aug. 31, 2021. https://www.youtube.com/watch?v=gef4n49MYvs.

Epstein, Rebecca, Jamilia Blake, and Thalia González. "Girlhood Interrupted: The Erasure of Black Girls' Childhood." SSRN Scholarly Paper, June 27, 2017. https://papers.ssrn.com/abstract=3000695.

Essien, Idara, and J. Luke Wood. "I Love My Hair: The Weaponizing of Black Girls Hair by Educators in Early Childhood Education." *Early Childhood Education Journal* 49, no. 3 (May 2021): 401–12. https://doi.org/10.1007/s10643-020-01081-1.

Evans-Winters, Venus E., and Jennifer Esposito. "Other People's Daughters: Critical Race Feminism and Black Girls' Education." *Journal of Educational Foundations* 24, no. 1/2 (Winter 2010): 11–24.

Ewing, Eve L. "The Quality of the Light: Evidence, Truths, and the Odd Practice of the Poet-Sociologist." In *Black Women's Liberatory Pedagogies: Resistance, Transformation, and Healing Within and Beyond the Academy*, edited by Olivia N. Perlow, Durene I. Wheeler, Sharon L. Bethea, and BarBara M. Scott,

195–209. Springer International, 2018. https://doi.org/10.1007/978-3-319-65789-9_11.

Field, Corinne T., Tammy-Charelle Owens, Marcia Chatelain, Lakisha Simmons, Abosede George, and Rhian Keyse. "The History of Black Girlhood: Recent Innovations and Future Directions." *Journal of the History of Childhood and Youth* 9, no. 3 (2016): 383–401. https://doi.org/10.1353/hcy.2016.0067.

Field, Corinne T., and LaKisha Michelle Simmons. "Introduction: Looking for Black Girls in History." In *The Global History of Black Girlhood*, edited by Corinne T. Field and LaKisha Michelle Simmons, 1–28. University of Illinois Press, 2022.

Finney, Nikky. *Love Child's Hotbed of Occasional Poetry: Poems & Artifacts*. TriQuarterly Books/Northwestern University Press, 2020.

Ford, Donna Y., Breshawn N. Harris, Janice A. Byrd, and Nicole McZeal Walters. "Blacked Out and Whited Out: The Double Bind of Gifted Black Females Who Are Often a Footnote in Educational Discourse." *International Journal of Educational Reform* 27, no. 3 (2018): 253–68.

Fordham, Signithia. "'Those Loud Black Girls': (Black) Women, Silence, and Gender 'Passing' in the Academy." *Anthropology & Education Quarterly* 24, no. 1 (1993): 3–32. https://doi.org/10.1525/aeq.1993.24.1.05x1736t.

Franklin-Phipps, Asilia. "Entangled Bodies: Black Girls Becoming-Molecular." *Cultural Studies Critical Methodologies* 17, no. 5 (October 2017): 384–91. https://doi.org/10.1177/1532708616674993.

Freeman, Cordelia, and Sydney Calkin. "Feminism/Feminist Geography." In *Encyclopedia of Human Geography*, 2nd ed., edited by Audrey Lynn Kobayashi. Elsevier, 2020.

Garner, Porshé R. "The Sounded-Word Aesthetics: Black Girl Covenant and the Fire Commandments." *International Journal of Qualitative Studies in Education* 34, no. 6 (July 3, 2021): 549–61. https://doi.org/10.1080/09518398.2020.1852487.

Garner, Porshé R., Dominique C. Hill, Jessica L. Robinson, and Durell M. Callier. "Uncovering Black Girlhood(s): Black Girl Pleasures as Anti-Respectability Methodology." *American Quarterly* 71, no. 1 (2019): 191–97. https://doi.org/10.1353/aq.2019.0012.

Gaunt, Kyra Danielle. *The Games Black Girls Play: Learning the Ropes from Double-Dutch to Hip-Hop*. New York University Press, 2006.

Ghebremedhin, Sabrina, and Christina Carrega. "Timeline: Inside the Investigation of Breonna Taylor's Killing and Its Aftermath." ABC News, November 17, 2020. https://abcnews.go.com/US/timeline-inside-investigation-breonna-taylors-killing-aftermath/story?id=71217247.

Gill, Lyndon K. "Situating Black, Situating Queer: Black Queer Diaspora Studies and the Art of Embodied Listening." *Transforming Anthropology* 20, no. 1 (2012): 32–44. https://doi.org/10.1111/j.1548-7466.2011.01143.x.

Gillam, Reighan. "Representing Black Girlhood in Brazil: Culture and Strategies of Empowerment." *Communication, Culture and Critique* 10, no. 4 (2017): 609–25.

Gilmore, Ruth Wilson. *Golden Gulag: Prisons, Surplus, Crisis, and Opposition in Globalizing California*. University of California Press, 2007.

Givens, Jarvis R., Na'ilah Nasir, kihana ross, and Maxine McKinney de Royston. "Modeling Manhood: Reimagining Black Male Identities in School." *Anthropology and Education Quarterly* 47, no. 2 (June 2016): 167–85. https://doi.org/10.1111/aeq.12147.

Goldman, Danielle. *I Want to Be Ready: Improvised Dance as a Practice of Freedom*. University of Michigan Press, 2010.

Gopinath, Gayatri "Diaspora." In Keywords Feminist Editorial Collective, *Keywords for Gender and Sexuality Studies*, 67–70.

Gottlieb, Eric. "The Role of the Page in Jazz: *dyke/warrior-prayers*' Theatrical Jazz Aesthetic; an Interview with Sharon Bridgforth." *Liminalities* 18, no. 2 (2022): 1–8.

Grant, Linda. "Black Females 'Place' in Desegregated Classrooms." *Sociology of Education* 57, no. 2 (1984): 98–111. https://doi.org/10.2307/2112632.

Green, Misha, writer. *Lovecraft Country*. Season 1, episode 3, "I am." Directed by Charlotte Sieling. Aired on September 27, 2020. https://www.imdb.com/title/tt9548458.

Griffith, Janelle. "Alleged Strip Search of 4 Black Middle School Girls Prompts Third-Party Investigation." NBC News, January 30, 2019. https://www.nbcnews.com/news/us-news/alleged-strip-search-4-black-middle-school-girls-prompts-third-n964856.

Gross, Kali Nicole. "African American Women, Mass Incarceration, and the Politics of Protection." *Journal of American History* 102, no. 1 (2015): 25–33.

Halliday, Aria S., ed. *The Black Girlhood Studies Collection*. Women's Press, 2019.

Haraway, Donna. "Situated Knowledges: The Science Question in Feminism and the Privilege of Partial Perspective." *Feminist Studies* 14, no. 3 (1988): 575–79. https://doi.org/10.2307/3178066.

Hartman, Saidiya V. *Wayward Lives, Beautiful Experiments: Intimate Histories of Social Upheaval*. W.W. Norton, 2019.

Hauser, Christine, and Patrick McGee. "Black Student's Suspension over Hairstyle Didn't Violate Law, Texas Judge Rules." *New York Times*, Feb. 22, 2024. https://www.nytimes.com/2024/02/22/us/darryl-george-locs-hair-trial-texas.html.

Hawthorne, Camilla. "Black Matters Are Spatial Matters: Black Geographies for the Twenty-First Century." *Geography Compass* 13, no. 11 (2019): e12468. https://doi.org/10.1111/gec3.12468.

Heitzeg, Nancy A. "Education or Incarceration: Zero Tolerance Policies and the School to Prison Pipeline." *Forum on Public Policy Online* 2009, no. 2 (2009): 1–21.

Hernandez, Jillian. *Aesthetics of Excess: The Art and Politics of Black and Latina Embodiment*. Duke University Press, 2020. https://doi.org/10.2307/j.ctv16rdct2.

Hill, DaMaris B. *A Bound Woman Is a Dangerous Thing: The Incarceration of African American Women from Harriet Tubman to Sandra Bland*. Bloomsbury, 2019.

Hill, DaMaris B. *Breath Better Spent: Living Black Girlhood*. Bloomsbury, 2022.

Hill, Dominique C. "And Who Will Revere the Black Girl." *Gender and Society* 35, no. 4 (2021): 546–56.

Hill, Dominique C. "Assata's (Groove[ing]) Daughter: An Embodied Lyrical Autoethnography of Resistance." *International Review of Qualitative Research* 14, no. 2 (2021): 337–43.

Hill, Dominique C. "Black Girl Pedagogies: Layered Lessons on Reliability." *Curriculum Inquiry* 48, no. 3 (2018): 383–405. https://doi.org/10.1080/03626784.2018.1468213.

Hill, Dominique C. "A Black Girl's Crown Changes the Game." *Gender and Society* (blog), July 15, 2021. https://gendersociety.wordpress.com/2021/07/15/a--black-girls-crown-changes-the-game.

Hill, Dominique C. "BLST/SWAG 246 – Introduction to Black Girlhood Studies." Syllabus, Amherst College, Amherst, 2017.

Hill, Dominique C. "Rethinking Spaces of Confinement Through Black Girl Embodiment." *Oxford Research Encyclopedia of Education*, March 25, 2021. https://doi.org/10.1093/acrefore/9780190264093.013.1321.

Hill, Dominique C., and Durell M. Callier. "Troubling Innocence: Staging Scenes of Black Youth Pleasures and Possibilities." In *Refusing the Limits of Contemporary Childhood*, edited by Julie C. Garlen and Neil T. Ramjewan, 219–40. Lexington Books, 2024.

Hill, Dominique C., and Omi Osun Joni Jones. "'Put on Your Good Bra!'" HowlRound Theatre Commons, April 13, 2017. https://howlround.com/put-your-good-bra.

Hines, Dorothy E., and Jennifer M. Wilmot. "From Spirit-Murdering to Spirit-Healing: Addressing Anti-Black Aggressions and the Inhumane Discipline of Black Children." *Multicultural Perspectives* 20, no. 2 (April 3, 2018): 62–69. https://doi.org/10.1080/15210960.2018.1447064.

Hines-Datiri, Dorothy, and Dorinda J. Carter Andrews. "The Effects of Zero Tolerance Policies on Black Girls: Using Critical Race Feminism and Figured Worlds to Examine School Discipline." *Urban Education* 55, no. 10 (December 2020): 1419–40. https://doi.org/10.1177/0042085917690204.

Hobdy, Dominique. "Florida School Threatens to Expel African-American Girl for Wearing Natural Hair." *Essence*, October 27, 2020. http://www.essence.com/2013/11/26/florida-school-threatens-expel-african-american-girl-wearing-natural-hair.

Holsinger, Kristi. "Confinement, Girls." In *The Encyclopedia of Juvenile Delinquency and Justice*, edited by Christopher J. Schreck, Michael J. Leiber, Holly Ventura Miller, and Kelly Welch. John Wiley & Sons, 2017. https://doi.org/10.1002/9781118524275.ejdj0082.

hooks, bell. *All about Love: New Visions*. William Morrow, 2018.

hooks, bell. *Teaching to Transgress*. Routledge, 1994.

hooks, bell. "Visionary Feminism." In *Feminism Is for Everybody: Passionate Politics*. Pluto Press, 2000.

HuffPost. "Vanessa VanDyke [sic] Could Be Expelled after Having Her Hair Mocked." November 26, 2013. https://www.huffpost.com/entry/vanessa-vandyke-expelled_n_4345326.

Hull, Gloria T., and Barbara Smith. Introduction to *All the Women Are White, All the Blacks Are Men, but Some of Us Are Brave: Black Women's Studies*, 2nd ed., edited by Gloria T. Hull and Barbara Smith, xvii–xxxii. The Feminist Press at the City University of New York, 2015.

Jacobs, Harriet. *Incidents in the Life of a Slave Girl*. Dover Publications, 2001.

Jarmon, Renina. *Black Girls Are from the Future: Essays on Race, Digital Creativity and Pop Culture*. Jarmon Media, 2013.

Jefferson, Andrew, Simon Turner, and Steffen Jensen. "Introduction: On Stuckness and Sites of Confinement." *Ethnos: Journal of Anthropology* 84, no. 1 (February 2019): 1–13. https://doi.org/10.1080/00141844.2018.1544917.

Johnson, E. Patrick. "Black." In *Keywords for American Cultural Studies*, edited by Bruce Burgett and Glenn Hendler, 30–34. New York University Press, 2014.

Johnson, Jasmine Elizabeth. "A Politics of Tenderness: Camille A. Brown and Dancers' BLACK GIRL: Linguistic Play." *Black Scholar* 49, no. 4 (October 2, 2019): 20–34. https://doi.org/10.1080/00064246.2019.1655366.

Jones, Chenelle A., and Renita L. Seabrook. "The New Jane Crow: Mass Incarceration and the Denied Maternity of Black Women." *Race, Ethnicity and Law*, vol. 22 (2017): 135–54.

Jones, Joni L. "Making Space." In Jones, Moore, and Bridgforth, *Experiments in a Jazz Aesthetic*.

Jones, Joni L. "Performance Ethnography: The Role of Embodiment in Cultural Authenticity." *Theatre Topics* 12, no. 1 (2002): 1–15

Jones, Omi Osun Joni L. Introduction to *love conjure/blues*, edited by Sharon Bridgforth. RedBone Press, 2004.

Jones, Omi Osun Joni L. *Theatrical Jazz: Performance, Às e , and the Power of the Present Moment. Black Performance and Cultural Criticism*. Ohio State University Press, 2015.

Jones, Omi Osun Joni L., Lisa L. Moore, and Sharon Bridgforth, eds. *Experiments in a Jazz Aesthetic: Art, Activism, Academia, and the Austin Project*. University of Texas Press, 2010.

Jordan, June. "Civil Wars (1980)." In *Civil Wars: Observations from the Frontline of America*, 178–88. Simon and Schuster, 1995.

Jordan, June. "A New Politics of Sexuality." In *Some of Us Did Not Die: New and Selected Essays of June Jordan*. Basic/Civitas Books, 2002.

Jordan, June. "Poem about My Rights (1980)." In *Directed by Desire: The Collected Poems of June Jordan*, edited by Jan Heller Levi. Copper Canyon Press, 2007.

Jordan, June. *Who Look at Me*. Thomas Y. Crowell, 1969.

Jordan, June. "Wrong or White." In *Life as Activism: June Jordan's Writings from the Progressive*. Litwin Books, 2014.

Jordan-Zachary, Julia S., and Duchess Harris, eds. *Black Girl Magic Beyond the Hashtag: Twenty-First-Century Acts of Self-Definition*. University of Arizona Press, 2019.

Keywords Editorial Collective. *Keywords for Gender and Sexuality Studies*. New York University Press, 2021.

King, Deborah K. "Multiple Jeopardy, Multiple Consciousness: The Context of a Black Feminist Ideology." *Signs: Journal of Women in Culture and Society* 14, no. 1 (October 1988): 42–72. https://doi.org/10.1086/494491.

King, Wilma. *Stolen Childhood: Slave Youth in Nineteenth-Century America*. Indiana University Press, 1995.

Kwakye, Chamara Jewel, Dominique C. Hill, and Durell M. Callier. "10 Years of Black Girlhood Celebration: A Pedagogy of Doing." *Departures in Critical Qualitative Research* 6, no. 3 (September 1, 2017): 1–10. https://doi.org/10.1525/dcqr.2017.6.3.1.

Ladner, Joyce A. *Tomorrow's Tomorrow: The Black Woman*. Anchor Books, 1972.

Legal Defense Fund. "Natural Hair Discrimination: Frequently Asked Questions." NAACPLDF, accessed February 26, 2024. https://www.naacpldf.org/natural-hair-discrimination.

Legend, John. "Save Room." Track 1 on *Once Again*. GOOD Music, Sony Music, and Columbia Records, 2006.

Lewis, Janaka Bowman. *Light and Legacies: Stories of Black Girlhood and Liberation*. University of South Carolina Press, 2023.

Lewis, Sheri K., "Pushing the Limits in Black Girl–Centered Research: Exploring the Methodological Possibilities of *Melt* Magazine." In *The Black Girlhood Studies Collection*, edited by Aria S. Halliday, 157–80. Women's Press, 2019.

Lightfoot, Sara Lawrence. "Socialization and Education of Young Black Girls in School." *Teachers College Record* 78, no. 2 (December 1976): 1–18. https://doi.org/10.1177/016146817607800202.

Lincoln, Abbey. "Who Will Revere the Black Woman? [1966]." *Ebony*, February 12, 2013. http://www.ebony.com/who-will-revere-the-black-woman-405.

Lindsey, Treva B. *America, Goddam: Violence, Black Women, and the Struggle for Justice*. University of California Press, 2022.

Lorde, Audre. "Good Mirrors Are Not Cheap" in *Undersong: Chosen Poems Old and New*, rev. ed. Norton, 1992.

Lorde, Audre. *Sister Outsider*. Oxford University Press, 1983.
Lorde, Audre. "The Transformation of Silence into Language and Action (1983)." In *Identity Politics in the Women's Movement*, edited by Barbara Ryan. New York University Press, 2001.
Love, Bettina L. *We Want to Do More than Survive: Abolitionist Teaching and the Pursuit of Educational Freedom*. Beacon Press, 2019.
Malone Gonzalez, Shannon. "Black Girls and the Talk? Policing, Parenting, and the Politics of Protection." *Social Problems* 69, no. 1 (January 25, 2022): 22–38. https://doi.org/10.1093/socpro/spaa032.
Maparyan, Layli. *The Womanist Idea*. Contemporary Sociological Perspectives. Routledge, 2012.
Martensen, Kayla Marie. "Review of Carceral State Studies and Application." *Sociology Compass* 14, no. 7 (2020): e12801. https://doi.org/10.1111/soc4.12801.
McClaurin, Irma, ed. *Black Feminist Anthropology: Theory, Politics, Praxis, and Poetics*. Rutgers University Press, 2001.
McClaurin, Irma. "Black Feminist Auto/Ethnography That Makes You Want to Cry." *Insight News*, June 27, 2012. https://www.insightnews.com/news/local/black-feminist-auto-ethnography-that-makes-you-want-to-cry/article_50b309a6-8bb0-5ad1-9c8f-3a424ac3a020.html.
McKittrick, Katherine. *Demonic Grounds: Black Women and the Cartographies of Struggle*. University of Minnesota Press, 2006.
McQuade, Samuel C., James P. Colt, and Nancy B. B. Meyer. *Cyber Bullying: Protecting Kids and Adults from Online Bullies*. Praeger Publishers, 2009.
Mettler, Katie. "Mass. School Punishes Twins for Hair Braid Extensions. Their Parents Say It's Racial Discrimination." *Washington Post*, May 15, 2017. https://www.washingtonpost.com/news/morning-mix/wp/2017/05/15/mass-school-punishes-twins-for-hair-braid-extensions-their-parents-say-its-racial-discrimination.
Meyer, Elizabeth J. *Gender, Bullying, and Harassment: Strategies to End Sexism and Homophobia in Schools*. Teachers College Press, 2009.
Morris, Edward W. "'Ladies' or 'Loudies'?: Perceptions and Experiences of Black Girls in Classrooms." *Youth and Society* 38, no. 4 (June 1, 2007): 490–515. https://doi.org/10.1177/0044118X06296778.
Morris, Edward W., and Brea L. Perry. "Girls Behaving Badly?: Race, Gender, and Subjective Evaluation in the Discipline of African American Girls." *Sociology of Education* 90, no. 2 (2017): 127–48. https://doi.org/10.1177/0038040717694876.
Morris, Monique W. *Pushout: The Criminalization of Black Girls in Schools*. The New Press, 2016.
Morris, Monique W., Stephanie R. Bush-Baskette, and Kimberlé Crenshaw. *Confined in California: Women and Girls of Color in Custody*. African American Policy Forum, 2013.

Morrison, Toni. "The Site of Memory." In *The Source of Self-Regard: Selected Essays, Speeches, and Meditations*. Alfred A. Knopf, 2019.

Moten, Fred. "Blackness." In *Keywords in African American Studies*, edited by Erica R. Edwards, Roderick E. Ferguson, and Jeffrey OG Ogbar, 27–29. New York University Press, 2018.

Muhammad, Gholnecsar E., and Marcelle Haddix. "Centering Black Girls' Literacies: A Review of Literature on the Multiple Ways of Knowing of Black Girls." *English Education* 48, no. 4 (2016): 299–336.

Murray, Pauli, and Mary O. Eastwood. "Jane Crow and the Law: Sex Discrimination and Title VII." *George Washington Law Review* 34, no. 2 (Dec. 1965): 232–56.

Naimon, David. "Interview with Nikky Finney." *Between the Covers Podcast*, June 1, 2020. https://tinhouse.com/podcast/nikky-finney-love-childs-hotbed-of-occasional-poetry.

Nash, Jennifer C. "Unwidowing: Rachel Jeantel, Black Death, and the 'Problem' of Black Intimacy." *Signs: Journal of Women in Culture and Society* 41, no. 4 (June 2016): 751–74. https://doi.org/10.1086/685114.

Nashid, Laila. "Understanding Digital Narratives of Black Girlhood Through Social Media Aesthetics." *Girlhood Studies* 17, no. 2 (2024): 86–102.

National Women's Law Center. "DRESS CODED: Black Girls, Bodies, and Bias in D.C. Schools," NWLC, 2018. https://nwlc.org/resource/dresscoded.

Neal-Jackson, Alaina. "A Meta-Ethnographic Review of the Experiences of African American Girls and Young Women in K-12 Education." *Review of Educational Research* 88, no. 4 (2018): 508–46.

Neal-Jackson, Alaina. "Muting Black Girls: How Office Referral Forms Mask Dehumanizing Disciplinary Interactions." *Journal of Educational Administration and History* 53, no. 3, (2020).

NiaNow.com. "Nia | Dance Fitness for the Mind, Body and Soul." Accessed November 17, 2023. https://nianow.com

"Nikki Giovanni and James Baldwin in Conversation on 'SOUL!' (PART 2) | ALL ARTS Vault." *Soul!*, produced by Ellis B. Haizlip, WNET, 1971. Posted to YouTube by ALL ARTS TV, Dec. 16, 2022.

"Nina Simone – Here Comes the Sun (Francois K. Remix)." Posted to YouTube by jonathan moor, May 19, 2009. https://www.youtube.com/watch?v=jSVscnLdUxk.

Omolade, Barbara. "A Black Feminist Pedagogy." *Women's Studies Quarterly* 15, no. 3/4 (1987): 32–39.

Owens, Tammy C. "Black Sites of Speculation: A Case for Theorizing Black Childhood as a Subject in Black Adult Narratives." In *Children and Youth as Subjects, Objects, Agents: Innovative Approaches to Research across Space and Time*, edited by Deborah Levison, Mary Jo Maynes, and Frances Vavrus, 141–53. Springer International Publishing, 2021.

Owens, Tammy C., Durell Callier, Porshé R. Garner, and Jessica L. Robinson. "Towards an Interdisciplinary Field of Black Girlhood Studies." *Departures in Critical Qualitative Research* 6, no. 3 (2017): 116–32. https://doi.org/10.1525/dcqr.2017.6.3.116.

Parker, Pat. *The Complete Works of Pat Parker*. Sapphic Classics 102. Sinister Wisdom, 2016.

Parker, Pat. "Group." In *Movement in Black: The Collected Poetry of Pat Parker, 1961–1978*. Crossing Press, 1983.

Parker, Pat. "Revolution: It's Not Neat or Pretty or Quick." In *This Bridge Called My Back: Writings by Radical Women of Color*, 2nd ed., edited by Cherríe Moraga and Gloria Anzaldúa. Kitchen Table, Women of Color Press, 1983.

"Party Ain't A Party (Official Music Video)." Posted to YouTube by QueenPenVEVO, Nov 22, 2009. https://www.youtube.com/watch?v=CF-95dXw_1_c.

Patrick, Kayla, Adaku Onyeka-Crawford, and Nancy Duchesneau. "'And They Cared': How to Create Better, Safer Learning Environments for Girls of Color." Education Trust, August 20, 2020. https://edtrust.org/rti/and-they-cared-how-to-create-better-safer-learning-environments-for-girls-of-color.

Persch, Jasmine Aline. "Girl, 7, Switches Schools after Her Dreadlocks Are Banned." Today.com, September 6, 2013. http://www.today.com/parents/girl-7-switches-schools-after-her-dreadlocks-are-banned-8C11095779.

Pillow, Wanda. "'Bodies Are Dangerous': Using Feminist Genealogy as Policy Studies Methodology." *Journal of Education Policy* 18, no. 2 (2010): 145–59. https://doi.org/10.1080/0268093022000043083.

Pillsbury House and Theatre. "Theatrical Jazz Conference." Archived 2024 at https://pillsburyhouseandtheatre.org/homepage/theatrical-jazz-conference/

"Racist School Hair Rules' Suspended at SA's Pretoria Girls High." BBC News, August 30, 2016. https://www.bbc.com/news/world-africa-37219471.

Reagon, Bernice Johnson. "Black Women's Issues." Barnard College, Reid Lectureship Women's Issues Luncheon, November 11, 1980. The Internet Archive. http://archive.org/details/pacifica_radio_archives-IZ0711.

Reynold, Daniel. "Gay HS Senior Barred from Walking at Graduation for Wearing Pants." *Advocate*, June 2, 2020. https://www.advocate.com/youth/2020/6/03/gay-hs-senior-barred-walking-graduation-wearing-pants.

Richardson, Elaine B. *P.H.D. to Ph.D.: Po Ho on Dope: How Education Saved My Life*. Parlor Press, 2013.

Richie, Beth E. "Carcerality." In Keywords Feminist Editorial Collective, ed., *Keywords for Gender and Sexuality Studies*, 40–43.

Richie, Beth E., and Kayla M. Martensen. "Resisting Carcerality, Embracing Abolition: Implications for Feminist Social Work Practice." *Affilia* 35, no. 1 (February 2020): 12–16. https://doi.org/10.1177/0886109919897576.

Ricks, Shawn Arango. "Falling Through the Cracks: Black Girls and Education." *Interdisciplinary Journal of Teaching and Learning* 4, no. 1 (2014): 10–21.

Riddick, Breonna. "Searching for Home: Autoethnographic Reflections of a Black Girl." *Qualitative Inquiry* 28, no. 10 (2022): 1087–91.

Rosas, Debbie, and Carlos Rosas. *The Nia Technique: The High-Powered Energizing Workout That Gives You a New Body and a New Life*. Broadway Books, 2004.

Ross, Madeline. "Mother Accuses Catholic School of Having a Racist Hair Policy After Claimed Her Daughter Was Banned from the Playground and Canteen Because She Braided a Heart into Her Cornrow Hairstyle." MailOnline, January 19, 2023. https://www.dailymail.co.uk/news/article-11653975/Mother-accuses-Catholic-school-having-racist-hair-policy-daughter-banned-playground.html.

Royster, Francesca T. "Queering the Jazz Aesthetic: An Interview with Sharon Bridgforth and Omi Osun Joni Jones." *Journal of Popular Music Studies* 25, no. 4 (2013): 537–52. https://doi.org/10.1111/jpms.12049.

Scott, Jill. "Watching Me." Track 15 on *Who Is Jill Scott? Words and Sounds, Vol. 1*. Hidden Beach Recordings, 2000.

Shange, Ntozake. "Dark Phrases." In *For Colored Girls Who Have Considered Suicide / When the Rainbow Is Enuf: A Choreopoem*. Scribner Poetry, 1997.

Shange, Savannah. "Black Girl Ordinary: Flesh, Carcerality, and the Refusal of Ethnography." *Transforming Anthropology* 27, no. 1 (April 2019): 3–21. https://doi.org/10.1111/traa.12143.

Sharpe, Christina Elizabeth. *In the Wake: On Blackness and Being*. Duke University Press, 2016.

Shure, Lauren, Cirecie West-Olatunji, and Blaire Cholewa. "Investigating the Relationship between School Counselor Recommendations and Student Cultural Behavioral Styles." *Journal of Negro Education* 88, no. 4 (2019): 454–66.

Simmons, Aishah Shahidah. "Who Will Revere US? (Black LGTBQ People, Straight Women, and Girls) (Part 3)." *The Feminist Wire* (blog), April 25, 2012. https://thefeministwire.com/2012/04/who-will-revere-us-black-lgtbq-people-straight-women-and-girls-part-3.

Simmons, Maima Chea. "'There's More Than One Way to Be Black': The Literacy Experiences of Black African Immigrant Girls in the United States." In *Black Girls' Literacies: Transforming Lives and Literacy Practices*, edited by Detra Price-Dennis and Gholnecsar E. Muhammad, 98–112. Routledge, 2021.

Slate, John R., Pamela L. Gray, and Brandolyn Jones. "A Clear Lack of Equity in Disciplinary Consequences for Black Girls in Texas: A Statewide Examination." *Journal of Negro Education* 85, no. 3 (2016): 250–60. https://doi.org/10.7709/jnegroeducation.85.3.0250.

Smith, Barbara. Introduction to *Home Girls: A Black Feminist Anthology*, edited by Barbara Smith. Rutgers University Press, 2000.

Smith, Blair E. "Being in a With: Dreaming Black Girlhood Anew." Webinar, Colgate University, Hamilton, NY, April 28, 2022.

Smith-Purviance, Ashley L., Sara Jackson, Brianna Harper, Jennifer Merandisse, Brittney Smith, Kim Hussey, and Eliana Lopez. "Toward Black Girl Futures:

Rememorying in Black Girlhood Studies." *Girlhood Studies* 15, no. 3 (2022): 67–83.

"Solange – Don't Touch My Hair (Video) ft. Sampha." Posted to YouTube by solangeknowlesmusic, October 2, 2016, https://www.youtube.com/watch?v=YT-trnDbOQAU.

Spillers, Hortense J. "Mama's Baby, Papa's Maybe: An American Grammar Book" [1987]. In *The Transgender Studies Reader Remix*, edited by Susan Stryker and Dylan McCarthy Blackston. Routledge, 2022.

Spry, Tami. *Body, Paper, Stage: Writing and Performing Autoethnography*. Routledge, 2011.

Spry, Tami. "Illustrated Woman: Autoperformance in 'Skins: A Daughter's (Re)Construction of Cancer' and 'Tattoo Stories: A Postscript to "Skins."'" In *Voices Made Flesh: Performing Women's Autobiography*, edited by Lynn C. Miller, Jacqueline Taylor, and Heather Carver. University of Wisconsin Press, 2003.

"States with Hair Discrimination (CROWN) Laws in 2024: Interactive Map." GovDocs, September 23, 2024. https://www.govdocs.com/states-with-hair-discrimination-laws.

Stucky, Nathan, and Cynthia Wimmer. "Introduction: The Power of Transformation in Performance Studies Pedagogy." In *Teaching Performance Studies*, ed. Nathan Stucky and Cynthia Wimmer, 1–32. Southern Illinois University Press, 2002.

Taylor, Diana. *The Archive and the Repertoire: Performing Cultural Memory in the Americas*. Duke University Press, 2003.

Troutman, Stephanie, and Ileana Jiménez. "Lessons in Transgression: #BlackGirlsMatter and the Feminist Classroom." *Meridians* 15, no. 1 (December 1, 2016): 7–39. https://doi.org/10.2979/meridians.15.1.03.

Truth, Sojourner. "Two Speeches (United States, 1851, 1867)." In *The Essential Feminist Reader*, edited by Estelle B. Freedman. Modern Library, 2007.

Urban Bush Women. "Summer Leadership Institute." Accessed February 26, 2024. https://www.urbanbushwomen.org/summer-leadership.

van der Kolk, Bessel A. *The Body Keeps the Score: Brain, Mind and Body in the Healing of Trauma*. Penguin Books, 2015.

Vilakazi, Thabile. "Students Protest School's Alleged Racist Hair Policy." CNN World, September 1, 2016. https://www.cnn.com/2016/08/31/africa/south-africa-school-racism/index.html.

Wald, Johanna, and Daniel J. Losen. "Defining and Redirecting a School-to-Prison Pipeline." *New Directions for Youth Development* 2003, no. 99 (2003): 9–15. https://doi.org/10.1002/yd.51.

Walker, Alice. *In Search of Our Mother's Gardens—Womanist Prose*. Harvest/Harcourt, 1983.

Watts, Jenisha. "7-Year-Old's Mother Speaks on Cut Braid." *Essence*, October 29, 2020. https://www.essence.com/news/seven-year-olds-mother-speaks-out-about.

"We Levitate: Saving Our Lives Hear Our Truths aka SOLHOT #Next Level." SoundCloud artist's page, accessed August 31, 2023. https://soundcloud.com/solhot-next-level.

We Levitate: Saving Our Lives Hear Our Truths. "Black Girl Insistence, or, When You Wanna Be in Conversation with Fred Moten about SOLHOT." Posted to SoundCloud by We Levitate, 2017, accessed on August 10, 2022. https://soundcloud.com/solhot-next-level/black-girl-insistence-or-when-you-wanna-be-in-conversation-with-fred-moten-about-solhot-fr.

We Levitate: Saving Our Lives Hear Our Truths. "Black Girl Jewelry Series Featuring BGGW 2016 Homegirls." Posted to SoundCloud by We Levitate, November 16, 2016. https://soundcloud.com/solhot-next-level/sets/solhot-we-levitate-presents.

We Levitate: Saving Our Lives Hear Our Truths. "To Be Honest." Posted to SoundCloud by We Levitate, 2016, accessed on August 10, 2023. https://soundcloud.com/solhot-next-level/to-be-honest.

White, Bianca A. "The Invisible Victims of the School-to-Prison Pipeline: Understanding Black Girls, School Push-out, and the Impact of the Every Student Succeeds Act." *William & Mary Journal of Race, Gender, and Social Justice* 24, no. 3 (2018): 641–64.

White, E. Frances. *Dark Continent of Our Bodies: Black Feminism and the Politics of Respectability*. Mapping Racisms. Temple University Press, 2001.

White, Evelyn C. Foreword to *Black Like Us: A Century of Lesbian, Gay, and Bisexual African American Fiction*, 2nd ed., edited by Devon W. Carbado, Dwight A. McBride and Donald Weise. Cleis Press, 2012.

Williams, Angel Kyodo. *Being Black: Zen and the Art of Living with Fearlessness and Grace*. Penguin Publishing Group, 2000.

Williams, Fannie Barrier. "The Colored Girl." *The Voice of the Negro* 2, no. 6 (1905): 400–403

Williams, Janice. "Black Girls' Hair Extensions Are a Distraction." *Newsweek*, May 22, 2017. https://www.newsweek.com/malden-ma-dress-code-charter-school-policy-613691.

Williams, Patricia. "Spirit-Murdering the Messenger: The Discourse of Fingerpointing as the Law's Response to Racism." *University of Miami Law Review* 42, no. 1 (1987): 127–57.

Wilson, Shawn. *Research Is Ceremony: Indigenous Research Methods*. Fernwood, 2008.

Winn, Maisha T. *Girl Time: Literacy, Justice, and the School-to-Prison Pipeline*. Teachers College Press, 2019.

Wright, Nazera Sadiq. *Black Girlhood in the Nineteenth Century*. University of Illinois Press, 2016.
Wright, Nazera Sadiq. "Black Girl Interiority in Toni Cade Bambara's *Gorilla, My Love*." *Black Scholar* 50, no. 4 (2020): 5–16.
Wun, Connie. "Angered: Black and Non-Black Girls of Color at the Intersections of Violence and School Discipline in the United States." *Race Ethnicity and Education* 21, no. 4 (July 4, 2018): 423–37. https://doi.org/10.1080/13613324.2016.
1248829.
Wun, Connie. "Unaccounted Foundations: Black Girls, Anti-Black Racism, and Punishment in Schools." *Critical Sociology* 42, no. 4–5 (July 2016): 737–50. https://doi.org/10.1177/0896920514560444.
Young, Harvey. *Embodying Black Experience: Stillness, Critical Memory, and the Black Body*. Theater: Theory/Text/Performance. University of Michigan Press, 2010.
Zaborskis, Mary. "Queering Black Girlhood at the Virginia Industrial School." *Signs: Journal of Women in Culture and Society* 45, no. 2 (2020): 373–94.

Index

adultification
  carceral mechanics and, 54–56
  coming of age and, 62
  educational institutions and, 117
  innocence and, 68–69
  prematurely knowing and, 65, 69–70, 93, 100
  wrongness and, 45
Ahmed, Sarah, 27, 76, 205n41
Alexander, Elizabeth, 94–95, 96
Alexander, M. Jacqui, 21, 161, 163, 164, 168, 189, 191
aliveness, 4, 14, 42–43, 111, 132, 153
All About Love (hooks), 179
Andrews, Dorinda J. Carter, 105
Annamma, Subina Ancy, 102
anti-Blackness
  educational institutions and, 100–107, 112–20, 125–30
  gaze and, 140–41
  gendered identities and, 3, 50–51
  global production of, 55–56, 127
  hair policies and, 98–100, 114–20, 218n21
  misogynoir, 47, 127–28, 145
Apugo,
  Danielle, 106
archive access
  archive as home, 146–53
  body-activation and, 141–43, 146–53

  the erotic and, 135–36, 139–40, 155, 157
  knowledge creation and, 153–55
  (re)memory and, 153–55
  mirroring and, 141–43
  pedagogical tools for, 143–53, 157–60
  performance and, 34–35, 138–39, 141–55
  repertoire vs archive, 153
  retooling archives, 39, 75, 128, 135–36, 140, 155–57
  touch and, 135–36
  transgression and, 27–28, 37
Ault, Stacey, 55
Austin Project, The (tAP), 24, 207n58
auto/ethnography
  use of term, 3–4
  Black feminism and, 31–33, 63, 188–92
  Black Girlhood studies and, 32–38
  bodily archives and, 32–38
  celebration paradigm and, 30–32
  collectivity and, 189–90
  embodiment and, 32–38, 188–89
  as methodology, 32–38, 63, 189
  performance and, 34–35
  as political project, 33–34
  positionality and, 30–32
  reliability work and, 32–33
  self-definition and, 34

auto/ethnography (*continued*)
  as spirit work, 33
  See also groove[ing]; (re)memory/remembering; transgressn texts

Bailey, Moya, 47
Baldwin, James, 42, 208n3
Bambara, Toni Cade, 14, 22–23, 29, 65–66, 111, 118, 135, 191–92
Barnwell, Ysaye M., 110–11
being in a with, 189–93. *See also* Reagon, Bernice Johnson; Smith, Blair E. (DJ B.E.)
Bell, Shamell, 69
Black, use of term, 5, 63–64
"Black Boy with Cow" (Finney), 78
Black feminism
  Africana feminism, 210n33
  auto/ethnography and, 31–33, 63, 189–92
  Black Girlhood studies and, 20, 32–38, 43–50, 66–67, 210n33
  Black gurl reliable and, 31
  collectivity and, 189–90
  educational institutions and, 48–50, 105–7
  knowledge creation and, 33, 108, 205n41, 209n5
  LUXOCRACY, 107–8
  (re)memory and, 29, 63
  mirror theory and, 107–11
  pedagogical tools and, 20–22, 28–30, 48
  positionality and, 30–32
  queerness and, 47–48, 58–59
  race for theory and, 31
  sounded-word aesthetic and, 61, 172–75
  spirit work and, 33, 34, 61
  womanism and, 107–8, 210n33, 214n84
  wrongness and, 18, 27–28, 38, 43–48, 209n5

Black Feminist Poetics and Performance series, 189–90
Black Geographies, use of term, 17–18, 186–87
Black Girl Cartography (Butler), 52–53
Black Girl Genius Week (BGGW), 4, 137, 162–64, 210n33, 221n86. *See also* SOLHOT (Saving Our Lives, Hear Our Truths)
Black girl/gurl, use of terms, 5–7, 201n8, 202n2
Black girlhood
  use of terms, 5–7, 202n2
  becoming Black girls, 11–12
  Black girl ordinary, 60
  "colored girls" and, 67–68
  coming of age and, 62
  gendered identities and, 70–71, 165
  girlhood *vs.* childhood, 64–65, 68
  immigrant Blackness and, 64, 149–50
  intergenerational praxis and, 11–12
  knowledge creation and, 10, 50–51, 52, 65–66, 71, 118, 170, 173
  misogynoir and, 47, 127–28, 145
  mythologies of, 94, 104, 135, 164–66
  queerness and, 69–71
  as space-making, 17–18
  as speculative freedom, 63
  as trans/disciplinary, 19–20
  translocality of, 52, 63–64, 71, 156, 190–91
  womnhood and, 70–71
Black Girlhood Celebration (Brown), 18–19, 30
Black Girlhood studies
  introduction to, 41–43
  autoethnography and, 32–38
  Black feminism and, 20, 32–38, 43–50, 66–67, 210n33
  carceral mechanics and, 54–56
  celebration paradigm and, 18–20, 226n20

corridors of understanding and, 20, 38–40
development of field, 49–54, 105–7, 127–28, 210n33
future political envisioning of, 66–71, 197–200
hip-hop musicality and, 51–52
identity attentive work and, 19–20, 70–71
intergenerational work and, 20, 70–71, 210n33
locating girlhood, 62–66
methodologies of, 51–54, 55, 63, 64
performance and, 32–38
as a political imagining project, 4, 18–19, 38, 40, 41– 43, 52–54
practicing Black girlhood, 56–59, 165–69
responsibilities of, 143, 166, 168–69
as singing a Black Girl's song, 41–43, 71–72
social projects and initiatives and, 51
wrongness and, 43–48
See also practicing Black girlhood; teaching Black girlhood
Black Girl Jewelry, 221n86
Black Girl: Linguistic Play (Brown), 60–61
Black Girl Magic (Jordan-Zachery and Harris), 63
Black girl ordinary, 60. See also Shange, Savannah
Black Girls Matter (African American Policy Forum), 54–56
Black gurl reliable
use of terms, 4, 6–7, 10
to be honest, 225n13
Black feminism and, 31
Black mattering and, 185–87
celebration paradigm and, 12
collective responsibility and, 4
homegirling and, 58–59, 70–71, 225n21

intergenerational work and, 4
mattering and, 185–87
as pedagogy of transgression, 28–30, 195–200
practices of interconnection and, 185–87
queerness and, 4
vulnerability and, 31–32
See also body-activation; teaching Black girlhood
BlackLight Project, The, 58. See also Cox, Aimee
Blackness, use of term, 5–6, 64
Black Woman, The (Bambara), 135
"Black Women's Issues" (Reagon), 188
bodily archives
auto/ethnography and, 32–38
body-activation and, 39, 141–46, 153–55
disembodiment and, 74
retooling the body and, 39, 75, 128, 135–36, 140, 155–57
transgression and, 27–28, 37
undressing in public and, 38
Body, Paper, Stage (Spry), 143–44
body-activation
accessing spirit and, 39, 158–59
archive access and, 141–43, 146–53
bodily archives and, 39, 141–46, 153–55
"Body Affirmations" exercise, 139, 157–60
capture vs., 156–57
confinement and, 153–55
disembodiment and, 74
embodiment and, 39
the erotic and, 135–36, 139–40, 155, 157
as experiment, 119–25, 135–39
Feels Like exercise, 39, 143–53
gendered identity and, 154
groove[ing] and, 135, 138–39
innocence and, 156

body-activation (*continued*)
  interiority and, 141, 155–57
  intimacy practice and, 155–60
  (re)memory and, 143–55
  reliability work and, 39, 136–37
  repertoire expansion, 39, 135, 141–43, 153–55
  retooling bodily archives and, 39, 135–36, 140, 155–57
  self-definition and, 141–43
  somatic awareness tools, 39, 137–38, 143–46
  spirit work and, 158–60
  touch and, 135–36, 140, 155–57
  transgression and, 147–53
  undressing in public and, 157
  vulnerability and, 135–36
  See also archive access
"Body Affirmations" exercise, 139, 157–60
Bound Woman Is a Dangerous Thing, A (Hill), 21
Breath Better Spent (Hill), 61
Bridgforth, Sharon, 24–25, 28, 32, 206n54
Brockman, Jeff, 147
Brown, Camille A., 61–62
Brown, Ruth Nicole, 18–19, 30, 52, 59, 173, 202n2. *See also* celebration paradigm
Butler, Tamara T., 52–53

Callier, Durell M., 47–48, 53, 130, 156, 179
Cammon, Lamya, 130
capture, use of term, 156–57
Carbado, Devon W., 69–70
carceral mechanics
  use of term, 15, 16–17
  adultification and, 54–56
  Black girl cartography and, 52–53
  Black Girlhood studies and, 54–56
  the body as, 46–47
  educational institutions and, 54–56, 98–107
  pedagogies of foreclosure and, 91–96
  punishment and, 15, 16–17, 60
  self-definition and, 7
  stuckness and, 16–17
  terrible educations and, 14, 22–23, 29, 111, 118, 161–62
  wrongness and, 45, 54–56
  See also hair policies
Carlos, Laurie, 23, 202n1
Caroll, Rebecca, 50
Castro, Andrene, 106
celebration paradigm
  auto/ethnography and, 30–32
  Black Girlhood studies and, 18–20, 226n20
  Black gurl reliable and, 12
  future political envisioning and, 66–71
  hip-hop musicality and, 51–52
  political projects and, 63, 66–71
  politics of tenderness and, 62
  transgression and, 70–71
  voice and, 59–60
  See also Brown, Ruth Nicole
Christa (pseudonym), 9–11, 145, 150–52, 153, 195–97, 202n1
Christian, Barbara, 31
citation practice, 141–42
"Civil Wars" (Jordan), 226n15
Clifton, Lucille, 109–10, 188
Cohen, Cathy J., 47–48
collectivity
  auto/ethnography and, 189–90
  Black feminist auto/ethnography and, 189–90
  Black gurl reliable and, 4
  Jordan on, 190–91
Combahee River Collective, 46, 54

confinement, geographies of
  use of term, 15, 16
  body-activation and, 153–55
  bound as commitment not confinement, 21–22
  Brazilian resistance to, 56
  chattel slavery and, 43–44
  criminalization and, 15, 100–107
  identity politics and, 33, 46–48
  retooling the body and, 3, 40, 187
  spirit-murdering and, 11, 15–16
  stuckness and, 16–17
  the translocal and, 51–52
  wrongness and, 46–48
  See also East Ferry Detention Center
Cook, Deanna, 130
Cook, Mya, 130
Cook, Tomasina L., 55, 102, 105
corridor metaphor, 20, 38–40, 43, 52–54, 66. *See also* carceral mechanics; practicing Black girlhood; teaching Black girlhood
Corset, 194, 195
Corset, The (Hill), 226n14
Cox, Aimee, 58, 67. *See also* shapeshifting
Crenshaw, Kimberlé, 130–31
CROWN Act (Create a Respectful and Open World for Natural Hair), 13, 128, 131–32

Daley, Lashon, 62, 63
"Dark Phrases" (Shange), 42
Deborah (pseudonym), 145, 147, 152, 153
Dillard, Cynthia, 29, 75, 76, 79
disembodiment
  use of term, 38
  body-activation and, 74
  forgetting and, 91–92
  hair policies and, 120–25
  retooling the body and, 119–24
  self-making and, 76–77
  spirit-murdering and, 91–92
  touch and, 91–92
  undressing in public and, 75–78, 82–84, 91–92
dissent practice
  as freedom practice, 187
  hair alteration and, 118–19, 128
  innocence and, 68–69
  sartorial choices, 55–56, 60, 99, 107–12, 118–19, 129–30
  transgression and, 68–69
  wrongness and, 49, 56, 67–68
DJ B.E. (Blair E. Smith), 4, 189. *See also* being in a with
Dougherty, Sharyn A., 106
Du Bois, W. E. B., 43–44
Durham, Aisha, 33
dyke/warrior-prayers (Bridgforth), 32

East Ferry Detention Center
  court documents, 80–81
  dialogue with Dom, 84–90
  exercise of (re)memory and, 73–74, 79, 91–96
  monologue on, 82–84
educational institutions
  adultification and, 117
  anti-Black school policies, 100–107, 112–20, 125–30
  Black feminism and, 48–50, 105–7
  Black girl cartography and, 52–53
  carceral mechanics and, 14, 22–23, 29, 54–56, 98–107, 111, 118, 161–62
  criminalization and, 100–107
  love and, 66
  premature knowing and, 100–101
  scholarship on Black girl experiences and, 49–54, 105–7, 127–28
  self-definition and, 100–107, 117–18, 188

educational institutions (*continued*)
  as site of practicing freedoms, 188
  terrible educations and, 14, 22–23, 29, 111, 118, 161–62
  See also pedagogical landscapes
"Education of a Storyteller" (Bambara), 22–23, 29, 111
embodiment
  use of term, 37–38, 201n1
  auto/ethnography and, 32–38, 188=189, 188–89
  body-activation and, 39
  embodied knowledge, 34–35, 52, 146–48, 154, 157
  embodied vulnerability, 26, 74, 135–36, 169, 186
  innocence and, 68, 156–57, 214n87
  intimacy practice and, 119, 201n11
  mirror theory and, 107–11
  performance auto/ethnography and, 34–35
  retooling the body and, 186–87
  self-definition as, 201n1
  theatrical jazz aesthetics and, 25, 26–28, 206n54
  transgression and, 37–38, 192–95
  voice and, 59–60, 61–62
  of wrongness, 16–17
  See also bodily archives; body-activation
Erie County Detention Home. *See* East Ferry Detention Center
erotic, the
  body-activation and, 135–36, 139–40, 155, 157
  capture *vs.*, 156–57
  intimacy practice and, 139–40
  Lorde on, 135–36, 139–40, 155, 157, 190
  retooling the body and, 135–36, 139–40, 155–57, 190
  touch and, 135–36, 139–40, 155, 157

Ewing, Eve L., 32, 180
experimentation
  use of term, 32–33, 40
  body-activation as, 119–25, 135–39
  intergenerational praxis and, 119–23
  as methodological approach, 26, 32–33, 39–40
  as pedagogical practice, 36, 37
  reliability work and, 32–33, 37, 39–40
  transgressn texts and, 37
  undressing in public and, 74–75
  See also theatrical jazz aesthetics; transgression, pedagogies of; transgressngroove

femininity, 6, 58, 60
Field, Corinne T., 51
Finney, Nicky, 4, 78, 137
For Colored Girls Who Have Considered Suicide/When the Rainbow is Enuf (Shange), 23, 41–42, 51
Fordham, Signithia, 50, 104
foreclosure, pedagogies of
  use of term, 11
  carceral mechanics and, 91–96
  foreclosure of self-definition, 186, 226n14
  forgetting and, 29–30
  hair policies and, 125–30
  juvenile detention and, 91–96
  mirroring and, 46
  muting, 77, 93–94
  racial-sexual tactics of, 11–12
  See also confinement, geographies of; pedagogical landscapes
forgetting, 29–30, 91–92
Foucault, Michel, 106
Franklin, J. E., 50

Garner, Porshé R., 53, 64, 143
Gaunt, Kyra D., 50, 52, 63–64

gaze, the
    Black aliveness and, 42
    external gaze/internal definition, 6, 39
gendered identity
    use of term female, 201n1
    Black and female as, 6
    Black girlhood and, 70–71, 165
    Blacklight Project, The and, 58
    body-activation and, 154
    "colored girls" and, 67–68
    expansive love and, 48–50
    femininity and, 6, 58, 60
    gender nonconformity and, 70–71
    intergenerational praxis and, 58
    Jane Crow oppression and, 17, 38–39, 99–100, 188
    misogynoir and, 47, 127–28, 145
    nonbinary discourse and, 17, 38–39, 99–100, 188
    performance and, 70
    practicing Black girlhood and, 70–71
    teaching Black girlhood and, 165
    trans girls, 70
    transgression and, 48–50
    See also womn/womnhood
George, Darryl, 131
Gilmore, Ruth Wilson, 15, 45
Giovanni, Nikki, 42, 208n3
girl/gurl, use of term, 6–7, 201n8
Girls Empowerment Project, 58
Girl Time, 57
Goldman, Danielle, 141–42
"Good Mirrors Are Not Cheap" (Lorde), 45–46, 108–9
Gorilla, My Love (Bambara), 66
Grandma Dorothy (Bambara), 22–23, 32, 111
Grant, Linda, 50, 104
groove[ing], 138–39, 188–89. *See also* transgressngroove

"Group" (Parker), 73
Gumbs, Alexis Pauline, 189

Haddix, Marcelle, 157
hair policies
    anti-Blackness and, 98–100, 114–20, 218n21
    body policing and, 112–20
    bullying and, 98–99, 113–18, 124–25, 131, 221n90
    CROWN Act, 13, 128, 131–32
    disembodying experiences and, 120–25
    dissent practice and, 118–19, 128
    hair adornment and, 99–100, 126, 221n86, 221n94
    pedagogies of foreclosure and, 125–30
    sartorial choices and, 99, 107–12, 129–34
    spirit-murdering and, 11
    #STILLGOTVOLUME, 130–31
    Vanessa's Essence, 129–30
    wrongness and, 98–99
Hamer, Fannie Lou, 191
Hartman, Saidiya, 55, 67
Hernandez, Jillian, 57
Hill, DaMaris B., 21
Hill, Dominique C., 179
Hines, Dorothy E., 106
Hines-Datiri, Dorothy, 105
hip-hop, 52, 63, 142
homegirling, 40, 58–59, 70–71, 163
Home Girls (Smith), 58–59
hooks, bell, 21–22, 48, 60, 66, 179
hopelessness, use of term, 55–56
Humility Mixtape (DJ Sarah Grace), 166
Hunt, Derrika, 63
Hurston, Zora Neale, 33
hypersurveillance, 54–56, 60–61, 93–94, 115–16, 119

identity attentive work
  attributive identity, 201n1
  Black and female as, 5–7
  Black Girlhood studies and, 19–20, 70–71
  confinement, geographies of and, 33, 46–48
  diasporic identities, 5–6
  identity politics and, 33, 46–48, 164–65
  practicing Black girlhood and, 70–71
  teaching Black girlhood and, 165
  wrongness and, 33, 46–48
Incidents in the Life of a Slave Girl (Jacobs), 65–66
innocence
  adultification and, 68–69
  body-activation and, 156
  dissent practice and, 68–69
  embodiment and, 68, 156–57, 214n87
  groove[ing] and, 188–89
  innocent eyes and, 156
  prematurely knowing and, 65, 69–70, 93, 100
  reframing of, 68–69
  stuckness and, 69
  transgression and, 68, 156, 214n87
intergenerational praxis
  Black girlhood and, 11–12
  Black Girlhood studies and, 20, 70–71, 210n33
  Black gurl reliable and, 4
  childhood *vs.* girlhood, 68
  experimentation and, 119–23
  femininity and, 58
  freedom possibilities and, 70–71
  gendered identity and, 58
  Grandma Dorothy/li'l Toni, 22–23, 32, 111
  raising Black children and, 57
  Reagon on, 188
  reliability work and, 4
  retooling the body, 186–87
interiority, 14, 29, 65–66, 94–95, 141, 155–57
intimacy practice
  Black feminist auto/ethnography and, 31–33, 63, 189–92
  body-activation and, 155–60
  embodiment and, 119, 201n1
  the erotic and, 139–40
  eye contact, 157–60
  methodological approaches and, 25–26, 33, 156, 157–60, 186
  performance and, 34
  shapeshifting and, 186
  theatrical jazz aesthetics and, 25–26
  touch and, 139–41
  undressing in public as, 42, 93–94, 95–96
  vulnerability and, 186
I Want to Be Ready (Goldman), 141–42

Jacobs, Harriet, 65–66, 69, 100–101
Jane Crow oppression, 17, 38–39, 99–100, 188. *See also* Murray, Pauli
Jiménez, Iliana, 48
Johnson, E. Patrick, 63–64
Johnson, Jasmine Elizabeth, 62
Jones, Omi Osun Joni L.
  on form and training, 138–39, 142, 153
  on love as transgressive, 48–49
  performance ethnography and, 34
  putting on a good bra and, 202n1
  theatrical jazz aesthetics and, 24, 26, 27, 70
  See also theatrical jazz aesthetics
Jordan, June
  aliveness and, 42, 111
  "Civil Wars," 226n15
  "Poem About My Rights," 44
  "Some of Us Did Not Die," 131

"Wrong or White," 44–45
juvenile detention. *See* East Ferry Detention Center

Kent, Sabrina, 112, 118, 119, 126, 129–30
King, Deborah K., 101
King, Wilma, 68–69
knowledge creation
  archive access and, 153–55
  Black feminism and, 33, 108, 205n41, 209n5
  Black girlhood and, 10, 50–51, 52, 65–66, 71, 118, 170, 173
  cultural knowledge, 147–48
  embodied knowledge, 34–35, 52, 146–48, 154, 157
  repertoire and, 142–43
  somatic knowledge, 147–48
Kwakye, Chamara Jewel, 179

Ladner, Gloria, 38, 43, 50
Latina girlhood, 57
Learning to (Re)member the Things We've Learned to Forget (Dillard), 75, 76, 79
Legend, John, 224n11
"Lesson in Black Girlhood Rigor, A" (Hill), 181–83
Lewis, Janaka Bowman, 69
Lewis, Sheri K., 58
Lightfoot, Sara Lawrence, 50, 51
li'l Toni (Bambara), 22–23, 32, 111
Lincoln, Abbey, 12, 19, 47
Lindsey, Treva B., 55
Living a Feminist Life (Ahmed), 76
Long Walk Home, A, 58
Lorde, Audre
  the erotic and, 135–36, 139–40, 155, 157, 190
  on mirroring, 45–46, 108–9, 111
  raising Black children and, 57
  on silence, 173
  on visibility/legibility, 117
love, 48–50, 57, 66, 179–80
love conjure/blues (Jones), 48–49
Lovecraft Country (tv show), 10–11
LUXOCRACY, 107–8. *See also* Maparyan, Layli

Malone Gonzalez, Shannon, 100–101
Mama Crystal, 191
"Mama's Baby, Papa's Maybe" (Spillars), 45
Maparyan, Layli, 107
Marshall, Paule, 50
mattering
  aliveness and, 4, 14, 42–43, 111, 132, 153
  Black Geographies and, 17–18
  Black girls and, 12–14
  Black gurl reliable and, 185–87
  interiority and, 14, 29, 65–66, 94–95, 141
  pedagogical tools and, 29–30
McBride, Dwight A., 69–70
McIntyre, Diane, 23
McKittrick, Katherine, 29, 46–47, 71, 77–78, 79
McLaurin, Irma, 33
melt methodology, 58. *See also* Lewis, Sheri K.
Messiah Borne (pseudonym), 174–75
methodological approaches
  being in a with, 189–90
  Black feminist auto/ethnography, 31–33, 63, 188–92
  citation practice, 31, 141–42
  collectivity, 189–90
  documentation and, 206n54
  "Entering, Building, and Exiting" communities, 138
  epistolary traditions, 39–40, 192–200

methodological approaches (*continued*)
   the erotic as, 135–36, 139–40, 155, 157, 190
   experiments as, 26, 32–33, 39–40
   groove[ing], 188–89
   intimacy practice, 25–26, 33, 156, 157–60, 186
   melt methodology, 58
   (re)memory as data collection process, 29, 63
   somatic inquiries/workouts, 35
   tracing and, 5, 38, 63–64, 135–36, 141–42, 190–91
   See also teaching Black girlhood; transgressngroove
Meyers, 129–30
mirror theory
   archive access and, 141–43
   Black feminism and, 107–11
   embodiment and, 107–11
   Lorde on, 45–46, 108–9, 111
   pedagogies of foreclosure and, 46
   respectability and, 143
   self-definition and, 95, 107–12
   undressing in public and, 95
   wrongness and, 45–46
   See also visibility/legibility
misogynoir, 47, 127–28, 145. *See also* Bailey, Moya
Morris, Monique W., 55, 102, 105
Morrison, Toni, 29, 50, 65–66, 188
Moten, Fred, 110
Muhammad, Gholnecsar E., 157
Murray, Pauli, 17
muting processes
   foreclosure and, 77, 93–94
   (re)memory/remembering and, 93–94
   prematurely knowing, 65, 69, 93–94, 100–101
   surveillance, 93–94

Naimon, David, 78
Nashid, Laila, 60
National Black Feminist Organization, 46
Neal-Jackson, Alaina, 105
Nia technique, 25, 138
Nicole (pseudonym), 145, 147, 152
No Mirrors in My Nana's House (Barnwell), 110–11
nonbinary discourse, 17, 38–39, 99–100, 188
nonnormativity, 16–17, 24, 105

Oliver, Cynthia, 24–26, 169
Omolade, Barbara, 20–21
orientation/(re)orientation
   use of terms, 27–28
   capture and, 156–57
   (re)orienting tools, 4, 66–71, 192–93
   retooling the body and, 186–87
   teaching Black girlhood and, 168–69
   transgression and, 27, 49–50
   See also groove[ing]
osmosis, 75–76, 193–94
Owens, Tammy C., 53, 64

Parker, Pat, 2, 44, 73, 95–96, 191
Parker, Tiana, 130, 132, 218n21
"Party Ain't A Party" (Queen Pen), 166–67
Patel, Zulaika, 132
pedagogical landscapes
   use of term, 19–22
   Alexander on, 21–22
   Black feminism and, 20–22, 28–30, 48
   Black gurl reliable and, 28–30, 195–200
   engaged pedagogy, 21–22
   literacy enactments, 157
   pedagogical tools and, 28–30

performance-informed research and, 34–35
stuckness and, 21–22, 23
terrible educations, 14, 22–23, 29, 111, 118, 161–62
performance
  use of term, 3–4, 119
  accessing the archive and, 34–35, 138–39, 141–55
  auto/ethnography and, 34–35
  Black Girlhood studies and, 32–38
  documentation and, 206n54
  embodiment and, 34–35
  gendered identity and, 70
  groove[ing], 138–39
  intimacy and, 34
  (re)memory and, 79, 82–90, 93–96
  as pedagogical tool, 28–30
  performance projects, 58, 61
  Performance studies and, 34–35
  of protest/defiance, 11, 12–13
  queerness and, 70
  reliability work and, 40, 79, 185–86, 202n1
  transgression and, 34–35, 37
  See also transgression, pedagogies of
Perry, Brea L., 105
PHD to Ph.D. (Richardson), 74, 214n1
Phillipi (pseudonym), 148–50, 156
Pillow, Wanda, 101
"Poem About My Rights" (Jordan), 44
policy development, use of term, 41, 208n1
political projects
  auto/ethnography as, 33–34
  Black Girlhood studies as, 4, 18–19, 38, 40, 41–43, 52–54, 66–71, 197–200
  celebration paradigm and, 63, 66–71
  confinement and, 33, 46–48
  identity attentive work as, 33, 46–48, 164–65

politics of tenderness and, 62
transgression as, 48–50
politics of tenderness, 62. *See also* Johnson, Jasmine Elizabeth
positionality, 30–32
practicing Black girlhood
  use of term, 4–5, 20–22
  Black Girlhood studies and, 56–59, 165–69
  gendered identity and, 70–71
  homegirling and, 58–59, 70–71, 163
  identity attentive work and, 70–71
  reliability work and, 4–5, 165, 185–92
  SOLHOT and, 2–3, 4, 30–31, 59, 89, 138, 162–64, 193–95, 224n1
  as space-making project, 56–59, 68
  vulnerability and, 31–33
  See also reliability work; teaching Black girlhood
"Punks, Bulldaggers, Welfare Queens" (Cohen), 47–48
putting on a good bra, 202n1
Pyles, Nicole, 130, 132

queerness
  Black feminism and, 47–48, 58–59
  Black girlhood and, 4, 60, 69–71
  as formative geography, 69–70
  gender nonconformity and, 70–71
  performance and, 70
  queering/queer possibility, 47–48
  radical subjectivity and, 60
  theatrical jazz aesthetics and, 16–17, 24, 70, 105
  transgression and, 28
  as wrongness, 47–48
queer theory, 47–48

race for theory, the, 31. *See also* Christian, Barbara
racism, Gilmore's definition of, 15, 45

radical subjectivity, 60
Reagon, Bernice Johnson, 188, 190, 191
reliability work
   use of term, 1–5, 10
   auto/ethnography and, 32–33
   being in a with and, 190–92
   body-activation and, 39, 136–37
   experimentation and, 32–33, 37, 39–40
   Feels Like exercise and, 136–37
   homegirling, 58–59, 70–71
   intergenerational praxis and, 4
   performance and, 40, 79, 185–86, 202n1
   practicing Black girlhood and, 4–5, 165, 185–92
   retooling the body and, 191–200
   tracing and, 140–41, 190–91
   transgression and, 28–30, 195–200
   See also practicing Black girlhood; teaching Black girlhood
(re)memory/remembering
   use of term, 77–78
   archive access and, 153–55
   Black feminism and, 29, 63
   body-activation and, 143–55
   as border transgression, 95–96
   connection and, 5
   flooding as metaphor for, 188
   hip-hop musicality and, 51–52
   interiority and, 29
   as methodology, 29, 63
   as mode of healing, 29
   muting processes and, 93–94
   performance and, 79, 82–90, 93–96
   repetition and, 76–78
   retooling the body and, 77–78
   Richardson and, 214n1
   spirit murdering and, 77–78
   terrible educations and, 14, 22–23, 29, 111, 118, 161–62
   tracing process and, 5
   transgression and, 95–96
   undressing in public and, 73–74, 84–90, 93–97, 214n1
   voice and, 63–64
repertoire
   archive access and, 153–55
   body-activation and, 135, 141–43, 153–55
   knowledge creation and, 142–43
   repertoire expansion, 135, 141–43
   repertoire vs archive, 153
retooling the body
   accessing bodily archives and, 39, 75, 128, 135–36, 140, 155–57
   body-activation, 39, 135–36, 140, 155–57
   confinement and, 3, 40, 187
   disembodiment and, 119–24
   the erotic and, 135–36, 139–40, 155–57, 190
   homegirling and, 40
   intergenerational praxis, 186–87
   (re)memory/remembering and, 77–78
   orientation/reorientation and, 186–87
   reliability work and, 191–200
   shapeshifting and, 186
   somatic work and, 39, 75, 128, 135–36
   spirit work and, 120
   touch and, 140–41
   transgressngroove and, 27–28, 37
   See also undressing in public
Richardson, Elaine B., 74, 214n1
Richie, Beth E., 15
Royster, Francesca T., 138
"rupture" (Hill), 35–37
"Rupturing Silence" (Hill), 215n2, 226n14

sartorial choices, 55–56, 99, 107–12, 118–19, 129–30
"Save Room" (Legend), 224n11

Scott, Marian, 130
Sears, Stephanie D., 58
self-definition
  autoethnography and, 34
  Black girl hair and, 112–25
  body-activation and, 141–43
  Brazilian self-fashioning and, 56
  carcerality and, 7
  the Corset and, 194–95, 225n14
  educational institutions and, 100–107, 117–18
  as embodiment, 201n1
  foreclosure of self-definition, 186, 226n14
  journal writing and, 171–72
  love and, 49
  mirror theory and, 95, 107–12
  right-relationship and, 188–89
  sartorial choices and, 55–56, 99, 107–12, 118–19, 129–30, 145, 175
  saving room and, 171–72, 224n11
  self-recognition and, 147–48
  social media and, 60
  vulnerability and, 145
Shange, Ntozake, 23, 41–42, 51
Shange, Savannah, 60
Shapeshifters (Cox), 67
shapeshifting, 186. *See also* Cox, Aimee
Sharpe, Christina Elizabeth, 77
silencing, 194–95, 225n14
Simmons, Aisha Shaidah, 12, 19
Simmons, LaKisha, 51
Simmons, Maima Chea, 64
"Site of Memory, The" (Morrison), 29, 188
slavery, 43, 46, 65–66, 68–69, 77, 100, 102
Smith, Barbara, 58–59
Smith, Blair E. (DJ B.E.), 4, 189, 193
Smith-Purviance, Ashley L., 63–64
social media, 60

SOLHOT (Saving Our Lives, Hear Our Truths), 2–3, 4, 30–31, 59, 89, 138, 162–64, 193–95, 224n1. *See also* Black Girl Genius Week (BGGW); celebration paradigm
somatic work
  use of term, 5, 35
  agency and, 142, 143–44, 154
  body-activation, 39, 137–38, 143–46
  cultural knowledge and, 147–48
  education and, 147–48
  eye contact, 157–60
  Feels Like Exercise and, 137–38
  improvisation, 141–43
  Nia technique, 25, 138
  retooling bodily archives and, 39, 75, 128, 135–36
"Someday Is Today" (Hill), 175–78
sounded-word aesthetics, 61, 172–75. *See also* Garner, Porshé R.
space-making, 17–18, 56–59, 68
Spillers, Hortense J., 45, 67, 68, 202n2
spirit-murdering
  confinement, geographies of and, 11, 15–16
  disembodiment and, 91–92
  dress codes and, 11
  hair policies and, 11
  (re)memory/remembering and, 77–78
  undressing in public and, 91–92
  See also Williams, Patricia
spirit work
  auto/ethnography as, 33
  Black feminism and, 33, 34, 61
  body-activation and, 158–60
  embodied vulnerability and, 26
  retooling the body and, 120
  sounded-word aesthetic and, 61, 172–75
  voice and, 61
Spry, Tami, 143–44, 154, 141²

Stewart, Mary, 46
Stinney, George Jr., 78
Stolen Childhood (King), 68–69
stuckness
    use of term, 16–17
    groove[ing] and, 188–89
    innocence and, 69
    pedagogical landscapes and, 21–22
    wrongness, 16–17

tAP (The Austin Project), 24, 207n58. *See also* Jones, Omi Osun Joni L.
Taylor, Diana, 153
teaching Black girlhood
    belief introspection, 169–71
    Black gurl vernacular and, 172–79
    classroom exercises
    finding voice method and, 168–69
    gendered identity and, 165, 173–74
    homegirling and, 162–64
    identity attentive work and, 165
    "Introduction to Black Girlhood Studies," 165–79
    journal writing and, 171–79
    love and, 179–80
    (re)orientations and, 168–69
    personal narratives and, 165–69
    pleasure and, 166
    reflection and, 169–71
    reliability work and, 164–69
    responsibility and, 4, 166, 168–69
    rigor and, 181–82
    the rub and, 162–64
    self-identity and, 169–71
    "Someday Is Today," 175–78
    sounded-word aesthetic and, 172–75
    as spiritual process, 161
    temperature checks, 169–71
    touch and, 163–64
    undressing in public and, 163–64, 168, 169

    voice and, 161, 172–78
    vulnerability and, 164
    See also body-activation
Teaching to Transgress (hooks), 21–22, 48
terrible educations, 14, 22–23, 29, 111, 118, 161–62. *See also* Bambara, Toni Cade
theatrical jazz aesthetics
    use of term, 23–28, 206n54
    aliveness and, 4, 14, 42–43, 132, 153
    choreopoems and, 41–42
    embodiment and, 25, 26–28, 206n54
    finding voice method, 168–69, 188–89
    groove[ing] and, 188–89
    intimacy practice and, 25–26
    as pedagogical tool, 26–27
    queerness and, 16–17, 24, 70, 105
    transgressngroove orientation of, 27–28
    See also transgressngroove
Theatrical Jazz Conference (2024), 206n54
TikTok, 60
to be a witness, use of term, 4–5
"To Be Honest" (We Levitate), 180, 225n13
Tomorrow's Tomorrow (Ladner), 38, 43, 50
touch
    archive access and, 135–36, 141–43
    body-activation and, 135–36, 140, 155–57
    disembodiment and, 91–92
    the erotic and, 135–36, 139–40, 155, 157
    intimacy practice and, 139–41
    practicing touch, 140–41
    retooling the body and, 140–41
    rupture and, 140

"Towards an Interdisciplinary Field of Black Girlhood Studies" (Owens, et. al), 53
tracing process
  citation practice and, 141–42
  (re)memory and, 5
  methodological approaches and, 5, 38, 63–64, 135–36, 190–91
  reliability work and, 140–41, 190–91
trans, use of term, 19
"Transformation of Silence to Language and Action, The" (Lorde), 173
transgression, pedagogies of
  use of term, 11, 37
  archive access and, 27–28, 37
  to be a witness and, 4–5
  Black geography as, 186–87
  Black girlhood crossroads and, 187–92
  Black gurl reliability and, 28–30, 195–200
  "colored girls" and, 67–68
  dissent and, 68–69
  energizing voice and, 59–62
  Feels Like exercise, 144, 148–49, 151, 152
  groove[ing] and, 188–89
  as political framework, 48–50
  saving room and, 171–72, 224n11
  vernaculars of, 172–79
transgressngroove
  use of term, 37
  Back (to East Ferry Detention Center), 79–81
  "Body Affirmations" exercise, 139, 157–60
  "Echo" series, 82–90
  "Feels Like" exercise, 144, 148, 149, 151, 152
  "Introduction to Black Girlhood Studies," 165–79
  "Lesson in Black Girlhood Rigor, A," 181–83
  letter to Witness and, 1–5
  personal performances of, 3–4
  reliability work ruptures (letters), 39–40, 192–200
  "rupture," 35–37
  Scene 1/Scene 2 (Vanessa's case), 37, 119–25
  "Someday Is Today," 175–78
  theatrical jazz aesthetics orientation, 27–28
  transgressn texts, 37
  wrongness and, 27–28, 48–50
  See also groove[ing]
translocality, 52, 63–64, 71, 156, 190–91. See also Gaunt, Kyra D.
"Troubling Innocence" (Hill and Callier), 156
Troutman, Stephanie, 48
Truth, Sojourner, 43, 46
Tuck, Eve, 31

undressing in public
  use of term, 73–75
  bodily archives and, 38
  body-activation and, 157
  disembodiment and, 75–78, 82–84, 91–92
  dispelling of myths, 94
  experimentation and, 74–75
  forgetting, 74, 75–78
  as intimacy practice, 43, 93–94, 95–96
  mirroring and, 95
  (re)memory and, 73–74, 84–90, 93–97, 214n1
  silencing and, 94
  spirit-murdering and, 91–92
  surveillance and, 93–94
  vulnerability and, 26, 74, 94, 95–96, 169

Urban Bush Women Summer Leadership Institute, 24, 137–38, 157
"Uses of the Erotic" (Lorde), 135–36, 139–40, 155, 157, 190

Van Dyke, Vanessa, 39, 98–99, 112–20, 123–30, 132–33
Vanessa's Essence, 129–30
vernacular lexicons, 5–7, 172–79
visibility/legibility
    Black girl ordinary, 60
    Lorde on, 117
    making girlhood visible, 58
    space-making practices, 56–59
    vulnerability and, 117, 138–39, 141, 145, 156–57, 164
    See also mirror theory
Visionary Feminism (hooks), 66
voice
    celebration and, 59–60
    coming of age and, 62
    embodiment and, 59–60, 61–62
    energizing voice, 59–62
    groove[ing] and, 188–89
    (re)memory tools and, 63–64
    politics of tenderness and, 62
    spirit-work and, 61
    transgression and, 59–62
vulnerability
    Black gurl reliable and, 31–32
    body-activation and, 135–36
    embodied vulnerability, 26, 74, 135–36, 169, 186
    groove[ing] and, 138–39
    intimacy practice and, 186
    politics of tenderness and, 62
    practicing Black girlhood and, 31–33
    self-definition and, 145
    spirit work and, 26
    teaching Black girlhood and, 164
    transgression and, 26

undressing in public and, 26, 74, 94, 95–96, 169
    See also body-activation; intimacy practice
Walker, Alice, 50, 214n54
Wayward Lives (Hartman), 67
We Levitate, 180, 225n13
"What the Mirror Said" (Clifton), 109–10
White, E. Frances, 110
Who Look At Me (Jordan), 42, 111
"Who Will Revere the Black Woman?" (Lincoln), 12–13, 19, 47
Wild, 194
Williams, Angel Kyodo, 33, 144
Williams, Fannie Barrier, 67–68
Williams, Patricia, 15–16
Wilmot, Jennifer M., 106
Winn, Maisha T., 55, 57
Winters, Venus Evans, 50
womanism, 61, 107–8, 210n33, 214n84
womn/womnhood
    use of term, 6–7, 204n28
    Black girlhood and, 70–71
    "colored girls" and, 67–68
    decentered as aspiration, 70–71
    gender and, 204n28
    sexuality and, 204n28
    See also gendered identity
worldbuilding/worldmaking, 10–11, 69
Wright, Nazera Sadiq, 51, 65–66
wrongness
    use of term, 43–48
    adultification and, 45
    believability and, 45
    Black feminism and, 18, 27–28, 38, 43–48, 209n5
    carceral mechanics and, 45, 54–56
    confinement and, 45–48
    dissent practice and, 49, 56, 67–68
    embodiment of, 16–17
    hair policy and, 98–99
    identity politics and, 33, 46–48

mirroring and, 45–46
misogynoir and, 47, 127–28, 145
queerness and, 47–48
stuckness and, 16–17

transgressngroove and, 27–28
See also hopelessness, use of term
"Wrong or White" (Jordan), 44–45

www.ingramcontent.com/pod-product-compliance
Lightning Source LLC
Chambersburg PA
CBHW030533230426
43665CB00010B/868